Recon Trooper

Recon Trooper

*A Memoir of Combat
with the 14th Armored Division
in Europe, 1944–1945*

HUGH WARREN WEST
with JOHN SCURA

McFarland & Company, Inc., Publishers
Jefferson, North Carolina, and London

Photographs courtesy Alan West.

LIBRARY OF CONGRESS CATALOGUING-IN-PUBLICATION DATA

West, Hugh Warren, 1916–
    Recon trooper : a memoir of combat with the 14th armored
division in Europe, 1944–1945 / Hugh Warren West with John
Scura.
    p.   cm.
    Includes index.

    ISBN 978-0-7864-4812-8
    softcover : 50# alkaline paper ∞

    1. West, Hugh Warren, 1916–   2. United States. Army.
Armored Division, 14th.   3. World War, 1939–1945 —
Personal narratives, American.   4. World War, 1939–1945 —
Regimental histories — United States.   5. World War,
1939–1945 — Campaigns — Europe.   I. Scura, John, 1948–
II. Title.
D769.3053 14th.W47   2010
940.54'1273092 — dc22   2010014907
[B]

British Library cataloguing data are available

On the cover: Hugh West in Germany, 1945 (author's collection)

Manufactured in the United States of America

McFarland & Company, Inc., Publishers
  Box 611, Jefferson, North Carolina 28640
  www.mcfarlandpub.com

To my lovely daughter Carolyn,
and son Alan,
whose interests in family, friends,
and the preservation of history
have made all of this possible

Table of Contents

Preface
(John Scura)

If ever the phrase "good war" can be used, then it certainly must be applied to the conflict in Europe that took place between 1939 and 1945. The Nazi government in Germany had embarked on a mission of world conquest, taking into those conquered nations a policy of social Darwinism at its maddest and cruelest limits. The Germans had become enslavers, bent on the complete obliteration of entire peoples.

And yet, for two years, the United States sat on the sidelines. Its people overwhelmingly wished to stay neutral in what they considered a European affair. It took an attack on Pearl Harbor, followed quickly by a German declaration of war, to galvanize the American public for a fight.

Young men throughout the country enlisted in the hundreds of thousands. Hugh Warren West was not one of them. At twenty-six, he was married, paying a monthly mortgage and well into his lifelong career as a schoolteacher. He frankly admits that he was not eager to leave his life in Ontario, California, and undergo the rigors of military training to dodge bullets an ocean and two continents away from home.

But the draft yanked him out of that life and into the maelstrom. He became a cog in the great machine known as the U.S. 14th Armored Division, and underwent an almost unprecedented training period of nearly two years before crossing the Atlantic for France. He arrived as a member of Troop A, of the 94th Mechanized Cavalry Recon Squad, in 1944. His division took up its position on the front lines as part of the U.S. 7th Army, which held the extreme right of the broad Allied push toward Germany.

Over the course of the war, West saw action in Alsace, fought to cross the Rhine River, and helped to hammer through the German defenses along the Siegfried Line. He and his unit surged southward into Bavaria, through cities like Munich, freeing thousands of Allied prisoners of war along the way. By war's end, he had reached the Danube River and earned two Bronze Stars, two Purple Hearts, a French Liberator decoration and a Combat Infantryman's Badge. It was quite a performance for a young man who was reluctant to join the fight.

In 2008, West's daughter Carolyn hired me to write a book detailing her father's war experiences. We met frequently at the care center where he now lives, and I tape-recorded our interviews at his bedside. West was ninety-two years old at the time, but still possessed a sharp wit and an excellent memory.

This will be clear when the reader experiences the countless anecdotes in this book — some horrific, some hilarious.

After transcribing more than a hundred and fifty pages of interview notes, I interlaced West's memories with the official history of the 14th Armored Division to assure accuracy, and later had it fact-checked by a divisional historian. I trust that this eliminated most of the mistakes and rendered the book an accurate telling of West's war experiences, as well as an interesting read.

John Scura
Los Angeles, California
Spring 2010

West poses for his standard U.S. Army portrait.

HATTEN — The Ordeal

When I woke up, I didn't know where I was. It was dark. There was no sound. Not at first. The ground beneath me lurched. Small convulsions, like the earth had become spastic. Everything around me moved at irregular intervals. The air made me cough and choke. It seemed to be filled with some kind of dry powder, like talcum.

My eyes scanned the darkness. They burned as I looked up and found a point of light. It was a small opening, obscured by smoke and dust, but it promised fresh air. My only thought was to get to it, and out of this dark, asphyxiating place.

I tried to move. I couldn't. There was something wrong with my leg.

Panicked thoughts bombarded me. Am I paralyzed? No, I can move my other leg.

Have I lost my leg? No, I can still feel it. They say amputees still feel their severed limbs for months afterward. No, it's still there. I can wiggle my boot. I just can't lift it.

Maybe it's broken. Shattered. Maybe I'll have to lose it, anyway. No, I wouldn't be able to wiggle my boot if it was shattered. The pain would be excruciating.

But maybe I'm in shock, and can't feel any pain yet. No, it's sore, but it's not broken.

My hand reached downward and searched around in the darkness. It had to push through a lot of debris that felt like broken masonry and dirt. Lots of dirt.

I choked again in the dust- and smoke-filled air, as my memory synapses finally began to fire.

A basement. I was in the basement of a house.

I bowed my torso as much as I could, so that my fingers could reach my lower leg. It was nearly impossible to move at first, and I realized that I was covered in damp, cold earth. It had packed me tightly, like a baby in swaddling clothes. But I had to find out what was wrong with my leg.

I squirmed until I could free one arm. My fingers emerged from the cold earth pack and followed my leg downward until they hit something. I felt the rough surface of a large wooden beam. My boot was trapped beneath it. There was no way to move the beam. My fingertips barely reached it.

I tried sliding my leg back and forth, but it was stuck fast. The effort exhausted me. I straightened and lay back, trying to relax and remember. What house was I in? Where was it?

My head began to throb. The pain grew with each passing moment. I raised my hand to feel my forehead. It had a lump, but it wasn't wet. No blood.

Then it struck me that my head was bare. My steel helmet was gone.

I felt around in the darkness, my fingers sifting through the damp, cold earth that entombed me. They came upon something hard and icy cold. I grasped it, and with surprising difficulty, freed it from its burial place.

Holding it in the dim point of light, I inspected the helmet. There was a deep, horizontal dent in the forepart of its crown. Instinctively, I knew what caused it. The heavy wooden beam that now trapped my leg had bounced off my head. The helmet had saved my life.

There are moments in times of great stress when terror gives way to hilarity. I laughed, all alone and still not knowing where I was or whether I'd be dead soon. It came to me how I'd always hated wearing that damned heavy helmet, which never inspired me with any faith in it as a lifesaving device. To me, it was a glorified pot, which could be used in the field to boil water for coffee or whip up some scrambled eggs.

I remembered in basic training, the sergeant raging at us about cooking in our helmets over a fire, and how that weakened the steel and made the thing incapable of stopping a bullet. I ignored the advice, and the helmet saved my life anyway. I intended to share this with the sergeant when I got back home. If I got back home.

"Help!" I shouted toward the light above me. The effort brought on a fit of coughing. My voice sounded like it came out of a sealed room someplace far away.

There had to be someone within earshot. I hoped their hearing wasn't as impaired as mine at this moment.

"Anybody there? Help!"

Another coughing jag. The air seemed to be filled with the same dry powder, and it adhered to my throat and lungs with each breath.

There was a loud boom, and the ground beneath me bucked, freeing more dust into my tiny space. Artillery. I recognized it as a big caliber German gun.

The report seemed to knock the wax out of my ears, or maybe it was my consciousness returning to normal, because I began to hear a constant, irregular series of explosions. Some were far away. Others sounded like they were only yards from me. It was only a matter of time before one landed right on my head.

"Help!" I called out.

My puny voice had no hope of cutting through the din above me. If there was anyone around, he'd be burrowed into the ground like a mole, trying to avoid the concussion and flying steel in a world that had gone violently mad. He wouldn't hear my weak cry for help coming from deep in one of a hundred destroyed houses.

I began to remember this particular house. It was already blown to pieces, but the walls were still standing when we ran inside for cover.

We?

It suddenly dawned on me that I'd been in this place with someone. My brain groped for the memory like a blind man struggling to feel his way. Then I fastened on him. It was my friend, Bill Walby. I could see him.

Bill was a great big guy who wore glasses. I always felt safe with him, because he was fearless. It seemed like nothing ever could harm him, and if I stayed close enough, nothing would get me, either.

Bill and I had run into this house when the German attack hit us. Their artillery was blowing the hell out of the village. We scampered through the ground floor of the house, and I remember noticing that it was made of masonry and dirt, like so many other houses in the vicinity. The locals placed dirt between the floors for insulation.

We made a beeline for the basement. That was always the safest place, below ground. If you stayed low, you were much more protected from shrapnel and bullets. The only thing that could get you was a direct hit by an artillery or mortar shell.

I remembered spending a lot of time in basements over the past few weeks. This basement was like most others. It contained a wooden bin filled with raw potatoes. A lot of basements I'd seen in this region stored potatoes. I recalled eating them occasionally. If you're hungry enough, a raw potato is as good as a catered dinner. Sometimes, if you were very lucky, you'd find a basement that contained a barrel of pickles in brine. If the gods really were smiling upon you, there would be wine in the cellar, and other things a soldier was grateful to find.

But it was no time to eat. Bill and I were just trying to survive.

We pressed ourselves into the lowest corners of the basement, tight against the concrete foundation wall. The German artillery blasts walked closer. They sounded like 150s or bigger. They kept shaking the whole basement, louder and louder.

There is no way to describe the sense of helplessness you feel under a steady bombardment. It doesn't matter how many times you've been through it. You never get used to the inner terror and abject solitude that wells up inside you, no matter how hard you try to squelch it. Under bombardment, every man is alone.

You do learn to judge the sound of incoming shells. It's a visceral memory that has nothing to do with your brain. Your whole body remembers it.

I had heard the scream of a shell that I knew was headed right for me. I curled into a ball, trying to make myself insect small, and pressed even harder against the foundation wall.

The basement lit up like it had been struck by lightning. But the blast was oddly muffled. There was almost no shock wave from it. You always felt something. Even if the explosion was many yards away, you got a punch in the chest from the shock wave. This one landed practically on top of me, and I'd barely felt it.

Was it gas? Had Hitler finally unleashed chemical weapons?

I stayed in my tight ball on the basement floor, holding my breath until the dust cleared. The booming above continued, but it seemed to be moving away.

Like a ground creature peeping out of its hole after a tornado, I raised my head to take stock. First thing I checked was me. I felt no pain, but I still checked that I had all my limbs.

I saw no blood. Instead, I seemed to be covered in something soft, moist and cold. It was all over me, on my back, my neck, my behind — all of my parts that had been exposed to the blast.

My mind raced, counting the horrible possibilities as I scraped some of the stuff from the back of my neck and looked at it. Half expecting it to be flesh, my first instinct was to shake it off my hand in disgust. But for some reason, I looked closer.

Potatoes. It was only potatoes, blown into tiny, sticky chunks.

My eyes moved to the place where the bin had stood. It was gone. The shell had landed practically on top of it. I realized the potatoes had soaked up the shock of the explosion, even muffling the sound. My life had been spared by a pile of tubers.

"Get the hell out of here," I had heard Bill shout. "The goddamn building is coming down!"

I looked around to see Walby climbing what was left of the steps. Staring dumbly at him as he disappeared toward the ground floor, I noticed flames. The building was on fire.

I had risen on my shaky legs with the help of my carbine and headed for those stairs. But before I reached them, a terrible groaning assaulted my ears. It seemed to be coming from everywhere, the tortured whine and crack of splitting wood.

The whole house was collapsing. Everything around me seemed to be moving in slow motion.

I was at top speed, running for the stairs. There was a crash, like the crack of doom. I saw the ground floor buckle and drop. Then, darkness.

Now I was lying trapped in my tomb, buried alive.

"Help! Bill! You up there? Help me!"

No sound, except for the dull thuds of exploding shells above me.

Maybe Bill's dead, I thought. Maybe I'm the lucky one. Or maybe my death is ordained, too — a slow and more torturous death by fire and asphyxia.

I still could see the flames above me. The upper parts of the collapsed house seemed to be in a raging fire. I felt the heat from it. It felt good on this cold winter day.

At least I'll die warm, I thought. I never liked the cold. I remembered when I was a kid, how sure I was that I'd rather roast to death than freeze to death, if I had to choose such a thing. They always said in books that freezing to death was the most peaceful way to go, because it was like falling asleep and never waking up. I knew that wasn't for me. I thought only about the torture of being cold. Being from the American Southwest, my constitution wouldn't tolerate it.

Perhaps my childhood preference was being granted. Lying there packed in dirt, I concluded that I wouldn't be burned after all, because fire always travels upward. As I lay beneath the flames, I realized that I'd probably just choke to death on the smoke.

"Help!" I shrieked. I was getting frantic.

I barely could hear my own voice above the raging flames and the roaring battle. How could I expect anyone up there to hear it?

It occurred to me that I would die here, in this strange place a whole ocean and two continents away from my home. I would never see my wife Pauline again. She probably wouldn't even know how I died, senselessly, miserably entombed in a cellar.

The Army probably would send her some nonsense about how her husband, PFC Hugh Warren West, had perished bravely in battle. That's what they wrote when soldiers didn't die bravely in battle. That's what they said when the real cause of death was something stupid, like crashing a jeep while drunk, or picking up a souvenir that was booby trapped.

Or smothering under a house that fell on your head. They'd never tell her that's how I died here. And where was here?

I realized that my final resting place would be Hatten, a quaint Alsatian farming town near the French-German border. More properly, the town was called *Hatten d'Alsace*. It was part of the property that had passed back and forth between Germany and France several times between 1871 and now.

The ancient enemies treated Alsace like a bone of contention, fought over by two snarling dogs. Otto von Bismarck forced France to cede these lands to Germany after his armies had crushed theirs in 1870. He rubbed it in their faces by proclaiming the new, united nation of Germany in the hallowed Hall of Mirrors built by Louis XIV at Versailles.

Less than half a century later, Alsace was back in French hands, the result of Germany's defeat in the Great War. The government of Monsieur Clemenceau couldn't resist returning Bismarck's gesture, brokering that treaty at the same Versailles of the Sun King. The German government signed the treaty in a simple railroad car, which the French parked at Compiegne. *Revanche!*

Twenty-two years after that, Alsace returned to Germany once again, along with the rest of France. The surrender documents were signed in that same railroad car in Compiegne. Then Hitler had it burned. Hell hath no fury....

I knew all of this before I arrived in Hatten, because I had to. I was a schoolteacher back in the States, but I'd never dreamed that one day I would have such a direct and intimate sabbatical in this historic place.

The first time I saw Hatten was when our unit, Troop A of the 94th Mechanized Cavalry Recon Squad, 14th U.S. Armored Division, rolled in on our half-tracks, peeps, and armored cars. Division always sent us way out ahead of the heavy stuff, the tanks and mechanized artillery. It was our job. It was what we'd been trained to do.

The town was almost totally intact when we arrived. That was because our planes had merely ringed the place with bombs, careful not to drop any into the town itself. We usually did that to make a point — don't resist us — without harming any of the people or the buildings.

We never were sure whether German units might be hiding in any town we entered, so we all were like cocked triggers when we entered a new place. Hatten was no different.

We'd learned to read the unmistakable signs. If the townsfolk hung white sheets out of their windows, there were no enemy troops around, and we could enter with some confidence. If, instead of the sheets, we saw townspeople running for cover, there was going to be a fight. In this instance, we saw white sheets.

The people of Hatten were friendly, and openly glad to see Americans. Most of them were French, and spoke the language with a peculiar provincial accent. One and all, their hatred for Germans was consuming. And yet, they had lived prosperously under German rule for the past four and a half years. It made me wonder about them, because there was something disingenuous about their brazen anti–German pose.

The first thing I noticed was that the town was populated by women, boys, girls and old men. There were no young men.

It didn't take long before I learned that the men of military age were serving in the *Wehrmacht*. The people insisted they'd been pressed into service, but I learned later that many had volunteered after Germany invaded Russia. Anti–Communism was an even stronger current than anti–Germanism among some of the people in this part of Europe, and many young men from Hatten had joined the Great Crusade against godless Communism. Most of them never saw Hatten again. Some of them may even have fired at me.

Mixing with the women and children in the town square, we were glad to give them small offerings from our knapsacks — canned rations, soap, chocolate. They treated the pitiful gifts like they were made of gold. Chocolate almost caused fainting spells. There was none to be had for a very long time. Many of the kids had never even tasted it before.

The town mayor, who was still referred to in the German title of *burgomeister*, made a very pompous, ceremonial speech, thanking us for sparing the town and its inhabitants from our bombs and shells. He reminded me of our politicians at home, eager to make a speech whenever more than four people are gathered. Dressed in his threadbare suit covered by a silk sash, he reminded me of a burlesque emcee introducing the next act. Unfortunately, the next act was written in blood.

When we left Hatten, we thought we were leaving it forever. Our unit, like the rest of the U.S. Army in Europe, was heading for the Rhine River. Our sights were set on a body of water that, once crossed, would probably result in the end of the war.

But the German army had different ideas. Its troops launched a powerful counterattack in the Hatten-Rittershoffen sector. Our little village was the linchpin at a key crossroad and railroad line.

The enemy sent everything they had — panzers, artillery, mortars, crack ground troops with automatic weapons — and fought their way into Hatten. The town became a cauldron of close battle, mixed with the unbroken blasting of shells.

My unit received orders to return to the once peaceful and unblemished little town. It was an invitation to hell.

The enemy would push us into a corner, and we'd push them back. This went on for days. At one point we were surrounded. Orders came down to counterattack. We moved from doorway to doorway along the street. My carbine was slung crosswise over my shoulder and around my neck, because I toted a clumsy bazooka in one hand and a bag of bazooka rockets in the other. It was my job to use this glorified plumbing pipe whenever we got into a firefight.

Shouts came from everywhere. The shouting closest to me came from a colonel, who already was running for cover in one of the houses that lined the street.

I trudged like an old man under the weight of my weapons, and headed for the building where the colonel had disappeared. Machine-gun bullets raked the houses along the street.

There was a crack, and another explosion. I peered in that direction, and through the smoke I saw a panzer at the end of the street. It was a German Mark V tank, a Panther. It would be a bastard to knock out with a bazooka. You just couldn't do it unless you hit the tread and crippled it. The armor was so thick, bazooka rockets just bounced off or exploded harmlessly.

Hiding in the doorway, I felt a tug on my sleeve.

"Let's go, soldier. I'll be your loader."

I turned to say, "Are you nuts?"

But before I could spit it out, I saw that it was the colonel talking. He nodded forward with his head, clearly urging me to move in on the tank. What else could I do?

I moved out of the doorway, hugging the front of the houses as I ran in short bursts. At the end of each burst, I ducked down and waited a moment. The colonel caught up with me each time I stopped, as if nudging me forward.

Forward we went. That's when it all went bad.

And now I lay here under the earth, warmed by a raging fire above me. It dissolves the cold of winter.

I realize it's January 1945. That's the date they'll put on my gravestone, I thought.

If they ever find my body.

Arizona—Family Beginnings

When my family moved to Prescott, Arizona, from Grand Saline, Texas, I was only three years old. I almost didn't make it to four.

We were in a three-car caravan. I was in the first car with my father, my mother Eula Mae, and my younger brother Kenneth, who was just a year old. My grandmother, Laura West, rode in the second car with the Martin family, and in the third car rode a mechanic and his family. It was 1919, and if you planned to drive any distance in the cars we had back then, you brought your own mechanic.

Somewhere en route, during one of our many roadside stops, I left the car and went exploring. There was a deep gully beside the road that seemed inviting, so I climbed into it.

I didn't notice the dark storm clouds hovering in the distant hills, but my mother did. Her years in Texas had taught her that such clouds could mean tornadoes and flash floods, so she didn't hesitate. She dragged me out of that gully just as a wall of water washed through it. That's how I spent the first of my nine lives.

It possibly could have been my second life, since I also dodged the fearsome influenza pandemic that swept through Texas just before we left Grand Saline. This worldwide disease claimed more lives in nine months than were lost by all combatants during the four years of World War I. The influenza was especially deadly to children, and my mother was deeply worried about my brother and me. That, and other health-related issues, were part of the reason we left Texas.

But my family apparently is well entrenched in Texas lore. They claimed that one of our ancestors, "Redneck" West, fought in the battle of San Jacinto, which gave Texas its independence from Mexico in 1836. Later, our family received a land grant from Sam Houston himself, shortly after Texas achieved statehood. There are tales also of earlier ancestors who came to Texas from Tennessee, part of the way by boat, and that one family member hid his gold in his boots. He fell overboard, his treasure dragging him to the bottom, forcing his wife and children to go on without him.

My grandfather, Sam West, was a cotton farmer and a businessman. He owned a large farm outside a place called Ben Wheeler, which was en route to Canton.

My dad's father had the wisdom to insist that all of his children receive strong educations, including college degrees. This was just after the turn of the 20th century, when college educations were an exception rather than a rule for young Texans. But all four of his sons not only graduated from college, they each received degrees from the University of Texas law school.

Like all the men in the family, everyone called my father, Joseph Andrew West, by his middle name, Andy. He was the oldest boy, so he led the way, graduating first from Sam Houston Normal Institute in 1904. One of his classmates there was Sam Rayburn, who would become the most influential U.S. congressman of his day, Speaker of the House, and mentor to Lyndon Johnson.

After graduating, my father entered the University of Texas law school, paying his tuition with a teaching job until he received his law degree in 1910. He was the first, but certainly not the last, of his siblings to achieve important goals. Even his sister Ruth became editor of the *Houston Gargoyle* magazine, and later she held a chair in the English department at New York University.

When my parents met, my mother was a teacher, and my father was the city attorney of Grand Saline. They married in 1915, and my father continued his legal work for firms like Morton Salt and the Texas & Pacific Railroad. Already an active Mason, he was deeply involved in community work, and during the First World War he was credited with having sold more Liberty Bonds than anyone else in the county.

I was their first child, born on what would become Income Tax Day, April 15, 1916. It took years for me to realize why everyone always seemed so depressed on my birthday. And I never had a real birth certificate. I still don't know why, but this would cause me a good deal of trouble years later, first when I entered the military, and again when I retired.

I was born in our Grand Saline house, which was located above the caverns of the Morton Salt mine. I remember being able to see the scaffolding of that mine in the distance from our porch. I used to sit on that porch and look skyward at the biplanes that buzzed past, and for some reason I called them "fligers." I would have other names for them when they were strafing me a couple of decades later.

Grand Saline was proud that silent movie actress Louise Fazenda was born in the house down the street from us. She would go on to marry film producer Hal Wallis.

My mother couldn't shake her concern about the fierce storms in Texas, however. Not only would those concerns save my life en route to Arizona, they would provide the impetus for our move there. She told me that one storm left a neighbor's barn lying atop our house, with the neighbor's cow landing in our yard. That was enough for her.

Our family moved to Prescott in 1919. One of the main reasons we chose this town was its air. It was clear and dry back then, which would relieve my father's bouts with asthma and bronchitis. Prescott also had a veteran's hospital that was world renowned for treating tuberculosis. My father wasn't a veteran, but he managed to get treatment there, and at the Flynn Sanitarium as an outpatient. His health improved.

My dad's successful legal career in Grand Saline allowed him to join the firm of Norris & Norris in Prescott. While doing general law practice, divorces and litigation at the firm, he befriended the man who soon was elected mayor of Prescott. My father became his deputy county attorney, with an office in the courthouse.

It was an exciting job, because he prosecuted the headline-grabbing criminals, including murderers, bootleggers, cattle rustlers, horse thieves and even gunslingers. He actually used me in his investigations. We'd go to a crime scene to reconstruct a murder, and I'd have to lie down in the place where a dead body had been, posing exactly how it had rested. This would give my father an idea of what had happened. He was an intricate guy in that regard.

My dad kept a lot of the murder weapons from the cases he prosecuted. As I was a kid, this was a huge bonanza for me — I got to take those guns out and fire them. One time, he convicted a guy for murdering another man with a shotgun. The man's defense lawyer claimed that the accused didn't intend to shoot the victim, and that the shotgun fired accidentally. The state wound up executing the defendant.

After the execution, I took that shotgun out into the sticks and fired it. It did tend to fire accidentally. If you pulled the trigger very hard, it would fire even with the safety on.

"You guys should have tried the gun," I told my dad. "He told the truth about it."

He wasn't thrilled by my post-mortem investigation.

It wasn't long before my father earned a fine reputation in Prescott, which led to his appointment as city attorney. He held that position for some time, and then became chief counsel for the Prescott Industrial Finance Corporation, eventually moving up to its presidency.

My father wasn't strict with me, but he demanded that I get things done without procrastinating. He was big on "Do it now." But I was a pretty fair student as a kid. I went to

Hugh West (right) and his brother Kenneth pose for a studio picture taken around 1922.

Prescott High School and later transferred to Phoenix Union, the largest high school west of the Mississippi at that time.

Bill Mauldin, who became famous during World War II for his "Willie and Joe" cartoons about the lives of frontline infantrymen, went to that school. We weren't in the same class, but I knew him. He was a great guy, and even back then, he showed glimpses of the humor that would flash in his cartoons.

One time he was kicked out of school because he'd stuck a cigarette in the mouth of a skull in the biology laboratory. It was a precursor to the problems he'd have later with the U.S. Army brass, and especially General George S. Patton. The general was spit-and-polish, and therefore he despised the grimy, unmilitary bearings of Mauldin's cartoon characters. Patton wanted to reprimand Mauldin and discharge him from the Army, but General Dwight Eisenhower intervened and said, basically, "Forget it, George."

That episode typified to me how the American Army is constructed, with citizen soldiers on one end, and career military officers on the other. That system seemed to work better for us than for other armies.

But at the time of Mauldin's high school shenanigans, I had no clue what was in store for him, or for me. I was too busy being a kid, and making some of the mistakes that kids inevitably make.

History already was a fascinating topic to me, especially the Middle Ages, but instead of just studying it, I had to participate. I actually built working models of medieval war weapons, including a catapult. It could fling a stone several blocks. I knocked out a few windows with the thing, and hit a few people.

One Halloween, I moved the catapult to our garage roof with help from six of my friends. The garage had a Spanish roof with a parapet surrounding it, a perfect make-believe fort. We fired rocks from the catapult at anyone who came after us. We really let them have it. Inevitably, one of these rocks broke a neighbor's window. After that, I used large green fruit as my ammunition. It did just as much damage, but I could claim it fell from a tree.

Later, I built an even bigger catapult. We had a grease pit for automobiles in our garage, and it had a ladder. That's where I constructed the new monstrosity, which could fire a missile about a hundred yards. I shot it at a few guys I didn't like. It didn't kill them, but it knocked them flat.

I also made a giant slingshot out of a car tire inner tube, and used it in our neighborhood rock fights. There were always a few bumps and bruises, and every now and then the parents of a damaged kid would complain to the police. Luckily, with my dad being county attorney, the trouble would be limited to the chief of police telling him, "Your kid's in trouble again."

My father's solution to his troublesome oldest son was to send him off to a military training camp. The kid who lived next door to us was my good friend, and his father, Norman Wykoff, was a colonel in the U.S. Army Finance Corps. He got us both into Fort Huachuca in the Arizona boondocks, and we spent three summers there starting when I was eighteen years old. We called the place "Huka-Chuka," because we couldn't pronounce it the right way.

At Fort Huachuca, we had to dress in full uniform at all times. In those days, the standard Army uniform included wrapped leggings, which were an enormous bother to put on. But they had to be wrapped perfectly according to the Army manual, or you'd get grief from the officers at the daily inspection.

The leggings provided no protection from the rattlesnakes that were all over the campground. You had to watch your step day and night. That caused most of us to look down at the ground in front of us instead of ahead, during the marches and runs we had to endure. There was a lot of head bumping, but no snakebites.

I remember Colonel Wykoff telling us that we needed to get ready to go to war, because we were going to have to fight the Germans and the Japanese. That was prescient, considering that he started saying it in 1925. Many of our politicians still weren't convinced of it in 1941.

The fort was located right on the border with Mexico, and the nearest town was Nogales. A regiment made up completely of African American soldiers was stationed at the fort. They were a rowdy bunch, so unruly that we heard the Army couldn't control them anywhere else but at Fort Huachuca.

They had tried allowing those troops to take their leaves in Nogales, but inevitably they'd get into a brawl and come back knocked all to hell. So the Army finally had to establish a "city" next to the fort, and stock it with legalized, inspected prostitutes, and a saloon. That allowed them to keep this rowdy regiment under better control, but it was quite an education for a teenager.

When summers ended, I returned home for school. I had two brothers, one two years younger, and the other, ten years younger. We had plenty of scuffles and argued about everything, but overall we got along pretty well. As the oldest, more was expected of me. It never seemed fair, and I often wondered about it when I'd get correction for doing the same thing my brothers were doing.

"Why don't you tell them?" I'd complain to my parents, but it never did any good.

My mother had a system for keeping me in line. She had a cow bell placed strategically on our kitchen window. Whenever she wanted me to come home, she'd ring that bell. You could hear it from a block away.

When I was out of earshot, the kids who heard the bell would give me the message. I might be sledding down a snow-covered hill — Prescott, in the mountainous region of Arizona, had snowfall — and a kid would run to me, saying, "Hey, your mom's ringing her cow bell for you." That meant "Go home now."

And when the kid grapevine didn't pass me the information, my mom had another option. She'd send out our dog Touser with the cow bell in his mouth, and he'd find me.

My mother wasn't the typical stay-at-home housewife so common to those days. She was very active politically, and served as a delegate to the 1928 Democratic Convention in Houston, Texas. She went there from Arizona to vote for Al Smith, and it was my mother who put Walter P. Hunt's name up for nomination.

My dad also was active in politics, especially in Prescott. Back then, the city had a population of only around five thousand, but my father was partially responsible for its the eventual growth. He had the foresight to gain legal rights to the water supply from Ash Fork, where the Del Rio Springs were located, roughly fifty miles north of Prescott. This allowed the city to construct a pipeline, and that spurred rapid growth.

It made sense, as Prescott was the territorial capital back then. We had our own military base, Fort Whipple, and the father of future New York mayor Fiorello LaGuardia was a colonel in charge of the band there. Fiorello attended Prescott High School during his father's posting at Fort Whipple.

In 1932, the Olympic Games took place in Los Angeles, California. My father was so determined to attend the spectacle with his family that he bought a house at 2323 South Sycamore Street, not far from the brand new Los Angeles Coliseum. This house acted as headquarters for the West clan, not only our immediate family, but the family of Uncle William Ernest West. The three-bedroom house was packed with people sleeping on cots and in bedrolls.

It was my first experience with Southern California, and I loved it. I was sixteen, approaching the end of my high school days, and eager to explore this strange new city. I rode the old Red Line trolley system.

The Adams Street line took me downtown, where I enjoyed the Bimini Baths, a magnificent place with hot and cold water pools, a gym, a café, and a game room. There were no public swimming pools in Los Angeles at that time, so it was a great place for kids and teenagers to go.

I was impressed by the number of Hollywood movie stars that seemed always to be there. They stayed in nearby apartment buildings, and in an ornate hotel right across the street. Those buildings are still there, and although the Bimini Baths closed in 1950, the natural hot springs still exist beneath the street today.

The West clan drove or rode the street car to the Coliseum every day during the Olympics. The track and field events are what I remember most, along with the swimming. I saw Babe Didrikson win two gold medals for the hurdles and javelin events. I watched Eddie Tolan win the one-hundred- and two-hundred-meter sprints. I cheered on Helene Madison while she won three gold medals in swimming.

Those Olympics helped people forget that the country had entered a terrible economic depression, although my family was fortunate not to be suffering like so many others.

When the games ended, my father rented our clan "headquarters" to another family, and eventually sold the house.

But that wasn't the end of our California connection. A few years later,

Seated at left is Eula Mae West and Pauline. Lying at Pauline's feet is dog Buck. Standing behind them is Hugh. At right, standing: Eula Mae's father Steve Howard and Clarence. Seated, left to right: Laura (in small chair), Hugh's father J. Andrew West, Bonnie (on the ground), and Kenneth Andrew West holding Kenneth, Jr., on his lap.

my dad bought another house, this time in North Hollywood. We enjoyed the new address, 10418 Whipple Street, because of our connection with Fort Whipple in Prescott. My father actually transported the fort's flagpole to this new address, and erected it in the front yard. Unfortunately, the L.A. zoning laws barred anything that tall, so we had to take it down and bury it in the backyard. For all I know, it's still there.

My folks split time between the new home and the one in Prescott for a while, until they made North Hollywood their permanent residence during the war years. But before that commitment, they still had to raise three teenage boys.

Like his own father, my dad insisted that all of his children go to college. I attended a community college first, before transferring to Arizona State University.

It was a completely different experience, living away from home in a college dormitory. I stayed in the East Hall dorm, but that soon became too confining. The school kicked us out of there, and my classmates and I had to stay in the Casa Loma Hotel in Tempe.

The activity I remember best from that stay in the hotel had nothing to do with study or scholarship. It was poker.

We played the game like it was a holy ritual, often starting in the middle of the night. I became fairly skilled, and won often enough to keep myself in pocket money.

West (white shirt, pipe) plays chess with his buddies at Arizona State, January 1939. Gambling was how West earned pocket money during his college days.

To ensure that I would have more time to play and carouse, I decided to arrange my school courses toward becoming a teacher, and not a lawyer. This was a disappointment to my father, but to me, it seemed like the easiest way out. Besides, we had a lot of teachers in the family. My father had earned his way through college as a teacher, and my mother taught for a short time in Edgewood, Texas.

In addition to that, ASU wasn't even called ASU yet. It was the Arizona State Teachers' College at Tempe.

The study for a teaching credential wouldn't be too intensive, so I was assured of graduating on time. And when I enrolled, the student body was only about five or six thousand.

My first teaching job required me to instruct classes made up mostly of local Native American children. It was a tough maiden voyage for my career, because many of these kids were downright uncivilized. I actually wondered whether I'd made a big mistake in my career choice.

But one great event grew out of this. I started dating my future wife, Pauline.

I'd heard of Pauline in high school, so I already knew her when we finally met again on a bus bench a few years later. We both were returning from our student teaching assignments, waiting for the bus to return us to the college.

Pauline was twenty months younger than me, but we were in the same

West poses with his 1934 V8 Coupe near his home in Ontario, California.

college class of 1939. I gathered the nerve to ask her out, and that night we dined together for the first time at a Mexican restaurant.

On subsequent dates, I usually took her to dinner, but I never had much money. I had to play a lot of poker to afford it.

We both graduated in May 1939, with Bachelor's Degrees in Education. As the better student, Pauline achieved membership in the professional English fraternity, Sigma Tau Delta. She parlayed this into a teaching position at the Laguna School, outside of Yuma. It was one of those rustic, old schoolhouses with two rooms and real slate chalk boards on one wall.

Pauline shared a house with another teacher there. It was a decrepit old place that had a gasoline lamp for indoor light, and a kerosene stove for cooking. They actually had to travel into town to buy the gas and the kerosene. One time, someone put the fuels in the wrong containers and they nearly blew the place up. Aside from that, they only had to endure the frequent earthquakes and swarms of mosquitoes.

I soon received offers to teach in schools at Fort Huachuca, and Ontario, California. The better paying job was in Ontario, so I jumped at it. Having already experienced the joys of California, I knew it was the right move.

I told Pauline to give me some time to make my way, although she probably thought she was seeing the last of me. I didn't realize it then, but I would teach in Ontario for a total of thirty-one years, interrupted only by the war.

It was still 1939 when I arrived. Ontario was mostly orange groves back then. It was a delightful place. The food was good and the wine was cheap. I bought a used 1930 Model-A Ford with a rumble seat, and kept it for a couple of years, driving it between school and home. But every weekend I went to visit a lawyer friend in faraway Sherman Oaks, so I decided to get a faster car. I wound up with a V-8 red coupe, which was a very good little car. My wife drove that vehicle throughout the time I was overseas during the war.

My new students in Ontario were a dramatic change from the Native American kids I'd tried to teach in Arizona. These were nice, middle-class kids, and some of them were brilliant. I was living in a middle-class neighborhood just a few blocks from the school, and education was very important to those people. They made sure their kids were dedicated to school work.

I taught every grade, from sixth to ninth, during my tenure there. Many of my students were Latino, and they seemed to enjoy it when I embellished topics like history, to make the subject more interesting.

I remember one class I had in which there were thirteen kids named Jesus. They liked history, with the exception of Christopher Columbus. None of them understood why we celebrated Columbus Day, because they said he brought disease to the land.

In less than two years, I felt secure enough to get married. Pauline and I occasionally would meet in San Diego, and spend time together there, but since she was still teaching in Yuma, I had to make my proposal in a letter. My missive would have made Cyrano cringe: "I don't have much money, and I don't manage what I have very well, but if there's any way in the world we can get along on my salary, would you want to give it a try?"

I had to wait a while for her answer. The Laguna School was some distance from Yuma, in the middle of nowhere on an Indian reservation, so it seemed like forever before her response reached me. When it finally came, she agreed to marry me.

I went to Yuma and married Pauline in a little wedding chapel called Gretna Green on May 17, 1941. It was the quickie Vegas-style wedding and divorce establishment of its day. The ceremony was conducted by a justice of the peace named Reverend R. C. Robb. The first question he asked me was, "What's your wife's name?"

"Mrs. West," I said. Our relationship went downhill from there.

My honeymoon with Pauline also could be called a quickie. We drove straight to San Diego after the wedding, had dinner, spent the night, had breakfast and lunch, then went our separate ways. I returned to Ontario, and Pauline drove to her school in the Arizona boondocks, because we both had to finish teaching for the school year.

Less than a month later, we reunited and moved to Westwood, California, where we found an apartment on Barry Avenue. We spent a beautiful summer together while I attended some necessary courses at nearby UCLA, taking long walks through the Santa Monica bluffs.

When September arrived, and it was time for me to resume my teaching career, we moved to Ontario. We moved out of our apartment, and purchased a home at 119 East Carlton Street. We put down roots and started to deal with things like mortgage payments and other hurdles that newlyweds face. But it was one of the happiest periods of my life.

In late autumn of that year, everything changed. The news of the Japa-

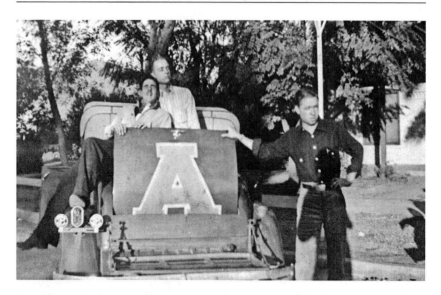

West, at right, poses near the rumble seat of his friend's car at Arizona State. The car was won in a poker game.

nese attack on Pearl Harbor stunned me, just as it stunned every other American. The country was at war suddenly, whether or not it was ready.

I was not keen on jumping into the fight. I had a wife and a mortgage to support, and two good jobs with which to do it. But I knew it was just a matter of time before I'd get the letter instructing me to report to my local draft board for a pre-induction physical.

This particular board did favors for certain guys to keep them out of the war. In fact, after the war I visited that draft board and noticed an inordinate number of fellows working in the place. I asked the retired colonel, "How do you manage to have so much help around here?"

"They're my boys," he responded.

"What do you mean, your boys?"

"I took care of them during the war," he said. "I requested they all be transferred to Ontario Air Base, where I was commandant."

It galled me that every one of those characters got to ride home each night on their bicycles while I was ducking bullets in Europe.

I received no preferential treatment, because the draft board didn't think much of schoolteachers. But I hoped to fail the Army physical, thanks to some leg injuries I'd suffered during my summers at Fort Huachuca.

No such luck. My draft notice came in November 1942.

The timing of the letter couldn't have been worse. Suddenly, I had to leave everything to my wife and fight on the other side of the ocean, perhaps never to come back. I don't mind admitting that it depressed and angered me.

My draft orders were to report to Fort MacArthur in San Pedro, Califor-

nia. Pauline drove me there in our little red coupe. We had to be at the fort by five o'clock in the morning. It was cold and damp that morning, a terrible day in every way. San Pedro seemed even seedier than usual.

Walking toward the fort's entrance, I wondered if I had made a terrible mistake in not taking the Army's offer to join the reserves. It didn't appeal to me at the time, because it was a ten-year commitment. I had a wife, a new house and a lifetime job, and I wouldn't trade all of that for a million dollars. So I had sweated out the draft, and now I was hooked.

I was a G.I. Government Issue. I wasn't a person anymore. I was property of the United States Army, and I didn't know what they had in store for me.

I found out soon enough.

West with Pauline at their Ontario home during his only furlough of the war, 1944.

CAMP CHAFFEE, ARKANSAS
—Basic Training

The words in the official document were flat and dull.

In accordance with General Orders, Headquarters, Armored Forces, Fort Knox, Kentucky, 1942, and pursuant to authority contained in letter, Headquarters, Army Ground Forces, Army War College, Washington, D.C., dated August 28, 1942, the 14th Armored Division is activated this date at Camp Chaffee, Arkansas.

Headquarters, 14th Armored Division, is opened at this station at 0001, November 15, 1942.

It was typical Army double-talk to announce the creation of a new armored division, but it settled my future.

I was processed at Fort MacArthur in San Pedro. This meant receiving a series of hypodermic shots that hurt like hell. The orderlies seemed to enjoy our discomfort. All of them probably learned medicine from Dr. Josef Mengele.

Following this, we received a short lecture on the articles of war, military courtesy, and sexual hygiene. Then we were issued our uniforms, and a motley collection of young men became indistinguishable figures in olive drab.

I received orders to board a train that would take me to a unit that barely existed, in a camp that was built just the year before in Arkansas. During the train ride, I tried to imagine what Arkansas would be like. I had only vague memories of Texas, which was the farthest east that I'd ever been. I figured Arkansas would be about the same. I would soon be divested of those naïve notions.

Camp Chaffee was near the western border of the state, which is separated from Oklahoma by the Arkansas River. It was just a few miles from the city of Fort Smith, located right on the river. The camp was named after Major General Adna Romanza Chaffee, considered an innovator in U.S. armored warfare, who died in 1941. Of course, none of that mattered to me, sitting in that train car crowded with other young men in ill-fitting new uniforms.

It struck me how young nearly all of the other guys on the train looked. It seemed like most of them were kids, teenagers or maybe a smattering of guys in their early twenties. I was twenty-six, and it made me feel alien. Many of the faces probably hadn't seen a razor yet. Most of the guys were away from their parents' homes for the first time in their lives. Some had never had a drink, or a woman. I was coming from a world of mortgages, career and marriage. One smart aleck already had called me "Pops."

The train stopped at a platform that seemed to be in the middle of nowhere. It was a sunny day, and somewhat warm when we debarked and formed into lines on the platform. There was an Army band playing to greet us. It made the whole scene surreal, hundreds of awkward, nervous young men standing stiffly to a bouncy martial tune. If the band was meant to make us feel welcome, it didn't work for me. I was more apprehensive about what would come next. It wasn't long before we all found out, as dozens of trucks came to take us away.

When I arrived at Camp Chaffee, the first thing I noticed was that nothing was flat. The whole vista rolled on mounds, set off against rocky hills and pitifully thin wooded areas of pine, birch and barren brush. I wrote off the barrenness to the fact that it was deep into autumn, but I figured the place was an eyesore no matter what season it was.

Our barracks resembled dwellings for California farm workers. Basically, they were four walls and a roof, divided into two stories with adjoining latrines. For many of us, including myself, using those open latrines took some getting used to.

The exteriors were whitewashed pine boards, so that they stood out starkly against the sparse, bare trees that surrounded them. Rows of thin cots and foot lockers crowded the interior, accommodating about forty men on each floor. The place reeked of damp new wood.

We made some clumsy attempts to introduce ourselves, as it was clear we'd be stuck with each other for many weeks, and perhaps much longer. But the informality didn't last long.

The drill sergeant was on us immediately. He made us stand rigidly in front of our cots while he delivered The Speech:

> This is the training ground for soldiers of the United States 14th Armored Division. It will be the most powerful, deadly, well-trained division in the history of warfare. And not one of you germs deserves to be part of it. You have to earn that right. And you do that by hard work, discipline and attitude. I'm not here to hold your hand. I'm here to turn you into soldiers. You will become killers, even if it kills you....

I don't remember much of what he said in the rest of that opening address. To a schoolteacher's ears, it sounded hollow and stupid. The Army wanted to treat me like a child. But I promised myself that I would go along. What else could I do? They had me cold.

Later, we received our general instructions: "The commanding general will not tolerate drunkenness.... Hitch-hiking will not be permitted...." And so on.

We recruits learned quickly that there was an "Army Way" to do everything. It had nothing to do with the right way or the wrong way. We learned to make beds the Army Way. We learned to peel potatoes and perform other KP duties the Army Way. We learned how to fall in and fall out. We learned about military courtesy — again. A lot of it made no sense, but you just had to conform. Anyone who didn't made the whole barracks suffer. That meant more exhausting physical training, called PT, more full-pack marches, and more punishment jobs. It was quite a system for straightening out the screw-ups, because the weight of peer pressure from fellow recruits is even greater than fear of the meanest drill instructor.

There were a couple of guys in our platoon who couldn't seem to get out of their own way during calisthenics, marches, and a lot of basic drills. I was thankful that I wasn't one of them. They immediately became favorite targets of the DI, who made their lives utterly miserable. He'd single them out every day, and it got to the point where they couldn't help screwing up, no matter how hard they tried. And that only made matters worse.

One of the guys actually broke down and cried like a child. I heard his loud sobs fill the barracks after lights-out, and they continued until one of the guys jumped up and made him stop. It wasn't pretty, and I felt awful for the guy. But at the same time, I was just as exhausted. All of us were. Our bodies ached for the sleep he was denying us.

We heard rumors about this guy or that guy who'd snapped under the fierce methods of a drill sergeant, and shot themselves with their service rifles. It was always in some other unit on the other side of camp, or something that happened before we arrived. There was never any corroboration, so I personally put it down as one of the many silly rumors that pepper camp life. There were more important things to worry about.

The man in overall charge of the 14th was Major General V.E. Prichard. Typical of Army structure, he was a vague figure rarely seen by enlisted men, but who had god-like power over our lives. Judging from the way his junior officers and NCOs worked on us, it was clear that Prichard made sure the division was preparing for one thing, and one thing only: combat.

"This is the 14th Armored Division," he told his officers. "It's going into combat as the 14th Armored Division, not as tank regiments, or infantry regiments, or artillery battalions. You have to know the other fellow's job, his business, and what he's going to expect from you."

That directive filtered down to us through the sergeants who trained us. We were expected to know all the jobs of the combat arm, in addition to our own. And the officers in the classification section told us what our jobs would be, based on simple questions like "What did you do in civilian life?" They also gave us aptitude tests, some of which were as simple as counting blocks. With more than ten thousand recruits pouring into camp, it was no surprise that their classification process had stuffed some round pegs into square holes.

Basic training settled into a monotonous, torturous routine. Each day began before dawn to the strains of a bugler's attempt at "Reveille," drowned out by the harsh barking of our DI. He burst into our barracks like a mad dog, shouting, "Up and at 'em, ladies," sprinkling in expletives that some of us had never heard before. We had to be fully dressed and standing to attention in front of our made beds in a preposterously short time, or suffer the consequences. Those consequences meant longer PT than usual. It made for a wild scramble, with guys banging into each other, hands being stepped on, curses being spat — a daily Texas fire drill.

The DI never was satisfied. He always found some mistake, or perhaps we just didn't finish in time. Because of this, we never learned what "normal" PT was, since the sergeant always punished us with extra calisthenics in the cold morning air. And the weather in Arkansas was beginning to get nasty.

One of our least favorite activities was to run in full gear to the top of Potato Hill, where the division did most of its artillery and mortar practice. The constant barrages had turned the hill into a pile of ashes, and after you spent some time crawling around on it, you were plastered from head to toe with the stuff.

Camp Chaffee featured another training facility, called Hitlerburg. It was a collection of abandoned homes a few miles away from division headquarters. The families that used to own them had moved out when the Army took over the area.

Hitlerburg was set up to train the infantry for house-to-house combat. Trip targets were set up in windows, doorways and alleys. When they popped up, the officers and sergeants expected them to be riddled with the live ammunition we used during the drills. It's dangerous anytime recruits train with live ammunition, but it's downright deadly when recruits have to fire their weapons instantly, without seeing whether some poor guy in the outfit might be in the way. It was a wonder half the recruits weren't shot in those exercises.

Our less colorful destinations included Spreading Hill, Central Road Range, and the 25th Street Anti-Tank Gun Range. None of us cherished going to any of them.

After morning PT, we marched to the cafeteria for breakfast. We already were so tired, we barely could chew the scrambled eggs that were the staple of the cooks. Then it was more marching, more calisthenics, more insults from screaming DIs.

The Army's idea of a reward was to let you ride in a tank. Every new man got a tank ride. When my turn came, I didn't see it as a reward. I never liked tanks. To me, they seemed like steel coffins. It was a crazy attitude to have, as I was part of an armored division, but there it was.

My tank ride was in a lumbering old M-3 medium tank. It was already obsolete, but the Army didn't know it, and would learn that painful lesson the first time an M-3 entered combat against German panzers. It was a ridiculously tall contraption, reminding me of a mechanized medieval siege engine.

I climbed up to the turret. It was like scaling a cliff. When I squeezed myself through the hatch, I immediately was overcome by a claustrophobic discomfort. The driver fired up the engine, which was deafening. He put it into gear and the tank lurched forward, whiplashing my head. It seemed like every bump in the ground was magnified, and right away the whole compartment stank of exhaust fumes. Soon, the heat of the engine made me break a sweat. My claustrophobia might have had something to do with that, too.

The tank commander told me I could look outside through the periscope, like he was doing me a big favor. I peered into the tube, and it struck me that this was the only visual contact with the world outside after the tank was "buttoned up" for combat. My claustrophobia sharpened. It seemed like a mad way to fight a war, and I decided right then that I would do everything I could not to be assigned to tank duty.

When the officers felt we were ready, they started putting us through maneuvers. Since we were an armored division, they'd assign us problems during war games. For those who aren't familiar with this quaint Army training method, units were divided into two teams, each bearing a specific-colored armband. The officers issued tactical commands, and the troops followed them, hoping to mimic real combat maneuvers. The only difference was that no one shot at each other. Military referees were on hand to declare whether your unit had won a skirmish, or had been eliminated.

My unit always thought it was very nice to get knocked out of the game early, because these things could last a whole week. They'd start on a Monday and go all the way to the weekend, so we liked getting shot out of it on Monday. And when we were in the field, we always made a point of bivouacking in a spot that was surrounded by civilian houses, so people would bring food to us.

Most of the time, we performed these maneuvers in rain. That winter, it seemed like it rained every day, and just about all the guys in my unit had a cold. The uniforms they'd supplied us weren't made for winter, so when we had to train in the mountains, it was a real hardship. Sometimes we'd be stuck in the field for ten or twelve straight days.

At one point during our maneuvers, I caught pneumonia. We were camped outdoors, and I crawled into a corn crib to find some kind of shelter and warmth. My friend, Ed Dean from Upland, California, found me shivering and curled up in a ball.

"You look like you're about gone," he said.

I told him I had a little cold.

"Cold, hell," he said, and dragged me to the division hospital.

The operating room was inside two or three insulated railroad cars, and they were all warmed by electrical heaters which they kept running all night. It was like entering heaven. I went from frigid, muddy and sloppy to fresh, clean and warm.

I remained in this Paradise for a few days, until they shipped me to a tent city that had been turned into a hospital. It was poorly heated by a collection of old pot bellied stoves, and we had to be careful not to set the tent on fire, while stoking the stoves to get warm. We only succeeded in not burning down the tent. It was miserably cold in there.

The doctor in charge of my tent poked and probed me. Then he made his diagnosis: Nasal Pharyngitis Catarrh Severe. Maybe he wasn't allowed to call it pneumonia, or maybe he just didn't want me to know what the hell I had.

Later, when we got into combat, the Army supplied us with uniforms much more suited to winter. They claimed the improved uniform was due to the lessons learned by the 10th Mountain Division when they were training in Alaska, but I liked to think that the Army also took the clue from how we suffered during that rainy winter in Arkansas.

Once I recovered from "nasal pharyngitis catarrh severe," I was back in the hands of the DI, marching miles with full packs. In my opinion, all of our DIs were jackasses. They'd make us take twenty mile hikes every now and then, toting fifty-pound packs. They usually filled our packs with rocks, so they'd weigh fifty pounds.

But there was one DI who was all right. He let us dump the rocks and fill our packs with newspaper, so they looked full. He was smart enough to know that no one in their right mind would be running around in Europe with a pack on his back. He also let us relax and play cards when we bivouacked in the woods. When we returned from one of these maneuvers, we marched past the officer's club shouting cadence lustily. They'd say, "My God, there goes that 94th outfit. They must be supermen."

This DI was a World War I veteran, so he knew what we would face when we got overseas. He's the man who warned us about heating our helmets. When we were in the field, we thought nothing of filling our steel helmets with water and heating them over an open fire for shaving. He told us that the heating would soften the steel, so it wouldn't stop a bullet. He also pointed out that the heating made the helmets black, and easy for enemy troops to see. I took his advice for the time being, but a lot of the guys continued using their helmets as pots, and then covered them with green netting to solve the blackening problem. A few of them would make the DI look like a prophet.

By December 23, the last of the new men arrived at Camp Chaffee, and the 14th Armored Division was up to full strength — 706 officers, 15,490 enlisted men. The next day, the whole division drew up in formation, all of us in drab overcoats to fend off the cold. It was a stunning spectacle, so many soldiers standing in perfectly ordered lines and columns. With everyone dressed alike, the formation looked like a massive block instead of a collection of individuals. And that's exactly the way the Army wanted it.

We had our first look at General Pritchard that Christmas Eve, as he stepped to a platform and spoke to us.

"You men here before me, new and old, are going into battle as the 14th Armored Division," he said. "Our trials will be bitter then, but even before that time, from now on, through all our training we shall have a hard and difficult time. You may look around and see the size and strength of the division. Activation was only six weeks ago. Very near this birth of Christ, with God's help, the 14th Armored will play its part in the struggle against the evil forces abroad in the world today."

After the speech, a quartet of soldiers sang "Silent Night," followed by a few tunes from some of the regimental bands. For the enlisted men, that was the extent of the Christmas holiday. The next morning, we all went on a dismounted march. Later, orders came for us to prepare vehicles and weapons for a command inspection.

For the great majority of the 16,000-plus men in camp, it was the first Christmas away from home. The brass tried to allay our homesickness by arranging an enormous Christmas dinner: fruit cup, cream of celery soup, roast turkey with dressing and gravy, cranberry and orange relish, celery, olives, pickles, radishes, potatoes, green beans, tomatoes, corn pudding, hearts of lettuce with Russian dressing, hot rolls and butter, mince and pumpkin pie, ice cream and spice cake, grapes, oranges and apples, nuts, mints, hard candy and coffee.

Typically, the food was plentiful, but not very good. The guys from the South who were used to going hungry were pleased with the bounty, but I thought the army cooks always butchered the food. They didn't know how to cook, and they just tossed it at you. Besides, many of us were too exhausted to enjoy it. They drilled us all of Christmas Eve and Christmas day.

One of the toughest and most demanding ordeals was the live fire exercise. It was just like the war games, only with live bullets, mines, artillery and tanks. There always were soldiers wounded, and sometimes killed in these exercises. The brass tried to hush it up, but we knew about it. We'd notice when someone was missing. But death and injury in an army training camp can have a hundred causes outside of live fire maneuvers. A lot more soldiers get hurt or killed in simple driving accidents. Once in a while, a guy would get drunk and run off the road. It was something you accepted after just a few weeks in camp.

But fear of injury didn't prevent the Army from making live fire exercises as real as possible. I remember how long it took me to get used to the concussion from nearby explosions. Sometimes it would nearly knock the breath out of me.

They made us crawl through fields where they'd pre-planted explosives, while firing machine guns over our heads. We had to learn to stay low as we crawled, because they were shooting the limbs off the trees above you. They'd planted sticks as reference points along the way, and we knew if we didn't stay below them, we'd get our heads shot off. It's amazing how soon you get used to bullets flying over your head.

They also had explosives hooked up to electric detonators, so as we crawled forward, evading the machine-gun fire, some guy would press a button and blow out the side of a hill right next to you. One time, this buried me in dirt, and I had to dig my way out. It gave me the feeling that it was the real deal, and that if I survived basic training, I'd really be prepared.

The exercise I hated most was lying in a field while the tanks ran over me. They didn't do it deliberately, but they were traveling thirty miles per hour in pitch darkness. With only a periscope to see ahead, the drivers simply couldn't make us out. The DIs told us to dig a slit trench, so we wouldn't be crushed by the tank tracks as they rolled past. If you dug deep enough, it allowed the tank to pass over without touching you. My slit trenches always were more than deep enough.

For some reason, I became a fairly good shot with a bazooka. We used disabled tanks as targets in these exercises, as well as moving targets. I learned to lead with my aim, and after that, it was simple. I'd rest the bazooka on my right shoulder while my partner behind me loaded a rocket into the rear of the pipe. When he pulled the wire that armed the rocket, he'd tap my helmet and I'd fire. For some reason, even though I always held the bazooka on my right shoulder, those exercises messed up the hearing in my left ear. Counting the pneumonia, it was my second patriotic sacrifice.

On the last night of maneuvers, I think the division fired everything we had. We were in Kentucky by this time, and it scared the local civilians half to death. We tried to limit the damage to local property, but sometimes it just happened.

The army was so determined that we'd be ready for combat, they kept us training at Camp Chaffee, as well as in Kentucky and Tennessee, for nearly two years. None of us dreamed we'd be kept in the States so long, but our general wanted the 14th to be an elite unit, even though it had no prior history.

The DIs and officers accomplished this by drilling us until we could handle our equipment like it was an extension of ourselves. At first, they issued us M-1 Garand rifles, and we learned to take them apart and put them back together blindfolded in less than two minutes. We even shouted odes to it as we marched. ("This is my rifle, this is my gun. One is for killing, one is for fun.")

The Garand was a fine rifle, a bolt action 30.6 caliber that was extremely accurate, and fired semi-automatic from a five-round clip. Later, I was issued an M-1 carbine, or more precisely, an M-2. It was much smaller and lighter, semi-automatic, with such a small kick that you could fire it from the hip or even holding it with one hand. It had the reputation of being less accurate than the Garand, but in the right hands, it was a great weapon. My own M-2 was manufactured by Remington Rand, the company that made typewriters and adding machines. It was just another company that had retooled its factories to make weapons of war, and I liked to think of my M-2 as a "business machine."

One day, I was firing the M-2 at the target range when a particularly nasty first sergeant approached me. I'd had a history of grief from this man, who assigned me to all the bad duty he could invent. I'd been shooting targets at rapid fire when the sergeant arrived and said he didn't like the way I held my rifle. I had the belt twisted around my arm to steady my aim, something I'd learned was most effective, but he shouted that no one could hit a target like that.

Since he wasn't my drill sergeant, I loaded a fresh twenty-round magazine and shot the whole clip rapid fire at the target with the rifle belt twisted around my arm. The target came back with 20 bulls-eyes. He never said a word. He just stalked away, looking for some other dog face to pick on.

My troubles with this man started when I was given the assignment to teach basic reading and writing skills to some of the uneducated enlisted men. Colonel Chamberlain, who knew I'd been a teacher before the war, had put me to work teaching English to a good number of soldiers—eighty or ninety in the classroom at first. He just wanted to be sure they could read the writing on boxes of ammunition and supplies, so they could function in the field.

All of the students were extremely eager to learn how to read and write. Some of them even had artistic ability, and I took advantage of this by getting them to draw pictures, and then making flash cards out of them. I'd hold up the picture, and they'd learn how to spell what it was. It was fun for many of them, but there were others who just weren't enthusiastic about learning.

Steadily, I noticed that the most unenthusiastic students stopped coming. When Colonel Chamberlain eventually asked how it was going, I told him it was a good class that behaved pretty well, but the number of students kept shrinking. He said it was because the division was putting some of our guys on shipping orders to serve in the Pacific. The division wrote off any soldiers who didn't show interest or enthusiasm, and sent them to fight in the steamy, malarial Pacific jungles. It was quite a disciplinary club to hold over our heads, because no one wanted to see Pacific duty.

To repay me for my teaching, Colonel Chamberlain issued me three-day passes. That's when my problems with the first sergeant began. He withheld my passes, saying he had orders that no one in our company would get a pass.

"Nobody gets a pass without my OK," he told me. "I don't care if you're Jesus Christ's best friend."

The guy was a jerk, pure and simple, and for whatever reason, he hated my guts. He warned me not to try going over his head to the captain or the colonel, and not to try leaving camp. I didn't intend to violate his orders.

One day I ran into Colonel Chamberlain, who asked me how I was enjoying my three-day passes. When I said I never got any, he promised to check into it.

"That probably will get me into trouble, sir," I told him, explaining the situation. Apparently, he heeded my warning, because I never got any of those passes.

Whatever passes I did manage to earn while at Camp Chaffee, I used to visit nearby Fort Smith. It was a small port city on the river, and a great place to relax. But with three entire army divisions stationed nearby, it was overflowing with soldiers. You barely could fit on the sidewalks due to all the enlisted men walking there. The military probably outnumbered the civilians.

But the locals were very friendly to soldiers. A lot of the men enjoyed spending Saturday nights at spots like the New Café, Playland, Pearl Harbor and the Hollywood. Some of the guys traveled all the way to Fayetteville, a

75-mile drive, to meet the girls on the campus of the University of Arkansas. Being military, we didn't have to worry about gas rationing.

During one leave, Pauline visited me in Fort Smith. I'd reserved a room for her in the Goldman Hotel. It's impossible to describe the joy I felt in being with her again, if only for a short time, and forgetting my military life for a while.

We had corresponded frequently since my arrival in Arkansas. I quickly learned the army procedure for mail, too. It was all spelled out for us on a bulletin board, beneath a photo of Betty Grable smiling over her shoulder. A giant poster displayed a model envelope, announcing, "This is now your correct address."

I suppose my letters were full of complaints about my new "correct address" and its miserable weather. Having been raised entirely in the Southwest, I had never seen so much rain in my life. And apparently, the locals hadn't seen as much either, because that winter saw record rainfall in western Arkansas.

I remember one day when an excellent officer, George England, arranged a big steak barbecue for our unit. He had some cows slaughtered and a lot of fires lit in preparation for our big feast. But it rained so hard and for so long that it put out all of the fires. That was the end of our steak feed.

We didn't know it at the time, but the storms pouring all of this rain on us also were piling snow on the Rocky Mountains, where the Arkansas River begins. With spring, those snows began to melt and by early May, the Arkansas River became a raging floodwater, swelling anywhere from a mile to fifty miles wide. It was like a long tidal wave, sweeping mud, bridges and houses with it, magically depositing everything into lowlands that had never seen water before.

No one in Fort Smith dreamed how bad it would be when the flood finally reached their city. Flood stage for that area is twenty-two feet, and by the first week of May, the waters had risen above that, with no sign of stopping. On May 12, 1943, Fort Smith was under more than forty-one feet of water. Cellars flooded. Bridges, highways and houses disappeared. It was the worst flood in the history of the region, and responding to the emergency, General Prichard called out the division.

Our first job was to rescue the people marooned by the rising waters. It was not unusual to see a house floating down the river with a lot of people standing on the roof. Livestock were everywhere, some swimming downstream, some floating, dead and bloated. We saw people in that condition, too. It was a bad situation.

Our division was equipped with seeps—amphibious jeeps—and they became vital in rescuing the stranded civilians. We also had the new DUKWs, larger-tracked amphibious vehicles that were designed to ferry men across rivers under fire. We even hooked motors to the back of pontoons, which barely could move against the current going upstream. Whole families, along with their pet dogs and cats, and their few most important possessions, crammed into anything we could find with a motor that could float.

In addition to bridges, the flood had washed out all the water and gas lines, so our engineers had to move quickly. We built all kinds of bridges, pontoon bridges, Bailey bridges, and we repaired the bridges that had been damaged. We had to do it quickly, so that trucks carrying food, medical supplies and precious drinking water could reach people.

Sometimes I had to stand guard on those bridges and abandoned properties. One bridge was a 1,065-foot steel and rubber span, anchored by three-quarter-inch cables, and my job was to knock off the debris that constantly crashed against it. The current was shooting by at twenty miles per hour, smashing trees and parts of houses into the guy wires and anchor ropes, making an ungodly racket.

I was fortunate not to be guarding the pontoon bridge downriver. The current snapped it, and the twenty-two soldiers and officers who happened to be aboard got the ride of their lives. We were amazed and thankful that no one was hurt. In fact, the only injury suffered by our division during the flood was when a bridge was being removed, long after the flood crisis.

In addition to bridge duty, I helped run the water and natural gas lines across the pontoon bridges to keep the city of Fort Smith supplied. It was a break from routine training, and I welcomed it. I didn't realize that it was training me for what I'd soon see in war.

Later, I heard some funny tales from other units involved in the rescues. One involved a 78-year-old woman who refused to let the engineers remove her from her flooded home. She said she'd lived there since 1868, and had no intention of leaving. The engineers said, "Yes, mother," and carried her out of there.

We had to call for water rationing as a precaution, while engineers set up water purification points in Camp Chaffee itself. We were allowed two gallons of water per man, per day. This included washing. Gasoline also was rationed, and none was available for anything but essential work.

I slept in small increments wherever I happened to be. It wasn't bad, as the spring sunshine had warmed the area. I grabbed food and coffee at little stands that popped up here and there.

By May 26, the river level had begun to drop. The crisis was over, and it was impossible to know how many lives the division had saved.

One guy who owned a milling company in Fort Smith was very thankful for the help we gave him. He was a World War I veteran, and he invited me to his house several times, where I enjoyed some good home-cooked meals. He even loaned me his automobile. It was a good feeling, knowing how much the civilians appreciated our help.

After the war, I was commissioned to write a plaque that would be bronzed and erected in Fort Knox, Kentucky, commemorating the work of our division in combat. I wanted to include mention of the help we gave during the flood, but the officers in charge wouldn't allow it. They wanted the 14th to be known as a fighting outfit, and not some WPA unit. I still don't agree with that decision.

The end of the flood crisis meant a return to training. I didn't welcome it, although we were finished with most of the basic nonsense, and were proceeding to combined arms training. By now we were well acquainted with our weapons, so we had a lot better chance of not shooting each other during the exercises. I even started to get used to bullets whizzing over my head as I crawled over the rough terrain, and to shells exploding just yards from me in the impact areas. It was the army's way of teaching you to know whether an artillery round is incoming our outgoing. Each has a different sound, and with time, you can recognize the caliber of the shell and the gun that fired it.

West poses for his basic training portrait in Camp Chaffee, Arkansas. Note the Signal Corps insignia on his hat.

By this point, I had been transferred to the Signal Corps. All the marching I'd done in basic training had aggravated a varicose vein condition in my leg that began long before, when I was slogging around in Camp Huachuca. The marching had broken down the veins to the point where my legs ached all the time. I had to check myself into the hospital again, where they operated on my leg. Once I healed, they transferred me out of the marching units, and into the communications end of the Signal Corps.

It was a huge relief, not only to be riding instead of marching, but to be away from the first sergeant who'd been bracing me so hard. I'm sure he was glad to get rid of me, too.

The Signal Corps was a comparatively plush outfit. Not only did you get to ride in armored cars, half-tracks, and peeps— armored division slang for the standard jeep — you were assured of mainly rear echelon duty in combat. The Corps usually was stationed a couple of hundred miles behind the front, which kept you far away from the bullets and shells.

Right away I noticed there was a lot less formality in the Signal Corps than in the unit I'd come from. Most of the officers were West Pointers who'd already seen combat in several places, so they were more realistic. They didn't want you to salute them, for instance, because they knew that would get them shot up in combat. For the same reason, they wore no insignias of rank, and more or less depended on one another.

What I did not like about the Signal Corps was learning to refine Morse

Code. In fact, I hated coding and encoding. It was dull work, transposing messages to the code in the book, and sending it out. I realized the importance of keeping the information hidden from the enemy, but it was a pain in the neck all the same. You didn't have to send messages word for word, so long as you got the gist of it right. Of course, you had to be precise about numbers, and if you missed one digit, the brass would barbecue you.

Being in the Signal Corps also gave me more time to visit the base library. I'd spent a lot of time there during basic training, because it seemed like the only civilized place in Camp Chaffee. There was no yelling, no abusive sergeant busting your chops, and even a few good books. The library clientele were more of my kind of people, and I made some lifelong friends there.

One day, the head librarian introduced me to another soldier, Robert Crossan. I was glad to learn that he was a Californian, too. Years later he received a Pd.D. in education and was a professor at California State University, Long Beach, for many years. Around this time, I also met Merrill Lipton, who became a psychiatrist after the war, and a good friend. Poor Merrill probably chose his future profession in reaction to basic training, during which he always seemed to draw the worst jobs.

The Californians in camp seemed to gravitate toward each other. I suppose it was because we couldn't stop bragging about our beautiful state, the weather, the movie stars and the relaxed lifestyle. Most of the guys from elsewhere became so tired of our home state pride, they stopped listening. But there were enough fellow Californians to fill the void.

My best friends during the war, Bill Walby and Ernie Wharton, were Californians. We were the three W's— Walby, Wharton and West. Even Ernie's army serial number was close to mine. I remember giving him a hard time about his dog tags, which, when turned over and upside down, spelled "Oh hell."

Friends brightened the otherwise tedious days of training. The Division was stressing combined maneuvers during the summer of 1943, which meant riding in tanks and vehicles of every kind on the dusty camp roads. And the dust at Camp Chaffee was like talcum powder. It got into your eyes and down your throat. The tanks churned tons of it into the air, so our maneuvers resembled the newsreel shots of Oklahoma dust storms during the previous decade. By the end of each exercise, everyone was plastered in chalky dust. We looked like ghosts, bearing only a hint of flesh color around the eyes of those men who were lucky enough to be issued goggles.

As cold as Arkansas was the previous winter, it blistered that summer. It never cooled off until very late at night, and everyone's uniform was dark with sweat by midday. We tried to keep our minds off the heat any way we could, including talking about the war. Since we already knew the 14th Armored was destined for service in Europe, that's where we focused our attention.

On July 9 that summer, Anglo-American forces invaded Sicily. They'd driven Rommel, von Arnim and their German-Italian armies out of North Africa during the previous months, bagging nearly a quarter of a million Axis prisoners, if the newspapers could be believed. Now the papers were lauding the early success of the Sicily landings. They didn't tell us that it was supposed to be a British show, and that the British had become bogged down in the Sicilian hills. To us, the German Army seemed to be in retreat everywhere, having just suffered a catastrophic defeat at Stalingrad. There was actually some talk among the guys that it might be over before we finished our training.

I wasn't one of those optimists. Having read so much history, I knew how many wars had been predicted to end quickly, and how few of them did. But I was thankful that the army was determined to elongate our training

Ernie Wharton, Bill Walby and Hugh West — the California contingent of Troop A — posing somewhere in Germany, 1945.

period, even though essentially it meant two stints in basic, along with protracted special training. The War Department had special plans for us, although we didn't know it at the time, and they wanted the 14th Armored thoroughly prepared for its mission.

Training Memorandum No. 98:

"The following will be stressed during this period: gunnery and combat firing; work in fortified area; communications training; make-up in all instruction missed by absentees; air-ground training; maintenance."

And so it went. There were inspections. We were quizzed. "What's the effective range of a bazooka?" "How often should you change the air filter in this half-track?" "How do you plot coordinates for an artillery bombardment?"

During all of this, guys were meeting girls from Fort Smith, falling in love and getting married in the camp chapel. There were boxing matches, softball games and swimming races. There were dances, card games, USO shows, and bingo nights. There were bond-selling tours. We even had an air show, a demonstration of the latest in Army Air Force fighters, dive bombers and heavy bombers, held at the Fort Smith air field.

I partook of only a few of these activities. I didn't care much for watching sports, and being married, the dances were occasions to hang with buddies instead of dancing with local girls. That pretty much left only the card games, which I enjoyed immensely. Not only did I get the chance to drink beer in good company, I supplemented my army pay with poker winnings.

Late that summer, the War Department reorganized all of the armored divisions, reducing their tables of organization and limiting their size to 10,000 men. We'd still be among the most powerful divisions in existence, in terms of tanks, mechanized guns and artillery, but the reduction in manpower made us more mobile and easier to supply. Our unit, the 94th Armored Reconnaissance Battalion, became the 94th Cavalry Reconnaissance Squadron, Mechanized. I remained with Troop A, but my friends in Troops D and E were transferred to other outfits.

The reorganization took a lot of time, but training continued. By October, we were deemed ready for our first big test. Dozens of high ranking officers, including General Courtney Hodges— then commanding the Third Army, to which we belonged— descended on Camp Chaffee. They watched us use every weapon we had, from artillery to bayonets, for five days.

94th
Cavalry Reconnaissance Squadron, (Mechanized)

The emblem of the 94th Cavalry Mechanized Reconaissance Squadron, West's outfit in the U.S. 14th Armored Division.

I was amazed at how much we had improved as a coordinated fighting division. We weren't the green kids of a few months ago, trying to learn how to aim a round at a moving target. Our tanks attacked cross country, our rifle platoon defense was crisp, our bivouacs and rail loading were fast, and our recon patrols were effective.

The brass was very impressed. Rumors circulated that we were going to be moved out of Camp Chaffee. In early November, rumor became fact when an advance detachment of the division left for the Tennessee Maneuver Area. It was the first time any part of the division had been moved, and we knew the rest of us would soon follow. Once we did, we'd have to live in the field constantly, just as if we were in combat. We would operate as part of an army, fighting other divisions. We would be using umpires instead of live ammunition, but the officers would make it as close to real combat as possible. And if we did well, we soon would be going overseas for the real thing.

When the rest of the division began to move from Camp Chaffee, it was an enormous undertaking. Every piece of unit property had to be accounted for, from tanks to typewriters. Every soldier's kit, from his rifle to his socks, had to be in good condition.

We left our vehicles to the 12th Armored Division, which was moving into Chaffee after us. Our new vehicles were waiting for us in the Tennessee Maneuver Area, near Lebanon Junction. No one knew what to expect there. We were going to a different state, with different weather, and different locals.

We boarded trains by company and battalion. My unit climbed into what was little better than a boxcar. We tried not to let in too many guys, so we'd have room to sit on the floor, which was filled with strands of hay and other debris from previous journeys.

It was quite a different ride from the train I took into Arkansas. On that train, I was surrounded by fresh-faced kids. Now I was looking at faces that were much wiser and harder. I wondered if I looked different, too. I certainly felt like a different man. I wasn't as apprehensive about the immediate future, even though I had no idea what that future held.

The train pulled out.

Tennessee—Advanced Training, Field Exercises

It was cold when our train finally stopped. We hopped from the boxcar to the platform in wet, miserable weather, knowing that we'd be living in it for at least the next few weeks.

We'd been dropped off in a place near Lebanon, Tennessee, called Carthage Junction.

"Here's your new home," someone said.

I looked around. There was nothing there. We'd have to build it.

Lebanon, the only civilization within miles, had a population of just more than forty five hundred souls, located in the north-central portion of Tennessee. It seemed like hillbilly country.

When I first entered our new barracks, I felt like turning around and setting up outside. The place was a pigsty. In fact, many of the guys were convinced that it had been a series of pig pens until very recently.

It was our job to clean it up. The only way that seemed feasible would be to completely tear it all down and start over. Fortunately, we didn't have much time to stew over it. The officers put us into maneuvers right away.

We bivouacked in a field outside of Lebanon, colorfully called Tucker's Gap. About eighty years before, I knew that soldiers of the Federal and Confederate armies had marched these same muddy fields in the rain and sleet. They were probably just as miserable as I was now, only they were also murdering each other in places like nearby Murfreesboro, which had become hallowed ground as a national monument to the Civil War battle.

The officers issued us new equipment, everything from vehicles to rifles. But all the light weapons were covered in Cosmoline, which was used to prevent corrosion while they were stored and shipped in wooden crates. It's a gelatin-like substance, but in the cold weather, it hardens. We simply couldn't scrape it off the rifles and machine guns with our bayonets, which is normal procedure. Someone finally came up with the bright idea of using gasoline. We poured it over the weapons, and it worked. After a few hours, the whole unit smelled of gasoline. It was a wonder that we didn't blow ourselves up.

Once we had the weapons cleaned, they issued us blank cartridges to make the maneuvers seem more realistic, and off we went. I tried to spend as much time as I could in the cab of the half-track. I generally tried to sleep there, listening to the radio monitor so I could hear what was going on. On the colder nights, I'd run the engine to keep warm, because the exhaust manifold was underneath the front seat.

When we traveled at night, we had to drive "blackout." This meant covering our headlights, so that only a thin strip of light illuminated the pitch black road ahead. It was tedium mixed with terror, trying not to slam into the vehicle in front of you while staying on a road you couldn't see. And some of the roads were roads in name only. We had to pass through quagmires, and avoid ditches that could swallow a tank.

The brass divided our maneuvers into eight "problems." My unit was in the "blue" force, and we all had to wear blue armbands, to differentiate us from the "red" force for the umpires. Our first "problem" was to take the high ground near a certain crossroad, and cover it. Naturally, we got lost. Rural Tennessee is conducive to that, because road signs were nearly non-existent. We had to rely on maps that looked like they'd been drawn by my grade school kids back in Ontario.

When we finally arrived at the crossroads, we were relieved to learn that members of our "blue" team had already taken the objective. We wouldn't have to listen to any lectures about screwing up.

Since it was Thanksgiving weekend, the cooks served us turkey dinner in the field. We had to wait until the day after Thanksgiving to eat it, but warm food was welcome, even though it was typically heavy Army fare. The officers seemed pleased with the outcome of this first "problem" in our maneuvers, so we got the weekend off. I went to Murfreesboro, attracted by its history. The town had a lovely rustic charm, and it was still very small, with less than eight thousand inhabitants.

But Murfreesboro wasn't a place that would please soldiers looking for a weekend of beers, movies and night life. For that, most of the men traveled to Nashville, the nearest city of any size. There, you could find a hotel room with a warm bed, and maybe even a girl. Nashville's streets were crowded with young men in olive drab uniforms every weekend.

The following week, my recon unit spearheaded the "blue" team as a screening force. We were on our way to the objective when the umpires suddenly told us to stop. I didn't quite understand when they announced that the tactical lessons of the problem had been accomplished, but it was good news just the same, because it meant the whole maneuver was finished. I suppose they thought we were getting the hang of coordinated movement as a division, and at times it was a majestic sight. Lines of medium tanks rolling across country, long rows of infantry supporting them along the roads, towed artillery being set up, engineers solving crossings, medics roaming along the lines, and an endless stream of two-and-a-half-ton trucks, the staple transport of supplies and men for our division.

One by one, we maneuvered through the "problems," sometimes making a mess of things, and sometimes not. By the fifth one, my unit was assigned to a task force headed by Colonel Huddleson, with orders to capture a bridge over the Cumberland River. When we arrived on the high ground above it, the "red" team looked like they would blow the bridge before we could capture it. Of course, they wouldn't really blow up a bridge so important to the local population. It was up to the umpire on site to decide whether they were successful or not.

For some reason, they delayed, and Colonel Huddleson ordered us to charge. We swarmed among the "red" soldiers and crossed the bridge. It was a holy mess, which degenerated into something like the war games I played as a kid.

Two blanks fired into the air.

"You're dead!" shouted the corporal who fired them.

"The hell I am," answered the lieutenant from the "red" team.

"I shot you! You're dead!"

"You missed me! I'm blowing the bridge!"

"You can't blow the bridge! You're dead, damnit!"

"The bridge is blown," shouted the lieutenant with finality, pleased with himself.

"The hell it is," interrupted an umpire, who'd been watching the comedy. "You're dead. The bridge stays in."

And so ended our glorious victory at the battle of Cumberland Bridge.

The very next day, victory was snatched from us when a friendly "blue" plane flew over the bridge, and the umpire — mistaking it for a "red" plane — ruled the bridge destroyed. It was a lesson about the gods of war, who giveth and taketh away.

By the time we'd finished the exercise, it was Christmas week, my second holiday season away from home. The weather turned bitterly cold, and we were living in pup tents in a field just south of Nashville. They delivered our mail to us there. Pauline's letters warmed me, if only for a while. I wished I was with her in sunny California, especially after I learned that we were to have our second turkey dinner of the season in the field.

I decided one cold turkey dinner on a blanket inside a pup tent was enough for fiscal 1943, and managed to find a ride into Nashville. There, at least I could eat Christmas dinner sitting at a table. A lot of the guys in the division were like minded, so Nashville hosted a good portion of the 14th Armored that Christmas.

The weather grew even more miserable by New Year's Eve. General Prichard wanted to give us a break by ordering the division to a new bivouac area north of the Cumberland River, near Westmoreland, but we had to drive at night in a blustery ice storm under blackout conditions. Once again, I sat shotgun in the half-track, shouting warnings and instructions to the driver while I continually wiped fog off the inside of the windshield. The so-called defroster was useless, and the wipers couldn't keep up with the freezing rain. There was no way I was going to open the door window and stick my head out to see in that fierce downpour. It was as if we'd chosen death over discomfort.

The driver was even more nervous than me.

"I can't see!" he kept repeating.

"Keep driving!" I always responded.

We sounded like the priest and the altar boy in church, only our call and response was in English expletives instead of Latin. I knew if we stopped even for a moment, the vehicle behind us would slam our half-track into a ditch.

When we miraculously arrived at our fancy new bivouac, there was nearly a mutiny. It was a thin road, surrounded on both sides by steep hills. Like most of the vehicles, we parked our half-track on a hillside, leaning at a steep angle, and resolved to sleep in the cab that way. It was not comfortable, but it was a lot better than many of the other guys had it, trying to sleep in open vehicles. A lot of them just crawled under trucks, jeeps, even our half-track, and slept in the mud and water running down the hillside. Anyone trying to force their way into our cab that night probably would have been shot.

That was how I brought in the year 1944. I wondered how much longer the war in Europe would last, and hoped it might end before our transfer there. I kept track of the news. The Russians had defeated the *Wehrmacht* in an enormous tank battle at Kursk the previous summer. The Germans had retreated hundreds of miles along the entire Eastern Front since then, approaching the Polish border.

Italy had surrendered, but the campaign there had slowed to a crawl. Everyone was talking about an invasion of France in the spring. It must have been the worst kept secret in history, and I pitied the guys who would be in the first wave of that show. Then it struck me that we might be among them.

When we tackled our final two "problems," many of us wished we were storming the beaches of France instead of shivering in Tennessee. By this time, it was snowing heavily, and temperatures plummeted. Tanks froze into the ground, and we had to thaw the tracks loose with anything we could think of. Many times, there was no point to it, because the tankers couldn't start their frozen engines. And trying to do any kind of work with frozen hands and numb fingers was practically impossible.

Again, we were lucky in the half-track. We'd stored a bottle of brandy behind the front seat, and the occasional sips kept my innards warm.

One of the geniuses among the brass decided that this was a good time for the division to run a malaria control "problem." We had soldiers stumbling through blizzard-like conditions wearing mosquito nets over their helmets and down to their shoulders. The medics had to dispense atabrine, which we tossed out as soon as no one was looking. Our tents had to be set up with mosquito bars placed over the stiff-frozen canvas. It amazed me that the organizers of this nonsense even knew that mosquitoes spread malaria. No mosquito in his right mind would be out in this weather. We were the only creatures dumb enough to do that.

When we finished the last "problem," everyone went wild. We fired off every weapon we had, blank cartridges, fake grenades, anything that made noise. It didn't matter to me that cleaning my rifle after shooting blank rounds is a much bigger problem than after shooting live ammunition. I needed to blow off some steam.

The generals seemed to understand, so they gave the division a weekend leave. The celebration continued through Sunday night, with the inevitable episodes of rowdiness. The MPs had a busy couple of days, and there were a lot of hangovers when we returned to work Monday to prepare a move to our next stop: Camp Campbell, Kentucky.

We all knew that this would be the last leg of our training. When we finished there, we would ship overseas, where no one used blanks.

KENTUCKY—Further
Advanced Training, War Games

My first view of Camp Campbell made me think I was back at Chaffee in Arkansas. The place was built after the war began, with the familiar two-story barracks of raw pine, freshly painted. It wasn't very inviting, but it promised a roof over our heads instead of a canvas tent, a greasy vehicle, or the cold sky.

We were allowed to gather ourselves after we arrived, before proceeding with gunnery practice, and some of the other drills we needed to perfect. This meant cleaning up the half-track, working on the engine and making sure it was ready for action. We would undergo the thousand-mile and six-thousand-mile vehicle inspections, the latter meaning that we needed to lube the half-track in addition to basic maintenance.

Leaves and weekend passes were issued generously. I took the opportunity to see the two nearest cities, Clarksville, Tennessee, and Hopkinsville, Kentucky. Suddenly I had a lot of time on my hands. I even found a few moments to peruse the division's official weekly newspaper, tragically titled *Turret Topics*. It was a good way to keep up on announcements. They usually included bulletins from our Special Service office about organizing baseball, basketball, softball, boxing, bowling, and ping pong sports programs for us. It also announced dances at the Armory in Hopkinsville, where a lot of the guys who didn't meet and marry girls from Fort Smith met and married the Kentucky locals. Even one of our captains from the 94th Cavalry married a local girl, and our commanding officer, Lieutenant Colonel Thomas McCollom, gave the bride away.

As usual, I wasn't too interested in the sporting events. I hated watching, and my leg wouldn't let me play worth a damn. Instead, I explored the local area, and even toured nearby Mammoth Cave. It was a habit I would continue throughout the war, which brought me to so many exotic and beautiful places, in addition to the ruins left behind by battle.

On February 3rd, the division announced that we would undergo Army Ground Force Individual and Unit Combat Intelligence Tests in April. To me, this meant we'd almost certainly miss the invasion, because there was no way to move ten thousand men and all their armored vehicles and equipment across the ocean that quickly.

In the meantime, we plunged into our advanced training. The tanks took gunnery practice. By this time, we were equipped with the M-4 Sherman tanks, whose 75 millimeter guns had a distinctive hollow bang. We were training with the first generation Shermans, which had proved no match against the German tanks in North Africa and Italy. Their guns couldn't penetrate the armor of any of the newer German panzers, because the barrel hadn't been designed for high muzzle velocity. We heard that the army had made improvements in newer versions of the Sherman, which had a longer barrel for better results in knocking out enemy tanks. There also were improvements in the shells, which were better able to pierce armor, and the armor of the Sherman had been thickened.

The most disturbing news about the early Shermans came from the poor guys who fought in them. They called them "Ronsons," after the cigarette lighter. It referred to the newspaper ad for that Canadian-based lighter company, which boasted, "Always lights on the first strike." It turned out that the early Shermans had been built with an unarmored stowage container for the main gun shells, so that any round hitting in its vicinity would set it off like a roman candle.

I felt real sadness for the young men who had to suffer excruciating deaths in combat due to these stupid design blunders. It made me wonder what other flawed equipment we'd been issued, and how we might not find out about it until it was too late. Fortunately, the newer Shermans had been improved so that by the time our unit arrived in Europe, that deadly design flaw was eliminated.

There was one piece of equipment I was sure of — the Browning .50 caliber machine gun. Many of the half-tracks had been equipped with at least one of these, sometimes ring-mounted on the cab hood. Some had twin machine guns on a rotating turret mounted in the rear compartment, and a .30 caliber machine gun on the cab roof.

During our gunnery trials, I had to fire both a .50 and .30 caliber Browning machine gun. It was part of our anti-aircraft exercise. I aimed skyward at targets. Sometimes they were towed aircraft, and sometimes they were radio-controlled planes. It was an unbelievable feeling of power, grasping the twin handles of those weapons while pressing both thumbs down on the trigger, and feeling the machine gun buck. The belt flew through its chamber, spitting empty cartridges in the air while I corrected my aim according to where the tracers flew.

Next on our training schedule was anti-tank machine gun practice. I fired at modified tanks, which had additional steel plates welded to their sides, front and back to protect the men inside. I wondered what it must be like to sit inside those tanks and take hundreds of .50 caliber hits, and I gave thanks that I hadn't been assigned to tank duty. I didn't know at the time that they were much safer than the half-tracks I'd been using. But it wasn't long before I started to hear that the soldiers in Europe referred to them as "Purple Heart boxes." It seems any shell heavier than a machine gun bullet could pierce the steel walls of the rear compartment, which often acted as a personnel carrier.

West poses next to his half-track, the vehicle in which he spent most of the war. The half-track couldn't stop much more than bullets, but in West's mind, it still beat walking. He is stopped here on the Autobahn.

Unlike the superior German half-track design, our walls were straight up and down, with no angling that would cause shells to ricochet. The vehicle was absolutely incapable of stopping any hand-held rocket-launched weapon like the German *panzerfaust*. In fact, the only real benefit to the thin skinned vehicle was that an 88mm round would fly right through the two rear walls.

But it had its more positive advantages, the main one being that I'd be riding and not walking. The cab kept you warm in the winter, and there was some storage room behind the seats, where I often stowed wine bottles, food, chocolate and whatever else I could scrounge in the field. It was like being in the old artillery detachments of the nineteenth century, which were the envy of every army, because they could carry so much contraband in their caissons.

Aside from additional training with my M-2 carbine and the bazooka, I relished taking target practice with the Browning Automatic Rifle. It was a relic, used in the latter stages of the First World War by our doughboys in France. The thing weighed more than twenty-five pounds, and was one of the first fully automatic assault rifles. But it fired a heavy 30.06 caliber bullet with incredible range and accuracy, which was something that a lot of machine guns lacked. And it was perfect for the soldier in the field, because it never jammed, no matter how much mud and water it encountered.

Our army continued to use the BAR because of its proven record in the field, and because we didn't have a suitable replacement until many years after the Korean War. I marveled at its simplicity, and thought Browning, its inventor, must have been a genius. He'd also invented our army's standard pistol, the Model 1911 .45 caliber automatic, which is still being used by American elite units like the Navy Seals and the Delta Force. I personally thought it had a little too much boom to be accurate, but it certainly had the one shot-one kill ability that every soldier wants when his life depends on it.

The rival assault weapon to the BAR in our arsenal was the Thompson sub-machine gun. This was the iconic weapon of choice by gangsters, boot-leggers and G-men during the Prohibition Era and throughout the 1930s. But its use in the field was limited mostly to officers. It had a variety of magazines instead of a belt, so its firing was limited to 30 to 50 rounds usually. After a magazine was spent, you had to eject it and pop in another, then rearm the thing. And firing it took some getting used to. It was a .45 caliber machine gun, so the muzzle tended to climb as you fired it in long bursts. You really had to grasp the front grip hard to keep it from climbing off the target. I wasn't that thrilled with the thing, but it was incredibly popular with the men because of its colorful history and frequent appearance in Hollywood movies.

A lot of our advanced training had to be done in the rain. As winter broke in Kentucky, it seemed to rain every day. I wondered whether we'd have to make a repeat performance as a civilian rescue division if the Cumberland River flooded. The rain caused cancellation of many divisional reviews, which was OK with me. I never felt that marching, standing at attention, and listen-ing to generals' speeches would help me to survive on a battlefield.

But the Army had a built-in aversion to idleness. Whenever a review or a gunnery exercise was postponed, the brass immediately thought of some-thing else to occupy us. Often, it was a simple "cleaning up" directive, which instructed every soldier to clean small arms, latrines, kitchens, and anything else they could think of.

The Kentucky rains eventually gave way to the heat of summer, and I learned that Camp Campbell was just as stifling as Camp Chaffee at that time of year. It reminded me of how lucky I'd been to live in California, where at least the heat was dry, and there weren't a myriad of mammal-sized insects and mosquitoes feeding on you.

Summer also brought tests and surveys to measure the technical readi-ness of every soldier in the division. All of our unit commanders were ordered to be sure that each man in their outfit had a complete record of his training, and to make a report on all men who required additional training. The spe-cialists in the division were to be tested to make sure they were fully trained to perform their duties in their Military Occupational Specialty (MOS). This meant testing for every occupation — mail clerks, blacksmiths, mechanics, tele-type operators, draftsmen, crane operators, dental technicians, meteorolo-gists, tank gunners, and hundreds of other specialized duties.

In my case, it involved testing for signals and code. I simply had to show them I could translate incoming codes to English, and sculpt outgoing English messages into gibberish. It was all part of the final preparation for a new acronym in our lives, one that had complete dominance over our futures: POM. Preparation for Overseas Movement.

The invasion of France had just occurred. Everyone was eager for information about this unit and that division involved in it. Spotty information about Omaha Beach gave us mixed signals. It was a cake walk. It was a meat grinder. Everyone had a different idea of how the invasion fared in Normandy. The only thing all of us knew was that the Anglo-American armies had grabbed a foothold on Fortress Europe.

And men of the 14th Armored Division were still honing their combat skills in the humid heat of Kentucky. On June 17, just eleven days after D-Day, the division began reinforced battalion exercises. My unit, the 94th, went up against the 125th. It was more of the same war gaming, only this time we were sweating instead of shivering. But even I could see that my outfit had become a slick, organized team in the field. Everyone seemed to know his job after so much repetition, and didn't have to think about it. Our cavalry recon unit seemed to operate automatically now.

On July 10, the whole division marched in review for General Prichard. It was to be the last time. He was leaving us, and we'd soon have a new commander in chief, Brigadier General A.C. Smith. My squad had the honor of escorting General Prichard to the division boundary, army ritual for the changing of the guard. We were saying goodbye to the man who had trained us so well.

All of us were curious about the new commander. We tried to form opinions from first impressions. General Smith was tall and stocky. His dark hair was peppered with some grey. He exuded a quiet confidence and determination. These attributes would serve him well in the year ahead, as he led us through combat.

Following the pomp surrounding our new commander, they sent us back into the field for more training. We were stressing air-ground cooperation now. Since my unit was destined to shoot ahead of the division to probe for enemy strong points and formations, coordination with the air force was going to be vital. All of us had to learn how to bracket targets from maps bearing numerical and lettered codes. The area in front of us was divided into target boxes, each with their own designations. Those targets were radioed or called by landline into air force command, which passed on the instructions to its planes. Even though the targeting calls were to be done by officers, all of us had to know how to do it. There was no guarantee in a hot combat situation that any of our officers would be alive.

These exercises in Kentucky were interesting, because for the first time I saw how devastating close air support can be. Once, my unit came up against an opposition strong point on a hill. We called in the target information, and in what seemed like seconds, a flight of P-47s swooped over our heads and dove on the hill. No bombs were dropped, of course, but it was invigorating to hear the roar of those airplane engines so close above me that my chest vibrated.

Mission accomplished. We received a nod from the brass for our work. We were starting to feel like an elite outfit.

In August, we had the climax of our training, a divisional firing exercise. We put on a real show — tanks, mechanized artillery, towed artillery, anti-tank guns, bazookas, machine guns, and small arms—for three days. It was an awesome display of firepower. Our division had become the most powerful mobile unit ever seen in warfare.

That same month, we read about the invasion of Southern France. That put our troops on both ends of the occupied country. We didn't know yet which end would be our entry point to the war, but everyone was sure that it wouldn't be long before we found out.

Early September witnessed a generous distribution of furloughs and passes. It was nice to get away from the training and the constant schooling for a couple of weeks. I took advantage of my time off by staying in a local hotel, eating restaurant food and enjoying the small-town Kentucky color. But like all vacations, it went too quickly.

I was back in Camp Campbell on September 20, and everyone was buzzing about the breakout of our forces from Normandy. All summer, our troops were involved in a torturous, slow slugging match, fighting from hedgerow to hedgerow in Normandy. Now they were out in the open, where their training and mobility was being put to use, finally. The German Army in Northern France simply wasn't prepared for the onslaught of air and armored power.

We watched it happen on the newsreels in camp, which always preceded the Army training films. These latter films were enjoyable, not because of their instructiveness, but because of their sheer stupidity. They were supposed to be teaching us things like how to behave if captured, how to recognize booby traps, how to recognize venereal disease, but the dialogue and the acting were so wooden, they were met with hoots from all of us. The titles were almost as silly: "Know Your Ally, Britain"; "Sucker Bait"; "Private Snafu"; "Kill or Be Killed."

The film that grabbed my attention was "What to Do Aboard the Transport." It dealt with our immediate futures, because the division already had begun marking everything from tanks to belt buckles for packing and shipping. We already knew our next destination, thanks to the new group of letters added to POM: NYPOE POM. New York Port of Embarkation. Preparation for Overseas Movement.

They told us what to take and what to leave behind. The instructions were explicit and detailed, down to the amount of underwear we had to pack. We were checked individually by the company commander for our property books and Government Issue forms. It was a logistical miracle, preparing more than ten thousand men and all divisional equipment for departure.

The personal belongings that wouldn't make the trip were to be sent home. I put together a package and sent it to Pauline, with another letter. It would be my last one from Kentucky.

Transportation units went to work. They blocked and chocked our vehicles, and loaded them on to railroad flatcars. It was impossible to count how many trains there were, and all of them seemed to stretch for more than a mile behind the locomotives.

Finally, the day came for my unit to depart. We dressed in our wool uniforms, our packs full of personal equipment, armed and helmeted, and marched to the train station. A transportation officer checked us on, name by name, while making little marks on his roster papers.

When I boarded the train, I was pleasantly surprised to see they weren't asking us to travel all the way to New York City in a foul-smelling cattle car this time. We had Pullman coaches, and they only squeezed three men into each compartment. As crammed as we were, it was almost luxuriant compared to what we'd been used to.

I spent a lot of time playing cards with the guys in my car during the trip. I won a few dollars, and had some laughs. But my favorite pastime was simply to stare out of the window at the passing countryside. I was struck by how green it became as we moved further east. It truly was a big, beautiful country. I let myself wonder whether I would ever see it again.

NEW YORK TO MARSEILLES—
The Difficult Atlantic Crossing

The first time I saw the New York skyline was from the train, my head sticking out of the open window. Everyone had seen it countless times in movies and magazines. None of that had prepared me for the majesty of those skyscrapers. I could easily see the Empire State Building, and nearby, the silver-topped steeple of the Chrysler Building. I ached to experience the city, but there would be no leaves granted now. We were here strictly on business.

The entire division had gathered in Camp Shanks by October 8. It was a bleak-looking place, but it served its purpose. This would be our final staging area before shipping out. Apparently, the guys who ran the camp were experienced veterans when it came to moving entire divisions on to transport ships, because they did it with almost factory precision.

We went through boat-loading drills. We went through abandon-ship drills. We practiced clamoring down the rope netting on the side of a model ship, while wearing full pack and rifle. It wasn't easy to haul myself down on sagging rope steps in full gear, because dozens of others were doing the same thing at the same time. The rope netting was in constant motion, swinging away from the hull and swaying side to side. A couple of guys fell and were banged up badly. Had this been over the ocean, they certainly would have drowned.

Our chief entertainment during all of this was visiting the PXs at Shanks, which were just tiny wooden shacks. But they sold sodas and hot dogs, and offered a place to relax and goof with your buddies. The 1944 World Series was blaring on all of the loudspeakers there. It was an all–St. Louis show that year, in which the St. Louis Cardinals played the St. Louis Browns—one of the rare times when both World Championship contenders played in the same park.

Cigarettes cost sixty cents per carton at the PX. Even though I wasn't much of a smoker, I loaded up. I knew they'd be handy as barter items in Europe, where niceties like tobacco and chocolate were almost extinct.

On October 13, we marched to the trains, carrying our blankets, musette bags, gas masks, weapons and duffle bags. They lined us up and checked us out to make sure we had all of our equipment. Then they loaded us again by roster into the train cars. This time, we were ordered not to remove our equipment. It would be a short ride to Weehawken.

A band played us out of the station at Shanks, and the crowded train bucked and rolled for half an hour before it stopped at the Weehawken terminal in New Jersey. When we climbed down the train steps to the platform, we already were on the pier. Small crowds of men, women and kids gawked at us, like we were another species.

When our turn came, we boarded a ferry that would take us to Staten Island. It was already night, so the New York skyline had become a beautiful panorama of vertical pinpoints of light. I made sure I was at the rail to enjoy it.

The ferry took us to the dock where our ship waited. It was the U.S. Army transport, *General James Parker*. But before we could board, we had to watch a procession of German and Italian POWs disembark. They were a miserable-looking lot, and there were hundreds of them. As ragged as they looked, every one of us thought they were the lucky ones. They were going to stay here in America, while we headed to Europe and combat.

When the POWs were gone, it was our turn to move. One by one, we were checked by name and serial number. Then it was time to climb the uphill grade of the gangplank and get aboard.

The *James Parker* was better than the Liberty ships the Army usually employed to transport soldiers across the Atlantic. It used to be the ocean-liner *Panama*, owned by the fruit exchange, and it had a slightly better setup for our quarters.

But it was incredibly crowded down below. My first impression of the compartment where I would spend much of the voyage was like something out of Dante's *Inferno*. It was a sea of bodies, ropes and hammocks. Everything was in constant motion, like an ant hill. The hammocks had been hung tautly throughout the compartment, and there were five levels of them. I made sure I grabbed one of the lower hammocks for myself, because if anyone rolled out of a top level hammock, the fall probably would kill him.

In addition to our recon units, we shared the ship with engineers and ordnance personnel. Most of the guys were college educated, and they seemed to blend better, which was going to be important under such crowded conditions. They were an intelligent bunch of characters, and they possessed many unusual skills and abilities that would serve the division well in the months to come. After all, we'd been training in the States for nearly two years, while the Army was sending other units overseas in masses. This long, specialized training kept most of our unit personnel intact, and created a strong bond throughout the division.

It was sunny and calm the day our armada pulled anchor and moved in line through New York harbor. I was on deck, like everyone else, for this important event. I inspected the face of the Statue of Liberty, its copper surface turned a beautiful green by the elements, as we slowly sailed past. When I looked around, all of the other men on deck were doing the same thing. An unusual silence fell over everyone as we glided past the iconic symbol of our nation, and it seemed that every man was moved by the thought that he was leaving its safety behind, perhaps forever. But I felt sure that deep inside, each man knew the sacrifice he was making had to be made, because across the ocean was a dark opposite to liberty that had to be obliterated.

Our convoy must have been a spectacle to everyone watching from the piers and buildings that lined the harbor. In all, thirty-five ships formed a procession out to sea, carrying all the men and equipment the 14th Armored Division would take to war. I watched Coney Island glide past, with its distinctive steel parachute ride jutting into the sky. I watched land recede, until there was nothing but open sea and growing darkness. We were on our way.

I soon learned to spend as little time as possible in my "quarters." The compartments below were hot, sweaty and foul-smelling. The heavy aroma of the bilges mixed with the ugly stench of hot oil from the engine room, formed a miasmic cocktail with the scent of sweating men. Since some of the guys began to be seasick, the tinge of vomit joined the mixture. It almost made me gag that first night, trying to sleep in a swaying hammock while the glare of bare light bulbs stabbed through my eyelids. The constant rumble of talking, snoring men didn't improve the ambience.

It turned out that, being amid ship, I was much better off than the poor guys who were stationed in the lower bow holds. The *James Parker* had many levels below deck, and the lower levels near the bow shot up and down like a carnival ride with every pitch of a wave. It took more than a week on land in Europe before the ground stopped rolling for those fellows.

I stayed on the main deck as much as I could. The fresh air was better, and it was so much cooler. The *James Parker* had air conditioning below decks, but it wasn't designed for seven hundred men. It worked fine for bananas, but not troops. And it didn't always work, either. There's nothing worse than to wake up in the middle of the night and find out that the air conditioning has failed. I used to wake up gasping for air, half punchy.

Not everybody could make it to the top deck. But I was determined to be one of the guys who did, so I marked all the exits immediately. I probably lost some sleep, but I made up for it with comfort.

Meals were an adventure on board, too. There was a large room below deck which served as our kitchen. Tables were built into the floor, but there were no chairs. We had to eat standing up, because there wasn't room to sit. Everyone became so used to eating on his feet that it took some time to learn how to do it seated when we hit dry land.

It seemed like the mess hall was open continuously. They served breakfast for five hours. The guys who weren't too sick to eat might have been sickened by the dehydrated eggs that were the staple on board. Lunch and dinner usually consisted of boiled potatoes and boiled hot dogs. Just about everything was boiled. Needless to say, the chefs weren't *cordon bleu* caliber.

When the mess hall wasn't dispensing gut-fill, we watched movies there. Most of them were B-grade titles that escaped from Hollywood. The only memorable part of those movies was that they always featured one or two beautiful women. This has a tremendous effect on men who've been crowded into a steel box with hundreds of other men. It's both a pleasure and a pain. For some, like myself, it only reminded you of the woman you loved, who you wouldn't be seeing. For others, it produced a frustrating sense of longing.

Each night at sundown, a voice on the loudspeaker announced, "Blackout. No smoking on deck. Close all ports." I usually was on deck at those times, and I watched while the naval personnel conducted their nightly boat drill, rotating and training their anti-aircraft and three-inch guns against imaginary planes and submarines. We were under orders not to talk to the ship's personnel, although I had several friendly chats during the voyage.

I also made a few new friends from among the engineers on board. I spent a lot of time with a guy who'd been a reporter for a newspaper in Green Bay, Wisconsin. He was a very knowledgeable person who could talk about almost everything. I had another friend who was in the beer brewing business. The war was just a temporary interruption of his career, and when it ended, he bought a German beer franchise and brought it back to the United States, where he sold the rights to the Miller Brewing Company. He was just one of a dozen interesting stories on board the ship, which was just one of so many similar ships. Our convoy spread from horizon to horizon, with the destroyers and destroyer escorts at the outer edges, blinking signals back and forth. Enemy submarines always were a concern, but no one in our division seemed to think about them. There was only one day when our ship had to maneuver, while the air force dropped depth charges on what they thought might be a U-boat. I imagine it was a false alarm, because we never saw any U-boats during the voyage.

It was clear the Navy, Merchant Marine and Army had become very organized in transporting troops and supplies across the Atlantic at this point in the war. The convoy followed a zigzag route, while the escorting warships flitted about its edges like highly trained sheep dogs.

None of us knew our destination, except that we were headed to Europe. There were dozens of rumors, though. Some said we were headed to England. Others said we'd be landed in Normandy, and trucked to the front lines from there. My reporter friend was convinced we'd land in Antwerp, Belgium, where new harbor facilities were supposed to be opening. Almost no one guessed southern France.

The one sure thing was that 14th Armored didn't spend all that time training and equipping with hundreds of tanks, armored cars, artillery, and half-tracks to be stationed in some safe rear posting. Every one of us knew that we were going to where the fighting was hot and deadly.

One day, all of the speculation ended. The loudspeaker announced that our destination was Marseilles, France. Marseilles. I knew it was the largest port city on the French Riviera. I'd heard of its reputation as a tough town with a long history of criminal activity. That was the extent of my knowledge about this first piece of Europe that I would experience.

On October 26, I was on deck again to watch the ship glide past the famous Rock of Gibraltar. I borrowed someone's binoculars so I could get a better look, and spied the guns of the British installations that loomed above the straits. Beyond it was the coast of Europe. Turning the binoculars to the other side of the ship, I could see the sandy shores of North Africa. The city of Tangier stood out starkly with its brilliant, white structures.

As the convoy turned into Marseilles harbor, small boats guided our ships through a channel that had been cleared of mines. From the sea, Marseilles looked like any other city, although its skyline wasn't close to that of New York. Instead, this skyline was mottled by barrage balloons drifting on their steel cables above the city. And high above them, American warplanes droned as they performed their combat air patrols.

We'd spent two weeks crossing the Atlantic Ocean — two weeks of salt water showers and cold water shaves on a hot, rolling bucket. I was ready for solid land. But it wouldn't be a simple matter of dropping the gangplank and walking on to French soil. The harbor was dotted with the hulls of sunken ships. The retreating Germans had sunk about eight merchant ships in the harbor where the loading and unloading takes place. They'd filled them with cement, so it would be impossible to move them. They counted on these obstacles to put the harbor out of commission. But they hadn't counted on American ingenuity.

Our engineers came up with the idea of using our Bailey Bridges, welding them to the hulls of the sunken ships, and making a road from one ship to the next. They built a zigzagging steel track on which all of our equipment, including our heaviest tanks, could drive directly from the transports to the dock. Counting the additional vessels that arrived in port behind our convoy, we must have unloaded about a hundred ships that way.

The Germans also had destroyed the harbor installations. I could see enormous tangles of twisted steel that once had been cranes along the docks. The warehouses were ruins, without roofs and in some cases, without walls. The repair work was underway, however, being carried out by German and Italian POWs.

When it was our turn to disembark, I grabbed my pack, rifle and duffle bag and joined the long line that walked the twisting bridge ashore. My first step on French soil landed on cobblestone. The streets of Marseilles were paved with the light-colored bricks that are always so pleasing to the eye.

Marseilles itself, however, was not so pleasing to the eye. It was a tough, dirty town. Not even the Gestapo could tame it, although they certainly tried. They couldn't handle all of the red light districts, and the criminals that populated them. There were a couple of streets right on the waterfront that ran for several miles, where the criminals and prostitutes were concentrated. When the Gestapo learned they couldn't clean it up, they decided to blow it up. They mined the whole area, giving its inhabitants twenty-four-hours notice before setting off the explosions. The buildings were obliterated. The streets were

Three enormous cranes jut into the sky above Marseilles harbor, where West's unit debarked following its trans–Atlantic voyage.

filled with rubble. And it took just one day for the criminals and prostitutes to return for business as usual. They lived there like rats. The Gestapo couldn't get rid of them.

And neither could we. Our MPs had a hard time keeping them away from the troops, despite the standing orders that we were not to accept gifts of any kind from the inhabitants. We assumed these "gifts" included venereal disease.

In addition to the civilians, the MPs were struggling to control the Senegalese troops. These African colonials fighting for the Free French Army were an unruly mob when they went on leave in Marseilles. They had a weapon that was like a knife, and the way they used it could cut off a man's head.

The Senegalese were causing a lot of trouble in the city, and when one of them killed an American soldier, the Army tried to hush it up. To avoid embarrassing questions and paperwork, the official note sent to the dead man's relatives claimed that he'd died of pneumonia in a combat zone. That avoided any investigations.

Our division had to bivouac about eight miles from the docks. We marched it, and I'm positive that every step was uphill. For whatever reason, it was hell. I'd been on much longer marches in training, but the two weeks spent on board ship must have weakened everyone's legs. My own legs weren't fit to march long distances, anyway, so I joined the chorus of complainers until we reached the bare hills outside of the city.

When we halted, I was too tired to pitch a tent. Big mistake. It started raining around midnight, and I had to roll myself in my two blankets close to a fire to keep from shivering to death.

The next day we started taking care of business, which meant re-equipping ourselves while the division unloaded its tanks and other vehicles. A lot of men were busy taking peeps out of crates and assembling them. More than a few guys simply hopped into a truck or a peep parked on the street, and drove it away. There was no such thing as grand theft auto in Marseilles.

I had the good luck to be posted on guard duty in Aix-en-Provence briefly. A coastal city less than 20 miles from Marseilles, Aix was once an ancient Roman settlement. It still had Roman baths. It was a delightful place to wander and sightsee, except for the bodies of French collaborators who'd been left hanging from the lampposts.

The first time I saw a man swinging limply, my brain couldn't process it. I looked around me, to see whether other people were cognizant of the hideous tableau. People went about their business, as if it was nothing out of the ordinary. For an instant, I wondered whether I was hallucinating the hanging man, because men, women and children passed without reacting to it.

As I moved closer, I saw there was a sign hanging from the man's neck. In French, it said, "This is what happens to traitors." I didn't dare move any closer than reading distance, and tried not to take in the bloated, discolored appearance of the corpse. It occurred to me that I would soon be used to such things, just like the people passing me in the street.

There were many cadavers hanging from telephone poles and flagpoles in the cities of France. It pointed up how ferociously the French people hated the Germans. This was underscored when I met the local historian of Aix, Madame Pomois. She hated the Germans with a rare passion. I was sure that I never would be able to reach that level of hatred.

Looking for a respite from those gruesome displays, I strolled the beaches near Aix. I had to admit that they were beautiful.

"These are almost as good as the beaches in Southern California," I said to a trooper who was accompanying me.

"Are you nuts?" he responded. "The French Riviera is one of the most beautiful places in the world. Why are you comparing it to California?"

"You haven't been there."

That was my stock response to anyone who doubted my state's beauty. I guess I was getting on people's nerves, but I didn't care. As far as I was concerned, Southern California was Paradise, and every other place was sorrowfully second rate.

I also spent a good deal of time in the Aix town square. It was November at this point, and getting cold, but it didn't prevent the town's elderly men from gathering in the outdoor cafes. They sipped their drinks and turned their heads to follow the progress of American troops speeding past in peeps and trucks. And above the ancient stone fountain hung another dead collaborator, his body slowly twisting in the breeze.

During the day, the sidewalks and streetcars were jammed with a kaleidoscope of nationalities—Berbers, Senegalese, British, American, soldiers, sailors, Red Cross girls giving away coffee and doughnuts, French women scrounging cigarette butts from the gutter, prostitutes with painted faces, dirty-faced children begging for chocolate.

At night, the streets were empty, save the constant roar of military trucks heading north. North, toward the war. Occasionally, there were air raid alarms, but the war never touched Aix again.

Through all this, the division reassembled all of its equipment, the millions of spare parts and details, as it gathered itself into a fighting force. Acetylene torches lighted the night, as men welded and hammered equipment into shape. We had only two weeks to reorganize, before heading to the front.

At the end of those two weeks, I hopped into the cab of a half-track. The driver ground it into gear and we moved out. It was time to see what we were made of.

Rhone Valley to Alsace
—Initial Fighting

Driving along the Riviera, I could see signs all around that this was the invasion area. Deep craters scored the beachfront, where large naval shells had landed. There were ruined houses all over the hills above the sea. Some bore signs saying, "For Sale" in French. Other signs were in German: "*Achtung! Minen.*"

We passed the burned-out hulk of a Sherman tank, its hatches opened. A truck moving in the opposite direction revealed its cargo, rows of dead American soldiers lying in its bed.

The road turned north, away from the shore. We drove through Nice and Cannes. I watched through the half-track window as French civilians lined the streets, cheering, waving, tossing flowers on the hood. I knew we didn't deserve the adulation. We hadn't done a thing yet. But it still felt good.

When we drove into the countryside of the Rhone Valley, I understood why our invading armies called this "the champagne campaign." Everywhere I looked, there were vineyards. It reminded me of home in Ontario, so I loved the Rhone Valley. It was a picturesque panorama that stretched out before us through the windshield, complete with castles and beautifully painted barns.

There were plenty of stops along the way. You don't move a whole armored division up a road at break-neck speeds. We took advantage of the pauses by mixing with the locals. It seemed as though every French farm had a wine cellar, and the locals were happy to hand out bottles to their liberators. The trip to the front was turning into a wine-tasting excursion.

I never considered myself a wine expert, but having lived in the wine country of Ontario, I knew a little. The French wines were excellent, but we had to be careful just the same. We used my friend, Ernie Wharton, as our official taster. Ernie loved to drink. He'd drink anything, and if Ernie could drink it and not drop dead in fifteen minutes, we'd all drink it, too.

This was an important advantage, because every now and then we'd get something that tasted awful and made us sick. Since the local farmers offered us a drink wherever we went, using Ernie's trailblazing gifts became SOP — Standard Operating Procedure.

The farmers of the Rhone Valley probably never changed their daily routines during the German occupation. As we passed farm and vineyard, they continued those routines under the eyes of American troops. They worked their fields from early morning to dusk. Their women worked alongside them. And when the work day ended, the men spent the whole night drinking in the local tavern. I couldn't help but like them. They seemed like a grizzly lot, but they were much different from the stuffy Parisians I'd meet later.

One morning, as our miles-long procession of vehicles crawled along the road, I peered out the side window and noticed several black dots in the distant sky. I didn't think much of them at first, as they progressively grew larger and took on the distinct shapes of fighter aircraft. I counted four of them, and when they came within a mile, they turned, revealing the black crosses on their wings. They were German Focke-Wulf 190s.

"Get the hell out!" my driver shouted.

I was momentarily frozen in my seat. It was my first contact with a hostile enemy. It was my first opportunity to be killed in combat. I was like a deer in the headlights.

The roaring buzz of the plane engines as they turned to strafe across our column finally knocked me out of my trance. I popped open the door, and like the sea of men around me, ran from my vehicle and threw myself into a ditch about forty yards to the side of the road.

The Germans wouldn't strafe our column lengthwise. We had too many anti-aircraft weapons, and they'd never survive it. Instead, they attacked from the side, and minimized their target profile. Their attack would only affect specific, small parts of our ten-mile-long procession. It was just my luck that I happened to be near one of those specific, small target areas.

I heard the machine guns rattle, and the rhythmic thud of the planes' *schregenmusik,* the 20-mm cannon embedded in the propeller nose. With my face buried in the dirt, I only heard and felt the strafing. The roar of the FW-190 engines increased. Bullets thumped the earth, followed by twanging ricochets. Then there was an explosion. I felt the shock of it in my chest. It made me look up, and I saw a column of black, oily smoke rise from one of our vehicles far ahead.

Just about every machine gun in our column was firing into the sky. Tank commanders stood in their hatches, rotating their .50 calibers left and right to rake the speeding bandits. The guys in the half-tracks were doing the same thing with their machine guns, mounted above the cab. There were quad-.50s in the backs of some half-tracks, rotating and pouring out an incredible amount of lead. One of the half-tracks had mounted a dual .50 caliber gun that was intended for a bomber. The gunner sat in the back of the half-track, rotating and firing the thing inside a plexiglass bubble.

Our bullets filled the sky, and it seemed impossible for even a mosquito to survive it. But the FW-190s banked unharmed, and turned for another pass at us. By now, every rifle and machine gun in the division was trained on them. I wished my half-track had a heavy weapon, but it was a personnel carrier, and for some reason the standard machine gun on the cab roof was missing. All I had was my carbine, a laughable weapon against planes swooping down at more than three hundred miles per hour. Still, I dropped to one knee, and aimed my carbine skyward, the way I'd been trained to do.

What happened next reminded me of a showdown in a Western movie. The two combatants stood in against each other, firing madly. The din of automatic weapons produced a wall of sound, and yet I could hear a voice shouting intermittently, calling into a radio microphone for air support.

The flying black silhouettes grew in size as they swooped down again. Their wings and noses spit deadly steel and lead which dug up great tufts of dirt and riddled vehicles. I fired my carbine, adding its .30 caliber bullets to the vast flood of lead already in the air.

The planes continued, apparently unharmed. We simply weren't leading them enough with our aim. They were close. I actually could see the face of the lead pilot in his cockpit. Beneath his wings hung two bombs. They jettisoned, barely two hundred feet above the ground.

I ducked, burying my face into the ditch once again. I tried to make myself as small as I could, and waited. Moments seemed like hours. I was tempted to lift my head. Two explosions shook me. I felt a rain of dirt clods hit my back and legs. The whining plane engines faded, replaced by a rumbling sound.

I looked up. The rumbling sound came from a raging fire. Several of our vehicles were burning. One of them was so twisted, it wasn't possible to guess what kind of vehicle it had been.

From the sky came new sounds. Like the rest of the troops in our column, I searched the clear blue vastness until I found the source. A flight of our P-51 fighters dove on the FW-190s. They were barely more than black dots in the distance. Soon, one of the German dots sprouted smoke. A cheer rose from the troops on the ground, now starting to stand and walk like human beings again.

"It's about f---king time!" I heard someone shout.

As I rose, my legs felt strange. It was like they didn't belong to me anymore. I climbed unsteadily to the road. My half-track was right in front of me, undamaged. But something made me walk up the column, toward the burning vehicles. The closer I got, the more pungent the stench of burning oil and rubber became.

I didn't go all the way. What I saw stopped me in my tracks. To the side of the burning vehicle lay three of our soldiers. One of them had been torn in half. His legs were stretched straight from the waist down. Several feet away, his torso was arched and burning furiously. The smell was thick and overwhelming. It would stick in my nose for days afterward, and its memory would never leave me.

I turned away from the gruesome sight, and looked at another soldier several yards away. He was lying on his side. There wasn't a mark on him. He looked like he was just a boy who'd decided to go to sleep. I had the urge to nudge his shoulder gently, to wake him. But I knew he would never wake again.

So this is how it is, I thought. I turned sadly, toting my carbine, and headed back toward my half-track. Behind me, I heard sergeants barking commands. Engines turned over. Burning and disabled vehicles were shoved to the side of the road, sometimes tipping over. Medics treated wounds. Officers snapped off the dog tags of the dead, and watched as they were placed into body bags and lifted into the back of a truck. We started driving north again.

So this is how it is.

The Luftwaffe visited our column a few more times on our way up the Rhone Valley, but our planes usually drove them off before they could do any damage. Still, it was an unnerving and helpless feeling to be attacked from above by such fast-moving machines spraying death. I knew I'd never get used to it.

We reached Dijon at night, during a storm. Rain was falling in sheets, and we were blacked out. I couldn't see the road, and I wondered how my driver kept us from plunging into a ditch. We had to bivouac in the city park, which was a quagmire. When we parked the half-track, I decided to relieve myself somewhere. I stepped down from the cab and immediately sank into the mud up to my knees. It exhausted me just to lift my legs high enough to turn around and sheepishly return to my perch inside the vehicle. Nature could wait. I got a few hours of sleep instead.

At dawn, I was awakened by the symphony of engines turning over and revving up. We were on the move again. Passing through the streets of Dijon in daylight under a light rain, I saw its inhabitants for the first time. Despite the wet weather and the early hour, the broad sidewalks were lined with civilians in their rain gear, smiling and waving. Behind them were rows of beautiful eighteenth-century apartment facades, undamaged by battle.

The same couldn't be said for the buildings of Charmes, further north. The Seventh Army had fought its way through this French town, and everywhere it bore the scars of battle. The sidewalks were piled with bricks and masonry that had been bulldozed out of the road. The once charming facades were skeletons, torn and roofless. There were no waving crowds of civilians to see us through this sad scene.

We kept rolling north. The character of the towns changed. It was farming country, and the towns retained the appearance they'd created long before, during feudal times. Often, the towns were nothing more than a few dozen stucco structures at a crossroad. All the homes were aged, and sat next to the obligatory barns. The farmers of every town instinctively seemed to organize their buildings in the same way — houses facing a central courtyard which contained a mountainous pile of manure. The aroma of these villages was so consistent, we called them "manure towns."

Some of our troops actually slept in these manure piles. It was frigid at night, and the manure radiated warmth. It was a comfortable bed, if you could stand the smell. I never could stand the smell, so I stuck with my half-track.

The rumor mill began to churn energetically as we drove further along the French country roads. We heard that the Seventh Army was fighting in the Vosges Mountains. They'd shot through the places we presently passed at the rate of forty miles per day, but the scuttlebutt said that they'd slowed almost to a halt. This meant we were catching up to them, and soon we'd be on the front lines. I tried not to dwell on it, although I couldn't help wondering how I would do once we were in the fight.

Our next stop was Epinal, where we bivouacked in a pine forest. It was colder in this part of the country, probably because we were in the hills. The forest was dark, richly perfumed by pine scent, and there was no underbrush. I was amazed to see how the trees stood in neat rows, which literally formed aisles as far as I could see. As I walked, I noticed that young seedling pines had been planted by the French farmers wherever an adult tree had been cut down. The ground alternated between the dry matting of pine needles and broad areas of swamp.

It never stopped raining. I spent most of the time under our tarp, which we extended out from the half-track on poles. We cracked open some of the wine bottles that the farmers had given us, and drank the robust libations with our C-rations. It was a crude delight, washing down spam and dried biscuits with fine wine.

We hadn't been issued sleeping bags. This nicety would come later in the war. For now, we had to scrounge whatever we could find for bedding. There was a very durable grade of canvas on the backs of most half-tracks, and we made use of ours. It was meant to be roofing material over the rear compartment, but we figured there were much better uses for it than to keep the guys we were taxiing all over France dry. We cut it up, the biggest piece acting as our tarp cover, and two smaller pieces that would be our bedding. We put the smaller pieces on the ground, and wrapped them around ourselves when we slept. It shed the rain very well.

But it didn't stop the rain. As we drove onward, the roads became a sea of mud. The constant passage of tanks, trucks, and thousands of other vehicles had made them impassable. Our engineers had to corduroy them, laying timber crosswise in close rows so the wheeled vehicles had something to grab besides muck. It hit me that the process was identical to what armies had been doing since the invention of the wheel. And here we were, the ultimate modern twentieth-century army, doing the same thing that Caesar's legionnaires did here millennia before us.

We were getting into territory where there was danger from mines. For the first time, our mine-clearing drills were put to the test under real circumstances. I was thankful that my unit wasn't at the head of the column, because they had to perform the dirty work. We had vehicles with special equipment that exploded mines safely, but occasionally men had to dismount and find the mines the hard way, crawling along the mud and probing it with their bayonets.

We'd been instructed about the wide variety of mines that crafty German developers had concocted. Some were designed to blow up a tank. Others were meant to blow off a man's foot, or hop up and spew shrapnel into his groin. There probably were about a dozen other types that fit between those two extremes.

But the mine clearing barely slowed our progress. The next time we stopped for the night, we could hear the booming of guns in the distance. The horizon flickered with light. We were close.

The officers ordered us to make a final maintenance check on our vehicles. I did what I had to do. I didn't like working in the half-track engine, but it beat walking. The half-track motor was a pain in the butt, and I never was any good at dealing with it. Fortunately, there were some guys in the unit who were decent mechanics, and actually enjoyed putting their heads under the hood and tinkering. This allowed me to avoid engine maintenance duty most of the time.

Whenever a vehicle broke down, a tank retriever vehicle towed it back to a rear maintenance area. We had whole units of tank retrievers, and we saw them in action for the first time during our trip through the Rhone Valley. But there weren't many breakdowns at this point. Those would come in time, when the vehicles would be stressed by battle. And that time was now at hand.

On November 20, we received orders to cross the Muerthe River and attack the German positions in the Vosges from the east. The Germans were holding mountainous terrain that was made for defense — narrow, winding roads surrounded by steep inclines. Every turn threatened an ambush. A roadblock could take days to break through. Men in the open were under constant threat from snipers. It was why the Seventh Army advance had ground to a crawl. It was time to call in the only armored unit in that part of the front — us.

As we moved forward, the tension built. I felt it. I knew everyone else felt it. But no one talked about it. It was our first experience with the anticipation of battle, which we'd learn is often worse than the battle itself. The endless waiting causes tension to build, until it's almost excruciating. Just to release it, we almost prayed for the fighting to start.

The detritus of battle was all around us now. Death is the signature of every war zone. I knew we were in one when we drove past a mottled row of dead soldiers. Most were German, lying alternately at tortured and peaceful poses in their field grey *Wehrmacht* uniforms. A few were Americans, lying similarly in their olive drabs. Further on, horses lay along the roadside. The wounded ones twitched and bucked, and they made sounds that I never dreamed could come from a horse.

We drove past a farm wagon, surrounded by French civilians. They were loading corpses into it, much like they'd load bales of hay. A few of them were inside the wagon, stamping the corpses down so they could fit more into it.

There were no sidewalk crowds greeting us now in the villages. Instead, we saw faces peering at us with blinking eyes through cellar windows. Fear glazed those eyes. This, too, is a signature of war.

Our column continued north, through Baccarat, then turned east at Blamont. We rolled through villages and towns — Cirey, St. Quirin, Abreshviller, Le Donon, Fontiane, Schirmeck, Urmatt, Mutzig — dots on a map that differed not at all in real life. Our tension built, and still there was no combat.

The division's tank units were at the point of our advance. We could hear the familiar thudding of the Shermans' 75-mm main guns in the distance. They were fighting through road blocks, ambushes covered by deadly 88-mm anti-tank guns, mines and mortars.

We turned south. We sensed we had moved behind the German lines. Obernai, Ottrot — the towns crawled past my window. All of them showed the scars of battle. All of them were littered with dead young men.

When we arrived in Obernai, the locals warned us that the enemy had set up resistance in the next town, Goxwiller. Division ordered our recon units ahead. This would be our first test against German ground units. It was what we'd been trained to do — probe ahead, draw fire, estimate enemy strength and positioning, and call in the tanks.

Our column rolled cautiously toward Goxwiller along the narrow Alsatian road, until we spotted a roadblock at the entrance of the town. It looked hairy, so we called for tanks right away. In minutes, I could hear the familiar clanking and growling as tank treads approached from our rear. I prayed they were ours.

They were. It was a section of medium tanks under the command of Sgt. Nolan Wesson. I watched them move past us. They only got about fifty yards beyond our position when all hell broke loose. The Germans sprayed them with machine-gun fire from their MG-42s. Their distinctive sound and deadly accuracy would be something all of us would learn to fear. They spit out lead so fast that they didn't go rat-tat-tat. They sounded more like fabric tearing.

I took cover and watched the lead tank blast the roadblock. It came apart like a matchstick structure, debris and men flying in the air. The German troops broke and ran. Apparently, they were joined by the rest of their comrades in Goxwiller, because our artillery opened up on the road beyond the town to hamper the German retreat.

Now our tanks took the point, and we rolled behind them as they slowly led the way through Goxwiller. White sheets hung from the windows. It was a relief to know there were no Mausers aiming at our heads as we drove down the main street.

Our column continued on to the next town, Gertswiller. It was a repeat performance. About two hundred yards in front of the town, the Germans had constructed another road block, defended again by their MG-42s. The tankers had to be cautious, because the makeshift fortification could have contained German anti-tank weapons. Their PAK guns were small and mobile enough for two infantry men to move into position, but the 37-mm gun was capable of disabling any of our tanks. We also had to be careful of their *Panzerfausts*, which were deadly at close range.

Wesson's tanks went at them again, but this time their 75-mm guns couldn't destroy the road block. The Germans kept returning fire, and we eventually had to call in our field artillery. The 105-mm howitzers opened up a barrage, and we walked it in by radio on to the stubborn fortification. A hole was blown into the roadblock, and the tanks charged through it.

I watched as the clanking machines continued their charge right into Gertswiller, firing as they went. It was a frightening display, the tanks rolling relentlessly as their turrets turned left and right, dispensing destruction wherever they pointed.

The enemy was on the run again, but this time they left a parting shot. A tremendous blast beyond the town sent great columns of smoke into the air. The Germans had blown the bridge that spanned a small rivulet, hoping to stop our progress. It didn't work for long, because we found a bypass.

But before we could cross in numbers, we had to make sure Gertswiller was secure. Our infantry dismounted, stripped off their heavy clothing and unnecessary equipment, and loaded up with grenades and small arms ammo. They formed into columns and proceeded down each side of the main street cautiously, moving from doorway to doorway. When the point platoons reached the far end of town without incident, they called up the rest of us, and we began to set up a perimeter defense there.

I watched one of our engineering units roll in next. They quickly set up a treadway bridge, despite sporadic German fire from the hills beyond. After that, they went to work on draining a street the Germans had flooded to prevent us from making a bypass. Again, the engineers had to work under fire. Some of them went down, and I learned firsthand what infantry engineers had suffered throughout centuries of warfare, taking casualties without being able to return the fire.

As darkness settled, the German artillery lobbed desultory rounds into Gertswiller. Most of it was mortar fire, but later that night, the enemy set up an 88-mm AT gun, and camouflaged it so well that we never saw it until it was too late. When our tanks were ordered to regroup at the edge of town, the gun opened fire at point-blank range. It hit one tank three times, obliterating it and killing its crew. Flames roared from its open hatches, fed by its ammunition cooking off.

The rest of our tanks began to withdraw, but Wesson's tank took a hit immediately after he gave the order. The concussion of the high velocity round knocked him out, and the rest of his crew dragged him to safety as they piled out of the burning tank. Right after that, the 88 claimed another tank. Again, the crew survived the hit and escaped, but it was pandemonium as the rest of the tanks sought safety.

Just about every one of our weapons in Gertswiller responded, and suddenly our ears rang with the uninterrupted roar of artillery and small-arms fire. It was a German counterattack. Some of them had leaked back into town, and our infantry had to go house to house again, this time lobbing grenades into windows and doorways. They were supported by tanks, which blasted the upper levels of suspect houses first, before slowly rotating their cannon down toward the basements.

At this point, it dawned on me that many Germans had never left the town. They hid silently in the cellars until darkness and then opened up on our unsuspecting troops. They were directing accurate mortar fire from their hidden perches, and we were losing men in the streets, as snipers picked them off.

Our tanks fired their 75-mm guns as fast as they could be loaded, and if a single German sniper was spotted in a top floor window, he got a round that blew him and the top of the building apart. Later, when we began to collect German prisoners, one of them asked me about this strange American habit of using a heavy gun to kill a single man. I told him we were there to do the job and save lives, and if it took a howitzer to kill every single sniper, we were glad to oblige.

The fighting lasted for what seemed like hours, although it probably didn't go nearly that long before it died down. Even at the height of the firing, our medics swarmed the streets to help the fallen GIs. They administered what first aid they could, and quickly moved the men out of harm's way to be transported later to a field hospital that had been set up back in Obernai.

It was astonishing to see the number of wounded American boys. I tried hard not to look at some of the worst cases as they were carried to the ambulances, but I couldn't help myself. It was like trying to look away from a traffic accident. Your eyes are drawn to the terrible vision like magnets, no matter how badly you try to avoid the sight.

There was a lull in the fighting that caused us to believe the Germans had packed it in. We were wrong. Their artillery started blasting the town again during the pre-dawn hours. While ducking the blasts, we heard the distinctive burping of German MP-40 submachine guns, which told us the enemy had infiltrated the town again. No one knew how far into town they'd gone, but it was time for every one of us to cover our behind as well as our front, because very often the enemy had moved around our outposts beyond the town. In a short time, those outposts had to be recalled, and we were back to hiding in the town's houses. This was no simple solution, since German patrols already were in some of those houses. On more than one occasion, our soldiers were cut down while trying to find shelter in an area thought to be safe.

All the while, German artillery and mortar fire increased. It got to a point where movement was suicide, and our troops had to hug the ground in any cover that was handy. I heard the cries of wounded men in the darkness. Some called for help. Others called for their mothers. It was a grim chorus.

Night fighting in a town is a mad exercise. You lie flat, burying your face in the dirt or some corner of a basement while machine gun fire rakes the world

Troop A enters a village in France, 1944. Villagers seem to be in shock, as the unit had just knocked out an enemy roadblock.

just over your head. When it ceases, you lift up and fire your weapon blindly at the place where you think you saw the enemy muzzle flash. Then you drop again. Sometimes you exchanged fire with a man just a few dozen yards away.

It was clear even to me that we were up against a major counterattack. I wasn't surprised when we got the order to retreat around dawn, and we had to return to Goxwiller. When we got there, I watched exhausted men drop where they stopped, leaning against buildings, and staring at the ground. Some of them lit up cigarettes. A few even tried to talk, asking about this friend or that person, hoping to hear they'd made it through the ordeal in one piece. Usually, such questions were met with silent shrugs from other soldiers, just as exhausted.

Our unit was one of the lucky ones during the retreat, because we'd been ordered to leave early. The units that brought up the rear were under heavy fire, because the Germans had set up machine guns on the hills flanking the road. They also blasted the road with artillery from Gertswiller. Our tanks stayed behind to cover the retreat, which could have become a rout were it not for the way our new, previously untested outfit comported itself. The two years of intense training already was paying dividends.

The next day, our battalion artillery hit Goxwiller with everything it had. We watched the columns of smoke rise high above the roofs, and knew we'd be following those shells soon.

The 94th Cavalry led the way back into Goxwiller this time. We had plenty of support from our tanks and infantry. The artillery barrage seemed to knock the fight out of the Germans, because we didn't receive the kind of resistance we expected. Our unit entered the town cautiously, and there was some firing, but most of the Germans had cleared out. We provided cover as the engineers once again put up a bridge where the previous ones had been destroyed. This time, we were in Goxwiller to stay. At least, that's what we thought.

BARR—Intense Battle

Barr was the next objective on our drive through Alsace. Our unit was ordered to lead the way again, followed closely by the 48th Tank Battalion. But before we reached Barr, our lead vehicles came under fire just outside a tiny hamlet. As usual, we took cover and let the tanks pass through to clear out the enemy.

I watched the tank column slowly crawl toward the first building, but progress stopped when the lead tank was struck by a *Panzerfaust*. As it sat burning, only one man crawled out of the hatch and began to run for cover. For some reason, he turned around and ran back to the wounded tank. I figured he must have been trying to help the rest of his crew escape. But as he climbed aboard the Sherman, a German artillery round exploded next to the tank, and he fell dead.

The rest of the tanks in the column pressed the attack, infantry men crouched behind the turrets with their rifles aimed. The new lead tank plowed into the hamlet, machine gunning a German squad in its path, until it encountered a road block. The tank never slowed down, but turned to get a shot at the road block from the side. I saw German soldiers scatter, most of them taking cover behind a large stone cross. A quick report came from the 75-mm barrel and the cross, along with the soldiers behind it, disappeared.

When the tanks completed their sweep of the hamlet, we continued toward Barr. Along the way, we encountered a few more road blocks. Some of them were undefended, but we still had to be careful. Other road blocks were held only by German small arms fire, so we rarely took longer than half an hour to clear them out of our path. The relatively light resistance didn't prepare us for what lay ahead.

The German army held Barr in force, with every intention of stopping our advance there. In addition to regular infantry, panzer grenadiers of the 10th Volks Division were present, supported by tanks, anti-tank guns, well-prepared road blocks, artillery and mortars. Of course, we didn't know that as we approached. It was the first of many cases in which our intelligence arm had grossly underestimated enemy strength.

But we knew there would be fighting in Barr, so our armored units led the way. In what would become a sad litany repeated again and again, our lead tank was slammed by an unseen 88. It lurched and stopped dead, issuing smoke and then a raging fire. Its crew never made it to the hatches.

The whole column of tanks went into action, deploying outwardly and firing their guns rapidly. One of their rounds landed in a German ammunition dump inside Barr, and the explosion sent out a shock that felt like a mule had kicked my chest. The explosions continued in an unbroken roar, sending black smoke skyward, and raining debris all over the surrounding area. Infantry men dove for cover, as the small-arms fire erupted from buildings.

Lieutenant John Kraker ordered us forward. We already respected Kraker as a good officer, because he always wanted to be where the action was hottest, and he never asked his men to do anything that he didn't do himself. He protected his men, and knew how to get them out of tough spots. He always lingered behind to check the rear, and it was common to see him venture into no man's land to collect our wounded when nobody else wanted that almost suicidal duty. Everyone looked up to Kraker.

We sped toward the town in our vehicles, but soon had to stop when a German 88 zeroed in on our supporting tanks. One of them blew up following a direct hit. Kraker directed our attack toward the 88, and one of our bazooka teams circled around for a clear shot, and knocked it out. For this action, and what would follow here, our New York–born Lieutenant Kraker would receive a Bronze Star. He later received the Silver Star.

But we were far removed from accolades as our units moved into Barr. What followed was an ugly slugging match, our tanks inching through the streets, firing their guns and receiving hits from hidden enemy anti-tank units. One tank platoon actually made it completely through the town, only to be fired on once they got to the town's outer edge by anti-tank artillery on both sides of them. Every one of the tanks took a hit, some of them repeatedly. One by one, they burst into flame. Their crews scrambled out of smoking hatches, only to be shot down by small-arms fire.

The battle inside Barr intensified into a maelstrom of flame, thunder and screaming men. Nearly every place above ground was riddled with flying steel fragments and bits of masonry and glass that would tear through human flesh like it was soft butter. Men lay beside their tanks, missing arms or legs. Some were not recognizable human beings. The firing became so intense that one of our companies had to pull back out of town, leaving behind their wounded. It was something that happened only in the most severe firefights.

Every house had the potential for a deadly ambush, and so every house became our target. This was underscored when we approached the town hospital along a cobbled street, and received fire from an anti-tank gun from inside one of its windows. One of our tanks immediately returned the fire, and blasted the hospital apart. There would be no buildings off limits in this fight. Chivalrous niceties about hospitals had been chucked aside.

Just moments later, that same tank suffered hits from two *Panzerfausts*, killing the crew. Its commander would receive a posthumous Distinguished Service Cross for staying inside and continuing to fire until he ran out of 75-mm ammunition. Then he crawled out of the turret and from behind it, fired the .50 caliber machine gun until small-arms fire cut him down. His name was Gable. He wasn't the only hero that day.

Posthumous awards went to a number of men who behaved the same way, firing from their disabled tanks until they ran out of ammunition. Their actions allowed medics to evacuate the wounded, and also wreaked havoc on the German positions.

Another outstanding officer emerged that day. Major George England, then Executive Officer of the 48th Tank Battalion, led his armored column into the town.

The newly appointed Capt. John Kraker, with his ever-present set of binoculars, poses near the German autobahn in 1945. As unit clerk, West had the privilege of writing up Kraker for the Silver Star.

But Barr would be a blot on the history of the 48th. The unit lost seventeen medium tanks in what seemed like moments. Major England's tank was among the first to go down, and he spent the entire night avoiding German patrols while trying to find what remained of his own outfit. The surviving tanks had to withdraw to avoid annihilation.

With darkness, we set up defensive positions in the town square, being sure to have cover from the continuing enemy artillery fire. It seemed as though the German troops were moving back. This was mostly due to the efforts of Major England. He'd found some of his remaining tanks and teamed them with an infantry battalion he'd bumped into. Then he led this tank-infantry unit back into Barr and proceeded to clean out the enemy troops.

The next day one of our units confirmed that the Germans had gone by searching house to house. Many of our wounded men who had spent all night behind enemy lines were overjoyed to see our ugly, dirt-streaked faces.

I joined a group of our men to help carry the wounded to the ruined hospital where the Germans had placed their anti-tank gun. It was filled with wounded men, both American and German. There were groans and background noises that combined to sound like a cattle pen. Doctors and orderlies moved quickly from cot to cot, sometimes delivering injections, sometimes cutting away limbs. They moved with a briskness and lack of emotion that reminded me of insects.

I was among the group charged with guarding the German wounded. Most of them looked just as pathetic as our guys, lying with dull stares and pained expressions, covered in dried blood on crusted bandages. A lot of them were not far beyond childhood. It made me realize that even children can be deadly with weapons in their hands.

We were in what had been a civilian hospital before the war. It was still run by the same doctor, who must have been overwhelmed by the sudden change in his hospital's routine. I chatted with him. He was an intelligent Alsatian man whose interests ran a wide gamut of literature and music. Now he was patching up broken young men torn apart in a war that left him numbed. But the war was leading me toward moments that were far from numbing.

Barr was the site of my first truly dangerous night patrol. We were tasked to reconnoiter the hills just beyond town, looking for trouble. The problem with that duty is, at night, trouble usually finds you first.

There is no way to describe the tension of a night patrol in totally alien terrain. First, you have to dismount and leave the safety of half-tracks, peeps, and armored cars behind. Then you walk into the blackest darkness you've ever experienced. Surrounded by woods on all sides, you never know who might be watching, drawing a bead on your head at that moment.

I stepped carefully through the underbrush, trying to be as quiet as a Comanche, but to my ears it sounded like a bull charging through the surf. In a moment when I could plainly hear my heart beating, the collective noise of our platoon resembled a cattle stampede to my hyper-sensitive ears. I hoped I was only imagining the level of noise.

Each step was terror. The ground was uneven, and I didn't know what might be one step ahead of me. I could fall into an open ditch, or tread on a mine. All of us could wind up in the middle of a huge enemy column, and not know it until we were riddled with bullets and shrapnel.

This is almost what happened to B Troop of our squad, which was performing a night patrol of its own on the east side of Barr. They were driving through the woods just north of Benfeld when they blundered into a minefield that was covered by enemy troops. As soon as the shooting began, they turned on the headlights of their lead peep. The beams revealed a German horse-drawn artillery piece pointing right at them. This was surrounded by enemy troops with machine guns.

Their armored cars fired at the Germans with 37-mm cannons, and blew up the artillery piece and its crew with the first round. The combatants were so close that another enemy artillery piece banged against one of our armored cars as the panicked horses ran off with it. B Troop then began to take fire from yet another enemy field gun that was hidden in a barn. Our guys had to call up an assault gun to take out the thing. It took only two rounds.

The skirmish developed into an all-out battle, with both sides firing furiously in the darkness, like blindfolded gunfighters. B Troop had to dismount, while their guys fired the .50s from the tops of the half-tracks. A platoon of our Shermans finally arrived, but that only intensified the German fire. Their mortars took a terrible toll. Their anti-tank guns knocked out several of our tanks. The smoke from battle only thickened the already opaque fog, and made the fight that much more blind and insane.

It went on like that all night, until our units finally had to pull back. The casualties were terrible. I heard all about it that afternoon from some of the B Troop survivors, so it was definitely on my mind as I tiptoed through the dark woods just hours later. We all knew the same thing could happen to us.

But it didn't. We failed to make any contact with the enemy, and as dawn approached, we remounted our vehicles and drove back to Barr.

Although the enemy had bloodied us at Gertswiller, Barr and Benfeld, our division continued to press its advance. We used the Corp's heavy artillery to blast positions where we knew German anti-tank guns and mortars were set up. It was a fearsome display, watching the eruptions made by the eight-inch guns firing from miles behind our front lines.

In closer were the 155-mm "Long Toms," which our guys had learned to use the same way the Germans used their 88s. These particular guns were towed by tractors, but they set up quickly and had an amazing rate of fire and accuracy. They launched a six-inch shell, which was a naval-sized weapon, equal to the main battery guns on our light cruisers.

It seemed like every time our barrages stopped, the German artillery answered with a barrage of their own — sometimes lobbing shells into the same place where ours had landed. It made me wonder about our targeting. But I guessed our big guns were doing some good, because our heavy tank and infantry units were moving ahead.

My unit remained in Barr during all of this, mainly performing security duty there. I noticed a growing number of German prisoners entering the town. We had to guard them. Although fraternizing with these POWs was forbidden, I used my smattering of German and some cigarette bribes to learn how things looked from their side of the war. They were a sorry-looking bunch, dirty, unshaven, and gaunt. It was like looking at the face of defeat. But I knew that just a day or so before, they'd been fighting us with a ferocity that few armies ever possessed.

One of the POWs expressed his amazement to me about the state of our army.

"You have no horses," he said in wonderment.

The German army relied heavily on horses to move their equipment. They even used horses to pull their tanks when moving to new fighting positions, because gasoline had become so precious in the Third Reich. But even when gas was plentiful early in the war, the *Wehrmacht* made liberal use of horse power.

"The American Army drives," I told him. "We don't trot."

He seemed to understand what it really meant. His army was hopelessly outclassed by our mobility.

Despite all shortages, the *Luftwaffe* continued to visit us. Their attacks were usually small in scale, but their fighters, Stukas, and light bombers made sorties against our front lines and rear areas. More often than not, our P-51s drove them off or shot them down before they could do much harm. But they still were killing our guys, and sometimes our own fighters simply weren't around to stop them.

We'd only been in the fighting for a short stint at this point, although it seemed like an age to all of us. I was ready for a break, and my prayers were answered.

On December 3, we received orders to join the rest of Combat Command A (CCA) in Corps reserve at Hochfelden. It was welcome news, especially after learning that CCA had made it to our Corps objective, a line between Schenviller and Eberscheim. The brass was giving us all a short rest before tossing us into the cauldron again.

My troop stopped in Waldersheim, and we were extremely lucky to find lodging in one of the houses. It belonged to the Gantzer family, and there I enjoyed one of the sweetest episodes of my entire time in Europe.

Mr. Gantzer took my whole squad into his home, and put us up on the second floor, while his family stayed on the ground floor. He was the community blacksmith, and his shop was filled with tools that fascinated me. Many of them were antiques. He also was the *burgomeister* of Waldersheim. One of his sons, Charles, had fought in the French army. Gantzer also had a beautiful little girl, and his wife was eager to take care of everyone, cooking the kind of meals that we hadn't enjoyed since leaving our own homes. There even was a funny dog in the house, named Floc. I felt at home there immediately.

Every night we had a little party where we'd play cards and drink schnapps. We'd tell jokes and practice our French while teaching English to the family members. They made us feel like part of their clan. It gave all of us a chance to regroup and gather ourselves again, following the harsh combat.

Mr. Gantzer also arranged to have the rest of my unit billeted in other houses in Waldersheim. The locals were cordial and friendly, and there was a nice little church in the town that was run by a priest who spoke English.

We spent some of the time in reserve doing maintenance work on our vehicles, while silently thanking God that we were alive and in one piece after our baptism of fire.

I noticed a lot of the tankers were busy welding racks on to the sides of their turrets and all around the base of their vehicles. They had stripped the metal for these racks from the disabled German vehicles that littered many of the roads.

"You expecting to carry a lot of luggage?" I asked one tanker.

"Naw," he drawled. "We fill these racks with sandbags. That way, when an 88 hits us, it blows the sandbags up, but doesn't enter the hull. It gives us an extra chance to keep going."

I looked down the long line of Shermans, whose supposedly improved armor still couldn't stop a direct hit from an 88-mm AT gun, a Panther or a Tiger tank, and saw that the entire battalion was welding on new metal racks. Some of them even welded racks underneath their Shermans, so the sandbags would cushion the explosion of a mine. There were so many amateur welders

The Gantzer family, posing outside the home where West and his fellow soldiers stayed during their push through Alsace in 1944. This photograph was taken after the war and sent to West during his long correspondence with his family.

at work that our Corps had an epidemic of arc-flash cases reporting to the hospitals.

Right away I took this bold innovation back to our unit, and we began welding metal racks to our half-tracks. When we loaded the sides with sand bags, we noticed a definite decrease in the vehicles' speed and performance. We'd probably doubled their weight with all that sand, but we didn't care. Half-tracks weren't famous for their speed, anyway.

The other common sight in reserve was the tank recovery vehicle. These tank transporters picked up any disabled armored vehicles which appeared to be salvageable, and hauled them back to the mechanics. They hauled Sherman tanks, Tiger tanks, Panther tanks, Mark-IV tanks—even Czech tanks. The machine shops in the rear were successful in getting a lot of them back in service, because in many cases, it was just a matter of replacing a tread that had been shot off. Of course, there were more grotesque salvage jobs, in which the mechanics had to clean away the remains of a crew that had been blown into a thick paste of flesh, blood and brains coating the interior.

The influx of restored non–American vehicles began to give our units a motley look, even though they were repainted olive green with a big white star. But they helped to fill out our units with vehicles that our supply system only partially replaced. Besides, a lot of these tanks actually were better than ours.

The IV Corps received new supplies of just about everything, from gasoline to belt buckles. This was when we finally got sleeping bags. They were dark, khaki-colored things that zipped all the way around. Right away, some wise aleck called it a "mummy case." The name stuck, because the bag conformed so tightly to your body, it made you look like something that came from King Tut's tomb.

A U.S. armored car parked outside a farmhouse in Gambsheim, 1944. Note the sandbags on the turret and the front, added by its crew for extra protection against enemy anti-tank weapons.

They were warm, because once you got into the bag, you could cover your head and leave just enough room to breathe. The new bags were great in the rear areas, but when we slept near the front, no one felt safe in them. You simply couldn't get out of one in a hurry if you had to. There could be nothing worse than to be immobilized from head to foot in a mummy case during a sudden enemy attack. That's why we eventually cut a couple of holes in the bags for our legs. We always slept with our shoes on in the field, and those of us fortunate enough to have a pistol, kept it handy inside the bag. It was probably a foolish solution, but it made us feel safer.

During our time in reserve, the brass took the opportunity to boost our morale. On December 6, we received a message from our Corps commander, Major General Edward Brooks, which was posted at key points among our billets.

"Since the beginning of military history in Europe," it read, "to force a successful passage of the Vosges Mountains had been considered by military experts an operation offering such small opportunity for success as to forestall consideration of such efforts.

"To march, supply and maintain a large body of troops through the natural obstacles, without hostile opposition, is a major problem in itself.

"To fight cross-country in the face of unreasoning, stubborn Nazi resistance, at times supplying over snow-covered roads and trails, through this region and at this season of the year, is a military achievement of which all who participated can be justly proud."

It went on to name the divisions that partook in the operation, including our 14th Armored Division, adding, "It is with pride and humility that I realize the pinnacle and the magnitude of this concerted achievement of American soldiery — your achievement."

I felt proud for about ten seconds. Then I realized it was buttering us up for the ordeal that was about to come.

TO THE RHINE—Initial Attempt, and Failure to Cross

Our outfit was transferred to Combat Command B (CCB), so we moved out to join it at Hochfelden. It was getting colder going into that second week of December, and I figured I would have to endure another winter of snow and sub-zero temperatures. It would be my third such winter in a row. I wasn't a South Californian anymore.

On December 6, we received orders to move forward and probe for enemy strong points. My outfit led the way, as usual. We reached Gambsheim, which is right on the Rhine River. We hoped the speed of our advance would allow us to steal across an undamaged bridge, because that would make headlines all over the world. All of us imagined the same screaming banner: "Troop A, 94th Recon Breaches Rhine." But our dreams died quickly. The Germans had blown all of the bridges.

We were under sporadic fire in Gambsheim from the enemy mortars and artillery across the river. It forced us to take cover in the cellars once again. From there we watched what was taking place around us.

In front of the house where I hunkered down was a road junction. We knew the Germans had planted a series of mines there, tied together with a rope. If you set one off, all of them would explode. The fire was too intense for any of us to risk exposure while digging out those mines, so we just warned everyone that they were there.

Unfortunately, there was a cow grazing in that minefield which didn't understand English. We tried shouting at it and threw rocks, but it just kept munching alfalfa. This led inevitably to the bloodiest event of the entire war. When the mines exploded, everyone ducked down in their cellars. Dirt, glass, rock and pieces of cow meat blew everywhere. After the dust settled, someone made a crack about steak dinners, but I'd lost my appetite.

We still hoped to cross one of the canals adjacent to the Rhine, so we could get into decent ground on the river. There were several islands in the river that were wooded and provided some cover. But our position on the river bank was badly exposed. That's why I couldn't believe it when we received the order to advance. It seemed suicidal, but we had to obey it.

We crossed an open field toward a canal, where there was an isthmus of dirt running next to the river. When I ran across that open field, I felt helpless. Dirt kicked up everywhere around me, as machine gun bullets tore into the ground. I had no idea where they came from. They seemed to be shoot-

A collapsed bridge over the Rhine River as it appeared when American troops arrived in 1945. The Germans were expert at demolishing their bridges to prevent the Allies from easy river crossings.

ing at me from every direction. I could hear the rounds whizzing past me. It sounded like an angry beehive, with occasional twangs from ricochets.

I ran in short bursts, taking cover where I found it. Then I'd pop up, run a few more yards serpentine, and hit the ground again, just like they taught us in training. I was sure that I'd be killed before I reached the safety of the river bank. It could come from any direction, because the shrapnel went everywhere.

The Germans blasted us with everything they had, and we started losing people. Shells from their 88s and even their vintage World War I 77-mm guns exploded among us. Mortar fire was killing a lot of our guys who thought they'd found cover. They were shooting at us from across the river in well-concealed positions, so we couldn't return their fire accurately. They'd had the ground we occupied totally bracketed and measured for their artillery long before we arrived. In short, they were ready for us.

We still didn't have a lot of combat experience, so we didn't accomplish much. We only had some bazookas, machine guns, and a handful of armored cars with short-barreled 37-mm guns. It was like returning deadly fire with spitballs.

But most of us reached the Rhine. We stopped there behind a riverbank with our legs deep in canal water. The water was freezing, but I was thankful that I was still alive to feel the pain of it.

Panting for breath, I finally looked around. I saw familiar faces pressed against the riverbank, wheezing for air like me. Their eyes had the cast of deep shock and fear. I wondered if I looked the same.

Bullets licked the bank above us, tossing dirt on our helmets and shoulders. Mortar shells exploded behind us. It only made us press more deeply into the earth. Popping up to return fire now would be stupid and pointless. We were just glad to be safe, even if only for a moment.

The moment was still too short. I heard a familiar drone, and didn't want to look to verify my suspicions. But I did, anyway. Messerschmitts. The *Luftwaffe* had arrived at the worst possible time.

I watched the two fighters roar toward us over the Rhine. Lights flickered from their wing machine guns. Their bullets splashed and foamed in the canal water, coming closer to me. I dove underwater and held my breath, waiting for the stream of lead to pass.

When I came up for air, I checked myself for blood. Nothing. Then I turned and watched the fighters screaming at us from the opposite direction. I ran to a different part of the canal and dived underwater again. I could hear bullets ripping through the dark, dingy water.

It went on like that all day, as the *Luftwaffe* sent wave after wave of its fighters and dive bombers at us. And all day, I kept diving underwater to avoid their strafing. I was shivering constantly. I didn't know whether it was from the cold or sheer terror. It probably was both.

I was never so happy to see the short daylight period of that December day end. I stayed in the freezing water of the canal until it was too dark for any German plane to see me. It didn't matter if I caught pneumonia again. Pneumonia would be a blessing, compared to being torn up by machine-gun bullets.

When it was dark enough, I discarded my bazooka and rifle, and started to crawl back away from the riverbank. Off toward the rear, there was a house that I'd noticed while we were being strafed. It looked like a short run at the time, but it might as well have been a thousand miles away, because I knew I'd never make it there in daylight.

We were still under fire from the other side of the river, so I had to keep crawling. It was miserably cold, and I could feel my wet uniform stiffening as it turned to ice. My combat boots already had frozen. Those things weren't made for water and mud, which was very stupid since that's where they usually were during combat. Later, the War Office would realize this, and replace the combat boots with shoe packs that were made of waterproofed rubber, with inner lining that kept your feet warm. But at this moment, I was working my way through mud in frozen leather boots that, if I took them off, would probably take my feet with them. It was like wearing refrigerators.

I was determined to make it to that house. It promised warmth, because smoke came from its chimney, and there was a bit of light peeking from the window shades. I crawled, ignoring the sharp pain in my frozen legs and feet.

When I tumbled through the door, I was shocked by what I saw. The room was filled with about thirty of our soldiers. They seemed to be having a feast. The air was thick with the beautiful aroma of cooking. It came from an old pot-bellied stove, on top of which was a skillet. In the skillet, pork chops cooked. Someone had slaughtered a pig, and thirty guys were eating pork chops. It smelled better than just about any cooking I'd even known. I realized suddenly that I hadn't eaten all that day.

With a little help from some troopers, I managed to peel off my wet uniform, and hung it next to the stove to dry. Then I backed my rear end beside the stove, and ate pork chops. It was the best meal I'd ever had.

When our bellies were full and our butts were dry, we started taking stock of what had happened that day. We weren't very happy about it, because we'd lost a lot of men. Our blame fell upon the commander of the 94th, Lieutenant Colonel Thomas "Corky" McCollom, because we felt he'd sent us into the situation as sort of a live ammunition "problem." We didn't appreciate being toughened up that way, especially since there was no discernable objective after we discovered the bridges had been blown. We couldn't have gone any farther, because we didn't have the engineers and bridging equipment with us. The Rhine was simply too big for us to fool with.

"It was probably some kind of stupid training mission," somebody said.

"Maybe we needed it," another voice supposed.

"For what?" I shouted. "Training us how to get shot up?"

I was angry. I had lost a few friends that day. It was always painful to lose somebody you knew, and I was just learning that. I didn't care how it happened. I didn't distinguish between dying a heroic death in combat, and dying in a bed from an infection. Dying is all bad. You certainly can't glorify it, and you have to respect everyone who has died.

Later on I was able to take the loss of a friend in battle and compartmentalize it in some quiet corner of my brain, so it wouldn't hurt so much. That way I never thought of them as being gone. Sometimes I'd be near a spot where a friend had died. I thought of him as still being there, in that spot. All the guys who died still had their spots. And all of us would keep our eyes on those locations and protect them, even though our buddies weren't buried there. Those spots still belonged to them.

Seeing guys I knew suddenly killed taught me how fragile life is. I carried that knowledge with me through all the years after the war. When I started raising my family, I always worried about my kids taking risks. I didn't like them climbing, because I was afraid they'd fall and break their necks. I always was afraid when they rode their bicycles, and later, when they drove cars. It was because I'd seen people fight hard to stay alive, and yet slip away so easily. I guess I burdened my kids with that.

The thing that bothered me most in the war was seeing a young child injured or dead, and I saw a lot of that in France and Germany. I'm sure that affected my behavior toward my family, too. Such horrible sights have lasting, as well as immediate, results.

My condemnation of our commander was a natural outgrowth of a very bad day in which so many of us had died. But later, I would learn that McCollom was just following orders that came down from division. And for all I know, division was passing along the order from higher up. Blame-placing was a pointless exercise in an army at war.

We didn't have long to mull over the point. The next day, we moved back to Hoerdt, where our unit was attached to the 313th Infantry. It was here that we were surprised by a German anti-tank gun. We weren't expecting any resistance, so it caught us completely by surprise when it fired the first round. It was at point-blank range, so they couldn't miss the lead vehicle. The blast killed one of our guys in an armored car, and gave another guy a concussion.

This also was the first place in which we experienced civilian resistance. An elderly gent in a suit fired a *Panzerfaust* at our column. Those things fired a rocket that looked like a toilet tank float, and when it went off, it shot fire in every direction. But it was more powerful than our bazooka, and could penetrate most of our armored vehicles.

After firing the *Panzerfaust*, the elderly civilian dropped the tube and ran, but our return fire killed him. We soon learned that he was part of the *Volkssturm* units that were stationed all over Germany. They were meant to be a "people's army," often farmers who lived in houses with their families. They stored their small-arms weapons and *Panzerfausts* right in their homes. I remember breaking into one house and finding an arsenal. I also learned to inspect the local graveyards, because many of the militia wrapped their weapons in oil slicker raincoats and buried them there. In Hoerdt, we found a spot of recently dug earth in the cemetery that was loaded with weapons— Mauser rifles, MP-40 machine pistols, Lugers, grenades, and mines.

You couldn't fault the *Volkssturm* as soldiers, because they did pretty well against us. They put up stiff resistance every time they could. I thought they were crazy to behave that way at this late point in the war. I told several of them that they ought to give up, adding that it was better to be a live coward than a dead hero. I sweetened my argument by saying the weather was much warmer in California and Arizona, where they would be sent as POWs. I promised them no cold winters and great food. This line of reasoning would come in very handy for me later.

Sometimes reasoning was just as effective as shooting. We tried any way we could to get the damn fighting over with. But most of the fanatics stuck to their guns. They were misguided politically. I didn't have any personal hatred for them, because I felt the wrong guy got control of their country. It taught me that we have to be careful about who we elect in America.

At first, we commandeered civilian houses in Hoerdt for ourselves. We'd take every other house, so the people we evicted could stay with their neighbors. This turned out to be a big mistake. Many of the people we turned out went into the fields and joined the *Volkssturm*. Then they'd come back and attack us in their houses.

After a few firefights, we changed policy. We made sure to keep the families in the houses with us. That way, the *Volkssturm* wouldn't be apt to attack us at night. It worked.

Troop A mixes with the villagers of a liberated French town, 1944.

One day in Hoerdt my attention was grabbed by the growling of airplane engines. I stepped outside and saw a squadron of our P-38 planes dogfighting with Messerschmitts. A few of the men from my outfit joined me, and we watched the deadly aerial ballet. Then we heard an ungodly roar behind us, followed by a loud bang. It sounded like a freight train making a crash landing. We looked around the house, and saw that it was an empty P-38 auxiliary gas tank. One of the pilots above us had jettisoned the thing, and it scared the hell out of everyone. After that, we limited our dogfight spectatorship.

Within a few days of our arrival in Hoerdt, we received orders to move up again. The whole division was going into an attack across Alsace and into Germany, with the objective of seizing crossings over the Lauter River, the border between France and the Third Reich in that sector. On the morning of December 12, it began.

Our unit rolled over the wet Alsatian roads into Hagenau, on the Moder River, and proceeded into the woods beyond the city. We met no resistance. Instead, we met civilians, men and women in their dark Alsatian clothes, lining the streets and roads. They wept. They shouted. The ladies threw kisses and waved handkerchiefs. I saw a few tiny French flags held high above the crowds' heads, waving madly, and wondered how long they'd been hidden until this day.

One of the men spoke in an unbroken prattle of Alsatian French, smiling broadly. He never seemed to take a breath. He ran to our half-track and handed me a bottle of wine and a bottle of schnapps. Then the man receded behind us before I had a chance to thank him, but I saw his face beaming and his eyes sparkle. We were liberators here.

Some of the civilians managed to interrupt their celebration with the warning that the Germans occupied the town of Buhl, a few miles ahead. I watched as troops from other units made the necessary detour toward Buhl, dismounting and moving toward it. Our unit stayed on the road leading to Surbourg, and for the first time I saw some of the old Maginot Line defenses.

The Germans were using those forts and pillboxes now. They'd just turned the guns around to the west.

France had invested a fortune in building the Maginot Line during the 1930s. It was a string of fortifications, connected by a labyrinth of underground tunnels, and chambers. These underground structures contained barracks, rail lines for moving supplies, men and ammunition, storehouses—even movie theaters.

The Maginot Line extended for scores of miles along France's border with Germany, supposedly providing an impregnable barrier. It was one big, costly insurance policy that allowed the French Army to degenerate from one of the world's finest fighting forces in the Great War to a midget-class military entity, rife with incompetence and corruption. All of France ignored that during the 1930s. The Maginot Line made the French people feel safe.

When the German Army invaded in 1940, they just went around this monument to military stupidity. France fell in six weeks. It was a lesson that seemed now to be lost on its German defenders. If great mountain ranges, rivers and seas can be crossed by armies, no man-made structure will stop a determined army for long. It's like the Great Wall of China. It looks pretty, but if you don't have every inch of it guarded, a good outfit will find a way to break through.

There must have been some corrupt contracting when the French built the Maginot Line, because right away we noticed that its concrete was not as well cured or as strong as that of the Siegfried Line, its German counterpart. This lesson probably wasn't lost on the Germans, either, because they didn't attempt to defend the Maginot forts with the same intensity as they did in their own fortifications. They probably knew from experience that the French-made concrete would blow apart easily under fire from artillery.

Whenever we came up against the Maginot forts, we simply called in our tanks. If they didn't destroy the emplacements, we brought up a 155-mm gun, lowered the barrel, and fired it at a flat trajectory to blast a pillbox. That usually blew it apart.

While our unit moved toward the border, we received our introduction to a monstrous 380-mm railroad gun that fired on the city from thirty miles away. It used to belong to the French Army, but the Germans captured it to bombard our positions. They usually fired it every Wednesday and Saturday night, like they were marking time for everyone within earshot.

Our forces had been trying for long time to locate this railroad gun. We sent out the air force and dozens of patrols, but none of them located it.

Within its range was the headquarters and position of the 136th Ordnance Battalion, and this behemoth had caused havoc there. One round landed right on a barracks, killing eleven men and wounding fourteen.

By questioning the local people, we finally found the gun. It was hidden inside a mountain tunnel, with its railroad tracks going downhill from there. The German gunners allowed it to roll down to a point and then fired it. The enormous recoil caused it to roll back into the safety of the tunnel. They repeated this process again and again, so the gun was rarely exposed.

I saw one of its shells hit a hospital. It was a five-story structure that was about a block long. The shell penetrated a wall at the top and went through five floors before exploding in the basement. It blew an enormous hole in the hospital. I never learned how many patients and doctors it killed, but it must have been an awful toll. Our side *had* to knock out that gun.

At first we tried bombing the tunnel from the air. This became unpopular, because it tore up the railroad tracks that our forces would need to use later. Then we went with the A-team. We sent a cavalry unit up that mountain on foot and in vehicles, and surrounded it. The Germans didn't have a large security force guarding the gun, and soon realized resistance was hopeless. They surrendered, and the railroad gun was ours. I wasn't part of the action, but I arrived in time to take pictures of our guys sitting on the barrel of that monster. It was long enough to accommodate an entire platoon.

Our progress never really was hampered by the railroad gun, however. The division kept pushing forward, often bypassing fixed enemy fortifications, leaving them to be cleaned up later by mechanized heavy artillery units that followed. By darkness, our forward units had reached the banks of the Lauter River. We were on the German border. The bridges had been blown, of course, so the units on the riverbank dug in. Engineers arrived a few hours later and threw together a Bailey Bridge in the middle of the night. A few of our guys crossed it, just to say they'd been in Germany.

Later we crossed the Lauter in force and set up several strong bridgeheads. Our recon units patrolled ahead, and we learned the Siegfried Line was just four miles away from the river.

It was mid–December, and I was in Germany. There would be no more cheering crowds, greeting us as liberators. We had become conquerors in a hostile land, filled with people who didn't want us there.

The Germans had been driven into their fortifications along the Siegfried Line, a couple of miles inside their homeland. It surprised no one that the German fortifications were much more formidable than the French forts. Unlike the Maginot Line, where you literally could kick the cement off the side of a pillbox, the concrete on the Siegfried Line was solid. In order to get at the pillboxes, you had to get through a wide band of "dragon's teeth"—reinforced concrete blocks a few feet tall, which were designed to hang up tanks that attempted to drive over them. Any tank caught on those teeth soon was destroyed by German AT guns placed everywhere.

All of the dragon's teeth were connected together below the ground, so you couldn't move any one of them. They were well anchored, and proved to be a difficult challenge for our engineers.

At first sight, the Siegfried Line was deceptively peaceful. From a distance, the dragon's teeth seemed small, and behind them lay a flat, open patch of country with a few scattered farm houses. But those farm houses had walls of reinforced concrete seven feet thick, protecting AT guns.

The Germans were demonically clever at disguising pillboxes. They even made trees into pillboxes. They erected bronze-cast trees in wooded areas, beautifully camouflaged so that our troops never could tell a tree from a strong point.

Any troops trying to assault a pillbox from its flank came under crossfire from two other pillboxes. The Germans were defending their "Fatherland" after all, so they spared no effort in building the so-called "West Wall."

Rather than make a costly assault, we dug in and watched as formations of silver B-25 bombers flew over the fortifications and dropped their deadly cargo. It was frightening to watch multiple geysers of flame and smoke arc high into the sky. I wondered how anyone could survive in that holocaust. As it turned out, nearly all the enemy troops did survive, retreating into underground bunkers that went several stories down.

When the bombers left, the German guns opened fire, almost as a demonstration of defiance. I looked at the scene through binoculars, and between the craters left by exploding bombs I noticed a patch of yellow snow. I pointed it out to one of the guys from another unit, who'd been up close to the Siegfried Line.

"That's where they piss," he said.

"They do it outdoors? With all this hardware pointing at them?"

"We give them a break," he went on. "Their latrine plumbing broke down in this sector. Every day they visit the same spot to piss and dump their bucket waste."

Chivalry was not dead, I realized, even in this "total war." I kept my binoculars trained on the same sector and sure

A collapsed railroad bridge squats in a river on the way to the Rhine.

enough, I watched a squad of ten or fifteen German soldiers crawl out of their fortifications toward the makeshift outdoor latrine. But this time, a bunch of our guys jumped them. They became prisoners, and marched to our POW stockade in the rear, where I imagined the latrines worked well.

My vantage point in a house near the edge of Kapsweyer gave me a panoramic view of the infantry attack that followed the air bombardment. Lieutenant Kraker led B Troop of the 94th toward the dragon's teeth in our sector, but the assault was general and included entire infantry and tank units on his flanks. The German counter-fire was murderous. Even I could see that the attack was a big mistake. Our troops were pinned down outside the dragon's teeth right away, and the supporting tanks were turning into blazing torches, one by one, as the enemy 105-mm guns fired with unbelievable accuracy. What tanks remained started to make a smokescreen to cover the infantry's retreat. The Germans continued firing everything they had into the cloud of smoke, and we lost dozens of men. Some of them were with the B Troop recon platoon, which was caught in the open by one barrage. Lieutenant Kirby went down, severely wounded.

The German guns followed our retreating soldiers with their barrage right into Kapsweyer. Suddenly, everything around me was exploding, and I looked for a cellar. Outside, it seemed like every vehicle that moved drew fire. I tried to stay clear of them and dove into a doorway. When I slammed the door shut behind me, I looked around and saw that my pal, Walter Blake, was in the room.

"All hell's breaking loose out there," he shouted above the unbroken din of explosions.

"Is there a cellar in this dive?" I shouted back.

Before Walter could answer me, we heard a loud knock on the door. Walter figured it must be another GI, trying to get to safety with us.

He opened the front door. An 88-mm shell flew through the doorway, zinged past both of our heads and blew out the back of the house. We didn't even have time to duck.

"Damn!" Walter shouted. "You try to be neighborly and let somebody into your house, and they blow out the back end!"

I didn't laugh. My hands were still shaking. If that shell had touched us, it would have torn our heads off. We were lucky that the shrapnel from the explosion seemed to go up and out the back, instead of into our exposed torsos. Now we had a bright view of the yard behind our house, which was filled with smoke from a fire.

Later, I thought about that incident often. It made me wonder about luck and fate, why some guys died and others were spared. We soldiers often talked of the bullet that had your name on it, how there was nothing you could do to avoid it. Every day, all of us wondered whether that would be the day when we met that bullet. And when the day ended, and you'd survived while watching some of your comrades die, you wondered why you were still around.

One of the guys in our outfit was a Rosicrucian. He often bragged that he had no fear of being under fire, because he believed in predestination. He had it all worked out in his mind that he was preordained to survive the war, and that he'd get all the help he'd need to do that without praying to God. That bothered me, and just about everyone else. A couple of the guys were superstitious, and told him to stay away from them. They didn't want to hear that kind of talk around them, because they were afraid it would jinx them.

One day we were in a house, and a mortar shell came through the roof and landed right on the Rosicrucian. There was nothing left of him. We couldn't find a trace. I figured the mortar round had his name on it, and that was all.

After the war, two of the guys in that house who witnessed the incident became ministers. It changed their whole lives, and proved to me the truth of the old saying, "There are no atheists in foxholes."

When the German artillery shifted from Kapsweyer, Walter and I emerged from our charmed shelter. It was a dark night, but I saw that our troops still were trying to breach the Siegfried Line. One unit brought up seven hundred pounds of dynamite to blow a gap in the dragon's teeth, but the German fire pinned them down short of their destination. They wound up withdrawing, dragging a kraut sentinel with them for questioning.

Our big guns, the eight-inch howitzers and 155s, peppered the German fortifications through the night. Bright orange flashes dotted the landscape, and I could feel the concussion of each explosion in my throat. Over the next couple of days, division held what they called a "turkey shoot," where every artillery piece, tank gun, assault gun, mortar and machine gun was directed at one specific enemy position. It was devastating. Said position soon disappeared in a wall of flame. Then our fire visited another position.

The weather had turned bitterly cold. It was common to see guys hop out of their tanks and run around them, so they wouldn't freeze to death. But the cold weather meant clear skies usually, which allowed our planes to fly against the Siegfried Line and add their donations to the general cacophony.

Our officer staffs were trying new tricks to breach the fortifications. I started seeing dozer tanks—Shermans with a bulldozer blade and operating mechanism welded on to the front end. We had one of these creatures in each battalion.

The brass had arrived at the simplest solution to the dragon's teeth. The dozer tanks were just to bury them, and create a path which the rest of the tanks could follow over the dragon's teeth. The Germans hadn't figured on that bit of ingenuity.

Our engineers came up with other ways to defeat the tank traps. They brought up Bailey Bridges to go over them, and dynamite to blast paths through them. The division clearly was preparing for another attack on the Siegfried Line. They would be part of an overall push made by the U.S. Seventh Army.

I was thankful that our outfit wouldn't be involved. Cracking fortified lines was not our specialty. We were recon cavalry. But even our light unit started to get more muscle. We mounted .50 caliber machine guns on the backs of our peeps.

Division later would supply us with tank destroyers, TDs, which were 90-mm guns mounted on tank chassis. We were one of the first cavalry outfits to get TDs, just in time for our eventual attack across the Rhine. We needed that heavier artillery. These would become our saviors in the weeks ahead. Whenever we entered a town where we thought we might meet resistance, we'd send a TD forward and fire a single round at the tallest structure. Usually, that was the top of a church steeple. We'd watch it fall, and wait a minute. We hoped and prayed that people would hang bedsheets out of their windows, which signified surrender. Sometimes they did. Sometimes they didn't. And sometimes we'd see the sheets and enter the town, only to have the enemy rise up behind us, trying to cut us off. That's another reason why we needed the TDs.

We didn't dare send dismounted troops into a town we thought was hostile. We'd send the TDs, and when we had tanks with us, we'd send them ahead, too. Sometimes the Germans set up an AT gun at a road junction. Occasionally, they used a disabled tank, which could still fire its main gun and machine guns. The intent was to cover two or three roads from the intersection. So it was obvious that cavalry recon units needed some extra punch from vehicles that could keep pace with us, and the TDs were an excellent solution.

But that wouldn't happen until we were across the Rhine. And the Rhine was still a tremendous barrier to our army at this time.

On Christmas Eve, our unit moved back into Alsace. It was nice to be around people who saw us as saviors instead of conquerors. The next evening, the local people got together and sang Christmas carols. They sang one of the songs in four or five different languages simultaneously. It gave us some semblance of a Christmas feeling, and we all appreciated their effort.

The church bells chimed throughout Christmas day. There was some beer, wine and schnapps to be had. Fir trees freshly cut from the woods stood decorated in the town square. Alsatian men and women, dressed in their best clothes, walked in a steady procession past my half-track, issuing holiday greetings.

The supply staff made a point of getting all of our mail to us by Christmas Eve. My wife had sent me some tobacco in the mail, so I smoked my pipe.

It was a peaceful little town in which I spent my Christmas 1944, although every now and then a shell came howling in from somewhere. We weren't directly involved in any fighting that day, which I considered the best Christmas present possible. It wasn't that we were behind the lines. Nobody knew where the lines were. Every time we pushed the lines ahead, the Germans would counterattack and push them back for a while. It was always flexible, and very dangerous.

The local civilians did everything they could to make us comfortable.

They shared what food they had with us, and we shared our food with them. Our rations delivery that Christmas included turkey and gravy with cranberries, and we had more than enough to feed the townspeople.

Our chocolate was a big hit. They were used to eating German chocolate, which was ersatz. German tobacco was nonexistent, and so was soap, so cigarettes and soap became the primary items of barter. I usually just gave them away.

I liked the people, and I thought their countryside was beautiful. The tops of the nearby mountains were covered with snow, and from the town you could see the tracks of the local wildlife. In some ways, the war had not touched that part of the country.

But nothing could substitute for being at home that Christmas. Home was six thousand miles away for me. I was in a place where people were dying, and I would see many more die before I was able to go home again.

Well northeast of our position, the German army launched a powerful counterattack, which would become known as the Battle of the Bulge. I heard all kinds of rumors about how far the *Wehrmacht* had advanced because the attack caught us completely by surprise. We simply didn't believe they had the armor to mount that kind of offensive. It was clear to all of us that we were in an emergency situation suddenly, which required extraordinary measures.

With General Patton's Third Army units pulling out of line to attack the German offensive in its southern flank, our Seventh Army had to make adjustments. The solution that command initiated was to form Task Force Hudelson, named after its commander, Colonel Daniel Hudelson. My unit was assigned to this task force.

We had a lot more ground to cover with the subtraction of Patton's forces to our immediate north, so Seventh Army had to man the line on an eighty-four-mile front. It was no secret that we were much thinner, and that would invite enemy attacks in our area. The big danger would be getting cut off from the rest of the Allied armies by a German attack through the Vosges Mountains, so our orders were to give ground rather than allow that to happen.

When the task force redeployed, it took over a ten-mile section of the front in the Vosges Mountains. Our unit set up near the town of Bitche. This place was destined to live up to its name.

We spent more than a week preparing our defenses. We dug trenches, and set up machine-gun and mortar positions with interlocking fields of fire. We built roadblocks. We buried mines, and arranged trip wires that would launch flares if the enemy tried to sneak up on us at night.

It was a strong position, located on a mountain ridge overlooking a valley. We fully expected the Germans to come through that valley when they attacked, so we had all of our heaviest weapons pointing at it. But the weather wasn't cooperating with us. It was foggy most days, with a mixture of rain and snow, so we couldn't see more than a few dozen yards ahead of us. The nights were about as black as I'd ever seen.

Despite all of our preparations, we couldn't seem to do anything right in Bitche. There were minor accidents with guys getting hurt left and right. Guys were coming down with frostbite from long exposure in outpost foxholes that served as our listening posts. We even had one guy who cut himself up badly by falling over our own barbed wire one night.

The capper came on New Year's Eve. Something hit our trip wire late that night, setting off parachute flares. We unleashed an unbelievable fireworks show. We blasted the valley with everything we had — mortars, 90-mm shells, machine guns, small-arms fire, grenades— until our ammunition was gone.

When daylight arrived, we saw that we'd mowed every tree down to about three feet high all along our field of fire. There was no sign of a German. Instead, we found one dead deer. That was what set off the trip wire.

We felt like idiots. It went down in history as the Great Big Battle of Bitche. Casualties: Bambi. It was some way to bring in the year 1945.

THE VOSGES—Fighting a German Counterattack

The Germans did strike our Seventh Army with a major attack launched just prior to midnight that New Year's Eve. It just wasn't in our area. They hit nearly all the other parts of our front with at least seventeen divisions. Practically all of the attacking troops were *Volksgrenadiers*, although there were two crack SS Panzer Grenadier divisions spearheading the offensive. They aimed for a breakthrough near the Hardt Mountains, where they intended to shoot a whole panzer division into our rear areas.

I guess we were expecting it, after all of our preparations. We'd even notched trees along the roads and set TNT charges on them, so we could blow them down as roadblocks when the attack came.

Our patrols were picking up German prisoners who seemed to bear a new confidence. One of them told me that his army was going to retake Alsace. It was all part of a plan they called "10 May 1940," named after the incredibly successful attack the *Wehrmacht* launched into France that day.

Our sector was quiet following our fireworks show. We huddled in foxholes with our carbines inside of our jackets to keep them from freezing and becoming useless. There was a definite feeling that we'd be needing them. I could hear a lot of firing in the sector next to ours. It was B Troop, getting the brunt of the fighting again. I felt sorry for them, and privately thanked God the Germans hadn't chosen our little patch of ground for their breakthrough.

During the day, we received orders to move back from our prepared positions. Apparently, our flank had become exposed after the Germans surrounded the company on our left. The roads were covered in ice, and the steel tracks on our vehicles skidded like they were on skates. We had to move slowly, to prevent accidents and losing vehicles in the ditches beside the roads.

The radio in our half-track barked with voices strained by fear. I heard calls for help. It shocked me to learn that an entire company had been surrounded in Bannstein. The radio voice begged for artillery support to stanch the German tanks that had entered the town. In the background, the noise of firing was constant. Next, I heard the voice announce that the whole company was retreating on foot, leaving all their heavy equipment behind.

There were distress calls from other units. One of them called for artillery support practically right on top of its own position. The German troops, clad in their white winter gear, were among them. They were firing wooden bullets, which were lethal at close range, but not dangerous beyond that. In this way, they killed Americans without endangering their own troops immediately behind our guys.

I prayed the Germans hadn't cut the road we were using. The radio reports indicated that our forces had pulled back to Sarreinsberg, which was several miles behind us. All of us were on edge, straining our eyes at the woods along the roadside, expecting the enemy to burst out at any moment. We'd heard reports that the Germans were using some of our own vehicles, which they'd captured. There also were instances where enemy troops donned the uniforms of dead American soldiers. I was prepared to open fire on just about anything that looked suspicious. I had a death grip on the handles of the .50 caliber attached to the half-track's side wall.

Fortunately, we didn't run into trouble on the road that day. But I learned later from a guy I met just how bad things were in places like Phillipsbourg. This guy was just a private, but he looked about eighty years old to me. Turns out he was forty-five, and he'd fought in the First World War. He said he'd re-enlisted so he could finish up in World War II.

And what a finish he made. When a German infantry unit entered Phillipsbourg with two Mark IV tanks, this old timer ran to his half-track and grabbed a bazooka. By himself, he loaded it and knocked out the lead tank. Kneeling in the middle of the street, with absolutely no cover from the hail of bullets coming his way, he kept firing until he damaged the second tank. When he ran out of bazooka rockets, he opened fire with his rifle grenades until the second tank was finished.

The old guy was just getting started. He ran back to his half-track, grabbed the .50 caliber machine gun and ammo, and returned to his perch in the middle of the street. From there, he cut up the enemy infantry and vehicles trying to rescue the two tanks. When his .50 jammed, he calmly fixed it while bullets tore away pieces of the cobblestone all around him, and he continued to fire. He pinned down the German troops, preventing their retreat.

There he stayed until supporting American forces came up and counter-attacked. He joined them, firing his .50 from the hip. When two U.S. tanks were disabled, he sprayed the Germans into seeking cover until the tank crews could escape to safety. But there was one tank crewman who was badly injured, and everyone could hear him screaming inside the burning Sherman. This old guy dropped his machine gun and climbed on the tank, trying to reach the wounded driver. He actually had hold of the man and began pulling him from the forward hatch, despite the fact that the turret was malfunctioning and revolved continuously. But the tank's ammo began to cook off, and the explosion knocked the old soldier on to the street, wounding him.

Despite his injuries, he refused to return to his unit and seek medical help. That night, he spotted a German patrol approaching the tanks he'd knocked out, and he directed fire on them, killing eleven, while forcing the remainder to take cover. The following morning, along with two other men, he assaulted the building where the surviving members of the enemy patrol had hidden. They captured four German soldiers, and both of the men accompanying the old timer were wounded in the firefight.

Later that morning, the battalion command post came under withering mortar fire, and the regimental medical officer urged that the severely wounded men be evacuated from the church where most of the rounds were falling. The old guy volunteered, hopping into a truck and driving it backwards up the street under fire. When he reached the church, he helped load four litter cases and eight walking wounded into the back of the truck. The Germans did everything they could to destroy that truck, but the old timer ignored it. He climbed into the cab and drove the truck through mortar shells and machine gun fire until he reached safety in the rear area.

For his unbelievable bravery that day, he was given America's highest battlefield award, the Medal of Honor. His name was George B. Turner. He'd certainly "finished up" what he began in the First World War. Seeing him, I never would have suspected the old man had that much bark on him.

Turner had been with the forward observer's section of Battery C, 499th Armored Field Artillery Battalion when he began his glorious chapter. He remained with this unit until the end of the war.

The 499th and other artillery units like it were breaking records in the numbers of rounds they hurled at the Germans during this offensive. The ammunition supplies coming from Marseilles allowed them to do this, and they were having an enormous effect. It was only after the war that I learned those ammunition supplies had nearly run out. The brass wisely had chosen to keep this unpleasant fact a secret.

When my unit took up its new position in the center of the task force line again, we started patrolling around Stockbronn. We came upon a roadblock made from felled trees, manned by enemy troops with MG-42s and burp guns, our slang for the MP-40 submachine gun. Even though these were lightly manned, we used the 90s on our TDs to blast them. We weren't eager to lose men by slowly escalating the conflict when we could finish them with our big stuff. Later, headquarters actually issued an order: "There will be no sniping with 75-mm tank cannon." Everyone regarded this as an elastic directive, to be obeyed only when necessary.

The Germans were patrolling, too. One of their platoons knocked out three of B Troop's armored cars. We'd constructed double apron fences to try to slow them down. One morning we found our fence had changed overnight. From a distance, it looked like it was hung with laundry. But as we got closer, we saw that it was a number of German soldiers hanging loosely over the top. We guessed our artillery had nailed them during the night. Now they were limp, collecting a light powdering of new fallen snow.

We'd hardly finished preparing our latest defensive position when we received orders to move again. Task Force Hudelson was being relieved, and ordered south to Reipertwiller. Many of the units had brought in the New

Year with ferocious combat. A lot of men had been killed and wounded. Colonel Hudelson himself almost was captured when German forces surrounded his command post. He was saved by the miraculous appearance of a tank platoon.

Our units took a terrible thrashing that New Year's Day, and nearly all of the 94th Recon troops saw intense action. All except my A Troop. We were the lucky ones so far.

Despite our severe losses, the German attack had gained only several thousand yards, and they paid a dear price in casualties and lost equipment. Some estimates claimed they'd lost more than fifteen hundred men.

But they weren't finished. They were determined to make a breakthrough. They reorganized, aiming at the route that would take them back through Hagenau and along the Strasbourg plain.

We had to prepare for continued attacks, even though Task Force Hudelson had been dissolved. The division reformed itself, and my unit eventually was sent to a quiet little burg on that Strasbourg plain. It had made it through the war without any damage. It was called Hatten.

HATTEN —
The American Stalingrad

The quaint, unharmed town of Hatten didn't stay that way for long. The Germans smashed into the 242nd Infantry troops who were stationed there on January 9. These troops were green recruits of the 42nd Infantry Division, stationed in Hatten because it was considered "safe" by the brass. The battle-hardened enemy forces cut them to pieces, decimating the three-thousand-man unit to a pitiful remnant. The carnage was horrible.

The battle report later stated flatly that the 5th Tank Battalion of the 25th Panzer Grenadier Division tried to surround Hatten with thirty Mark IV tanks and a company of infantry riding in half-tracks. But from where I stood in the distance, it was like a volcanic eruption. Shells of all calibers exploded everywhere.

It went on like that for days, with various relief units of American troops pouring into the cauldron.

On January 15, it was our turn. A Troop received orders to enter Hatten. I could see in the distance where the town used to be. No buildings were visible. The town was a massive wall of smoke, which seemed to be alive with the flashes of new explosions.

There was no way to approach that boiling storm in daylight. We waited until dark, praying for a moonless, overcast night. Then we began our approach, crawling on our bellies. We had to cover about a mile of snow-covered open ground like that. Machine-gun bullets and anti-tank shells whined just above our heads.

I desperately tried to flatten myself as much as I could. The cold snow burned my cheeks and hands, and it sifted through my collar and inside my tunic. I didn't care. All I cared about was staying flat, beneath the steel that was tearing through the air just inches above my head. All of us knew that if the Germans saw us, they would completely wipe out A Troop in this open, snow-covered field. We crawled more quietly than we'd ever done before.

Once we arrived at the edge of town, we met up with what was left of the 19th Armored Infantry Battalion. The roar of constantly exploding shells was maddening, and I noticed a look of madness on some of their faces. Combat veterans call that look "the thousand-yard stare." I couldn't blame them for being in a form of shock. Their unit had lost more than a hundred men in just a handful of hours. I didn't know it at the time, but my unit would lose half of its men in the coming days.

Our orders were to set up in positions alongside the 19th Armored Infantry, and to probe aggressively for any German troop concentrations toward the east. We'd heard rumors that the enemy was building strength for a renewed attack.

I helped to set up listening posts. It was murder trying to dig foxholes in the frozen turf. The weather was cold and snowy.

That wasn't our only problem. A Troop had been trained intensely for mobile reconnaissance missions. Now we were being asked to fight like regular infantry, even though we had neither the training nor the equipment. But no one complained. No one would have heard complaints over the din of a constant bombardment. We just checked our ammunition, armed our weapons and prayed that the division's heavy armor would arrive soon.

That relief wasn't immediately available, because the roads were ice coated. All of our vehicles had problems, but any vehicle that used steel tracks was fishtailing and swerving all over the roads. The army had improvised sand trucks that dusted the roads, but it didn't help very much. New snow covered it in just an hour. The only way to stay on the road was to drive slowly. That made all of our armor sweet targets for the enemy anti-tank gunners.

The area's topography didn't help, either. The terrain between Hatten and Rittershoffen was so flat and clear of trees that you could see one town from the other, even though they were nearly two miles apart. It was not a place any general would choose as a strong defensive position, and yet it would force our division to fight one of the greatest defensive battles of the war.

Mixed with the crash of artillery was the fearsome clanking of tank treads. Through the smoke, I could make out the silhouettes of Mark IV medium tanks, with enemy infantry crouched behind them like slithering shadows. They fired burp guns and hurled grenades. They poured into the village until they became mixed with us.

I fired my carbine from a window at fleeting images. I was never sure whether I hit anyone. I had to duck for cover too quickly. To remain exposed for a microsecond too long in that shower of lead meant certain death.

It seemed that our unit would be overwhelmed before the heavy armor of our division could rescue us. I prayed. I fired my carbine. It was all I could do.

Help finally came in the form of an artillery barrage. The explosions erupted in a tight arc around the outside of town, and when the smoke cleared, we saw wrecked German vehicles and soldiers strewn everywhere. Some of them still moved. Wounded soldiers screamed. Fires blazed in the twisted vehicles, sending up columns of black smoke.

The artillery had been perfectly directed by C and E Troops of our outfit, from their vantage points outside Rittershoffen. The information they forwarded to division artillery was a bull's-eye, and they would receive a Presidential commendation for it. They'd saved their brethren in A Troop—for now.

The enemy armor kept coming toward the town. By this time, our own armor was moving in along the single-track railroad that connected Hatten to Rittershoffen. It seemed like all of the Shermans fired their guns simultaneously, and in a couple of minutes, three German tanks were flaming hulks.

I heard cheers from our guys still hiding in the nearby houses, but they stopped when three of the Shermans blew apart. The enemy had them zeroed in with their AT guns, and the HEAT (High Explosive Anti-Tank) rounds were devastating. The rest of the tanks had to pull back out of harm's way, but by nightfall our lines had been reestablished.

The krauts didn't allow us any peace that night. They fired rockets into the village from their *Nebelwerfers*. We called them "Screaming Mimis," because of the shrieking noise they made on the way in. The rockets fired from simple tubes, and there were usually eight of them in a group. The *Nebelwerfer* rocket launchers were small enough for one soldier to pull them, like a shopping cart, but they saturated a small area with high explosives and steel fragments. When you heard Mimi scream, you ducked against a concrete wall and hoped they wouldn't land right on you.

Between blasts, I actually could hear the German vehicles gathering outside of town. I even could hear their troops talking from time to time. It was disconcerting, to say the least, and I wondered why our artillery wasn't targeting them.

The German artillery certainly didn't take the night off. At one point we had to take cover from a very heavy barrage. The ground bucked under what felt like naval-sized shells, and I wondered whether the enemy had moved up its huge 240-mm cannons. I could see from the glow outside that a fair number of houses had caught fire. The ground shivered with seismic intensity. No one got to sleep that night.

The morning light revealed a horrifying specter to our bleary eyes. Just beyond the edge of town I saw German tanks painted white to camouflage themselves in the snow-covered field. Their guns cracked at our tanks, which returned the fire. I saw a Mark IV flame up. Then another. And the German artillery opened up again.

Suddenly, our tanks started bursting into flames. One of them blasted its turret straight up to a crazy height.

The armored slugging match reached a crescendo so quickly, I couldn't keep up with the hits. Multi-colored tracers crisscrossed amidst burning tanks. The Germans were attacking again.

The single hour that battle took to complete seemed like a day to me. But when it was finished, the enemy had been repelled once again.

Our tankers had paid a terrible price, and the receipt was spread out on the snow for all to see. One platoon had lost all but one of its tanks. Another had lost all but two, and a third had just three remaining. The remainder of the tank company pulled back toward Rittershoffen, and my heart sank.

We did what we could to put out the fires and replenish our ammunition. I'd never been so thirsty in my life. My mouth and throat were coated with a fine powder, and I must have swallowed two canteens of water before I could breath right again.

I had no idea what I looked like, but I figured it was the same as the other soldiers I saw creeping out of the battered houses— gaunt faces covered in dirt and soot so that the eyes looked like headlights on a dark night; dust-covered uniforms that almost lightened their olive drab color to match the slushy snow on the ground; scraped and bloody hands gripping rifles like vises.

We heard a tremendous, steady rumbling from Rittershoffen, and we knew it was their turn. Our tank units fought from house to house to blast out the enemy troops there. We felt bad for our fellow troopers of the 94th — for about a second. We were thankful it wasn't us this time.

But our respite was short lived. The Germans kept attacking. We counted five separate attacks in two hours. Each one of them was beaten back by our division artillery.

If it wasn't for the wire crews keeping the landlines intact under constant mortar and tank fire, Hatten probably would have been overrun that day. Their work allowed spotters to accurately lay destruction on the attacking enemy units from all the guns of seven artillery battalions. In many cases, the shells landed a mere thirty seconds after they called for them.

The constant German pressure brought positive results for the enemy, however. Moving up house by house, they held most of the town, while we were forced into the western edge of Hatten. We received word that we were cut off. Their artillery from both sides of the town hammered us now. The once-unblemished burg was turning into a rubble pile.

The Germans set up anti-tank guns south of the village, and they blasted a tank column that was trying to break through to us. Again, the artillery dumped barrages right on the enemy AT guns. I saw them being destroyed, one after another. And yet they continued to knock out our tanks. We figured the enemy must be sending up new crews, or even new weapons, every chance they got.

All around me was the rapid staccato of burp guns. The German infantry kept moving in on us, shrinking our positions, house by house. There were times when American and German troops fought each other from different floors of the same house.

A platoon of tanks finally fought their way into town, bringing much needed supplies. That day the air force's C-47 transport planes had tried to drop supplies to us, too, but most of the goods wound up in German hands.

The tanks parked at a little rail station on the south side of the village, and I replenished by .30 caliber carbine ammunition and scored a bag of bazooka rockets. I put them next to my bazooka.

We did all of this under constant mortar and artillery fire. Darkness didn't interrupt the barrages. It was going to be another sleepless night in the bitter cold.

I watched dully as the medics arrived, gathering the wounded and loading them into the rear of the trucks and peeps. Some of the wounded were hideously torn up, and I tried not to look at them. I said a silent prayer that, if I was hit, it would finish me and not leave me like that.

More reinforcements poured into Hatten that night, infantry and armor. We had no trouble seeing them, as the town was ablaze. The enemy had no trouble either, lobbing round after round on top of the arriving troops. And wherever it was dark, the Germans lit up the night with their star shells.

The newly arrived infantry dispersed into the buildings we already occupied. We showed them the safest havens, the cellars. My unit was cramped into a tiny corner of the village, probably only one-and-a-half square blocks in all, adjoining the main street on the western edge. During the night, a German patrol attacked one of the houses. They used a flame thrower to set it ablaze, and our troops had to abandon the place. Bit by bit, our ring grew tighter.

They were using incendiary bullets, too—anything that would start the structures burning. In one house the enemy fired a flame thrower into the basement, where an Alsatian family hid. We heard their screams on the next block.

We learned about other infuriating incidents. In one of our houses that night, a German walked in the front door with his hands up to surrender, shouting, "*Kamerad.*" When one of our troops told him to enter slowly, he stood aside and another German soldier behind him opened fire. Tales like this caused the fighting to degenerate into a death struggle in which few prisoners were taken.

At daylight, our division's armor outside of Hatten resumed its counterattack. We pitched in by going after the Germans in the houses near us. We had to do it house by house.

I used the bazooka to make a hole in the walls of the houses. Then several other men tossed grenades into the hole and through the windows. There were a couple of tanks in the street behind us, blasting the houses ahead of us. It was an ugly kind of fighting, but despite my sheer exhaustion from sleeplessness, my senses were razor sharp.

We continued this way until after dark, at which time the Germans attacked again, and retook some of our hard-earned real estate. Once more, the medics used darkness to collect the wounded men.

One of our fast, light tanks ferried these men on litters from the forward aid station on the edge of town to the railroad station south of Rittershoffen. This had become our field hospital, command post, artillery spotting post, and basic lifeline. The light tank made thirteen trips carrying wounded to Rittershoffen that night.

It was no easy feat. The Germans had bracketed their guns on that route, and on just about everything else we tried to do. When we stockpiled our supply of rations in a small dump, the kraut observers located it in no time and directed fire on it.

In Hatten, it just wasn't safe to do anything. Sixty German batteries were firing at us. And during lulls, caused when our own artillery fired counter-battery barrages, the German gunners would drop a few shells on our positions, to make us think our guys were firing inaccurately.

The tank fighting in Hatten became cat-and-mouse. A Sherman would pull to a corner and stop, knowing that a Panther tank sat up the street. Both tanks sat still, protected from each other by that house on the corner. Eventually, they'd fire through the house, trying to score a lucky hit without exposing themselves. If one blew a hole that exposed the other, that tank would back out of harm's way.

At dusk, it was our turn to launch a big night attack. The lead tank platoon moved all of two blocks. It cost them three tanks. They seemed to be fighting blind in the smoke and darkness. It's hard enough to see what's happening around you in a tank during broad daylight. Under the conditions of that night, it was insane.

Something else happened that night. I noticed a certain numbness spreading inside me. It seemed to start in my brain. My responses to questions were slower. My words were clipped. I mumbled sentence fragments. The constant roar of explosions and screeching of rockets was battering my whole being, and it was getting inside my head. The heightened, uninterrupted state of fear was sucking the juice out of my brain. Somehow, I kept functioning. I followed orders, like an automaton.

We had orders to support the tanks on foot. We'd be in a house, separated from the house next door by a wall, and nothing but open sky above it. You never knew whether that next house was filled with enemy troops. We lobbed grenades over the wall and ducked until after the blast, just to make sure. Sometimes they would do the same thing to us. And through all of this, artillery shells never stopped exploding all around us.

The town no longer resembled a town. It was a rubble pile, punctuated by corpses. Germans. Americans. Civilians. Kids. I remember being annoyed at having to look at them all the time, as if the poor victims had any say in the matter. The stench of their putrefaction only added another ingredient to the overall miasma of burning gasoline, wood, steel and flesh. We'd all been breathing it for days. I barely noticed it any longer.

The Germans launched a new attack at dusk. This one topped all previous attempts to wipe us out of Hatten. As usual, it started with a big artillery barrage, followed by scores of crouched infantry in coal scuttle helmets, toting burp guns behind clanking panzers. And as usual, we met them with machine-gun fire and directed artillery. It produced a familiar wall of noise and concussion.

Tracers streaked through the dark streets, bouncing off walls and burned-out vehicles. Every now and then, an angry shout, or a wounded shriek, or a woman's scream would come through the noise.

Our tanks were using white phosphorous shells on the houses we knew to be German occupied. They didn't produce a large, destructive concussion,

The town of Hatten in ruins, following the fierce 1945 battle.

but they spread searing heat throughout an enclosed area, covering every-thing in a substance that burned like acid. God help anyone whose skin was splattered with phosphorous. The screams we heard inside those houses were more animal than human.

When the attack petered out, and the Germans withdrew what was left of their forward units to their own section of town, a quirky memory struck me. I thought of what the Duke of Wellington said after defeating Napoleon at Waterloo: "They came on in the same old way, and we beat them in the same old way." There was still some vestige of the history teacher left in my shell-shocked noggin.

I must be exhausted, I thought. It occurred to me that I'd only caught an hour of sleep here and there. I couldn't recall the last time I'd had hours of unbroken slumber. But that was the way things were. You grabbed a nap when you could, and you woke up when you had to. It wasn't odd to see a soldier asleep on his feet.

Eating was a matter of opportunity, too. You'd plop down behind a wall, open a tin of rations, and wolf it down. Sometimes you ate while bullets flew overhead and shells erupted nearby. Sometimes the contents had become so frozen in the cold weather you had to hack out pieces with the sharp back edge of your spoon, and suck on them like ice pops.

I usually ate in the cellars, where often I'd find a cache of produce like raw potatoes or vegetables. To me, they were just as good as K-rations. It was a fairly safe place to feed yourself, and grab a few moments of sleep.

That's what I was doing when somebody kicked my boot. I opened my eyes to see a sergeant standing above me in the cellar.

"Let's go," he said. "We're moving up."

I rose on my aching legs, grabbed my bazooka and its bag of rockets, and followed him outside with a couple of other men from our unit. From the noise, I could tell that we were counterattacking the Germans again. We moved down the rubble-strewn path that was once a street, past twisted, unrecognizable hulks of metal and frozen corpses, crouching against what cover we could find.

Overhead suddenly, there came a burst. I thought it was a time-fuse round. I hit the ground, knowing full well that a time-fuse round would kill me anyway. They were designed to explode in the air, and rain shrapnel down on anyone below. It didn't matter if you were in a beautiful piece of cover. If you didn't have cover from above, you were dead meat.

But this shell had a different kind of report. I'd never heard anything like it before. There was no loud explosion. Instead of fragments, bits of paper floated down on us. I picked up one of them. It contained a series of drawings and writing in English, informing me that my position was hopeless and urging me to surrender. The drawings demonstrated the proper way to achieve this. I actually chuckled before balling it up and tossing it. Hard to avoid the irony when an air-burst shell could have nailed me, and instead it showered me with cartoons.

We followed the sergeant until we reached the sector where some other American unit was pressing a counterattack. Just when we arrived, the whole area erupted under a barrage of mortar and artillery fire. The mortars were heavy 81-mm and 120-mm shells, some of them with delayed fuses designed to explode in our faces when we were sure they were duds.

Our men were inside a pocket that was about two hundred yards by four hundred yards, and the Germans were saturating it with artillery. All around me were houses that smoldered because there was nothing left in them to burn.

Peering through the smoke, I heard a crack. I looked in that direction and recognized a German Mark V tank, a Panther, at the end of the street. Then I felt a tug at my sleeve.

"Let's go, soldier. I'll be your loader," someone said.

I turned to see the voice belonged to a colonel. If it had been anyone but an officer, I'd have told him to go screw himself. No one charges a Panther tank out in the open with just a bazooka.

But I had no choice. I grabbed the bazooka from behind my shoulder, and followed the colonel. He urged me up the street toward the Panther tank. We moved ahead, spurting from doorway to doorway.

I handed him the bag of rockets and squatted in a doorway just a few dozen yards from the panzer. The colonel squatted behind me, shoved a rocket into the back of the bazooka tube that rested on my right shoulder, and patted my helmet.

I aimed through the clear plastic sight, and lined the cross-hairs up on the small area where the turret meets the body of the tank. That was about the only way I could disable the monster with a puny bazooka.

My hand squeezed the trigger and I felt the pipe lurch on my shoulder as it emitted flames from both ends simultaneously. It roared, and I watched the rocket approach the tank as if in slow motion. It hit exactly where I'd aimed it … and bounced off without exploding.

"My God, I think I forgot to pull the pin," the colonel shouted. "Let's take another shot!"

"Hell, no!" I shouted, not caring what rank the fool had. "That thing is coming after us!"

The Panther's turret turned, its long-barreled 75-mm cannon rotating toward me. I felt frozen in the moment, watching terrified as the gun's snout arced around. But before it could draw a bead on my head, the cannon barrel struck a telephone pole and stopped turning. I didn't have time to thank God or dumb luck.

"Let's get the hell out of here!" I yelled, and we ran like madmen.

I was afraid to look back when I heard the clanking of the Panther's treads. It was pursuing us down the street. It fired, blowing huge chunks of masonry out of a building just behind us. We zig-zagged along the street.

Blam! Another round shot past us and took out the corner building ahead. I turned that corner, panting like a dog. My bazooka was gone. I had no idea when or where I'd dropped it. I had only my carbine, strapped over my shoulder across my chest. I just kept running until I reached a group of guys who were manning a 155-mm gun behind a wall of rubble.

"Panther!" shouted the colonel, pointing behind us to the corner.

We took shelter in a doorway and watched the gunners slam a huge round into the breach. The barrel was down, level with the street. There was a crumbling noise as the Panther tank pushed through the corner of the building up the street, and came into sight. The 155 shot out a bright flame and there was a loud double thud. The second thud was the round hitting the Panther tank so hard that it knocked it sideways. There was no smoke, no fire, no noise at all from the tank. I eased my way up the street toward it. I had to see what had happened, because this was the same tank that had injured one of my friends during the firing on our column. His name was Bill, and he was badly wounded.

When I climbed aboard the Panther, I immediately saw that the 155-mm round had penetrated just above the driver's head, where the armor is thickest. It caved in the whole front end on the driver's head. There was no sign inside of the commander and the rest of the crew, just a greasy paste on the interior walls.

Later, I found Bill lying on a stretcher among scores of other wounded men, waiting to be trucked back to a hospital. I told him we got the guy who got him, if that was any consolation. He smiled thinly and squeezed my hand. He was just glad to get out of Hatten.

Bill spent two years after the war in Walter Reid Army Hospital, having all sorts of surgeries to heal what that panzer had done to him. But heal he did, and eventually he became a doctor. He married his nurse, and they raised six kids. At the aid station, I almost envied Bill, despite the severity of his wounds. I wanted to get out of Hatten, too. We'd been fighting nonstop for days in conditions that some would compare to Stalingrad.

I didn't realize then that I wouldn't have much longer to wait. On January 19, the enemy launched yet another attack. It was a major emergency. Even the medics grabbed rifles and fought beside the combat infantrymen. They had no option. They had to fight or else. Half of the medics in the 94th should have received combat infantry badges. When they weren't shooting, they were treating the wounded. The only wounds they attended at this point were those to the head and stomach.

In our pocket of the village, shells landed so thickly that no place but a cellar seemed safe. That's where I headed, following my friend Bill Walby. I knew that if big Bill thought a place was safe, it was safe.

We crouched against the concrete foundation, knowing the only thing that could harm us was a direct hit that brought down the whole house.

And that's exactly what happened.

"Help!" I cried, alone and buried under the house beam that trapped my leg.

I was hoarse from calling for hours. I didn't know how many hours it had been. Outside, amid the din of destruction, I heard a thin voice.

"Westy?" it yelled.

I thought I must be hearing things, but I shouted as loud as I could.

"I'm down here!"

"Hold on, Hugh! Hold on!"

It was a real voice, and not my imagination. It belonged to Walby. He'd made it out of the house as it fell down. Until that moment, I was sure he'd been killed. If he had been killed, that would have been the end of me, too, because he was the only guy in the world who knew where I was.

"Give me a hand here!" I heard Walby shout to someone above.

Between the crackling of small-arms fire and the booming of shells, I heard men digging. Walby and some other guys were pulling out chunks of masonry and heaving aside timber with a battle raging around them. I prayed they would get to me before anyone got hurt.

Walby didn't quit. He and his helpers scratched and heaved until they were in the shambles of the dark basement. Walby stood above me, looking bigger than ever.

"Don't worry, Westy," he said. "We're getting you out of here."

"Thanks," I mumbled weakly.

I noticed blood seeping down Walby's arm as he bent over and grasped the beam trapping my boot. It didn't register on me at first that he might be wounded, too. Everyone seemed to have blood on them.

Two other soldiers joined Walby and they lifted the heavy beam aside. There was no way I could walk. The soldiers grasped me under the armpits and followed Walby up the pile of rubble, dragging me into daylight. The smoke-filled air was like a breath of heaven after so many hours of entombment.

"Thanks," I muttered, looking up at Walby and the rest. It was all I could say.

The firing and bombardment was all around us as they pulled me toward the aid station. I was in such deep shock, I barely noticed the noise.

They placed me on a litter among rows of groaning, torn up men. It was just a few yards from where I'd talked with my friend Bill one day before. Now I was getting out of it, too.

The battle of Hatten-Rittershoffen would continue to rage for several days afterward. Four German divisions had attacked those towns, hurling in tens of thousands of artillery rounds and hundreds of armored vehicles in a desperate attempt to break through to the Alsatian plain, all the way to Strasbourg.

They smashed at the 14th Armored Division for eleven days. The 14th Armored Division blunted their attacks.

After surrendering, the Germans agreed that Hatten-Rittershoffen was one of the greatest holding actions of the war, based on the number of their casualties, and the number of artillery shells they'd fired at us.

My unit, the 94th Cavalry Recon, received a Presidential Commendation for this action. I received a Bronze Star and a Purple Heart.

I also received nightmares that have haunted me long after the war's end, and that continue to this day. I've often asked myself how and why I got through it.

But at that moment, when Walby loaded my litter into the rear of the half-track which would transport me to a hospital, I asked no questions. My battle of Hatten was over.

Nancy —
Hopitalized in the Rear

Bill Walby rode with me in the half-track that transported me to safety. We both were clamped down on litters in the rear compartment. He'd been slightly wounded, but I didn't really notice. I noticed very little at the time.

I don't remember much from that ride to the hospital. I have no idea how long it took. My first memory following the journey is in a hospital bed, looking around and seeing Walby in the bed next to me.

"Welcome to Nancy," he smiled.

My brain still wasn't functioning. Bill must have read it in my dull, confused eyes.

"Nancy, France," he continued. "We're in the hospital, Westy, the big one."

My brain groped through the crumbs of information Walby had just sprinkled. I couldn't quite grasp that I was in a safe place, deep in the rear. There would be no artillery barrages, no tanks shooting at me, no whining ricochets around my head. It wasn't possible for me to process that, after living in unbroken terror for so many days.

I automatically took stock of my physical situation. My head was sore, and I had a throbbing bump on my forehead where the wooden beam hit my helmet. It hurt when I turned my head, so I knew there was something wrong with my neck, too. The pain wasn't excruciating, but years later I would learn that I'd suffered some spinal damage.

Most of my pain came from bruises and burns, which seemed to be all over me. None were serious, but they all added up to bother me more than the bump on my head or the pain in my neck.

Random thoughts took stock of my situation: I was lucky just to be alive. I'd be dead for sure, if it wasn't for Walby. I have all my body parts. Everything hurts, but I'm going to be OK.

That much I knew in my dazed state.

What I didn't know at the time was that the doctors didn't admit me to this hospital for my wounds. None of the wounds was serious, and taken all together, they wouldn't have qualified me to get out of combat.

They were treating me for shell shock. That's what they called it back then, before someone invented the medical term Post Traumatic Stress Disorder, or PTSD. The doctors still were learning about it, and how to treat it. Until the First World War, medicine didn't even recognize it as a disorder.

Funny how shell shock coincided with the advent of big artillery barrages in 1914. The two definitely are connected.

It's hard to describe how it feels. You just freeze mentally, and can't get unwound. Most of the time, you don't even realize there's something wrong with your thinking. You become delusional. I guess it's the human brain's way of protecting itself when it's been overloaded with fear and tension.

I kept my confusion to myself for a few days, as they fed us warm hospital meals on trays, with real plates, knives and forks. The food was great, but I didn't trust them. I was sure they were setting me up for something.

One day, I leaned over to Walby in the bed next to me, and whispered my suspicions.

"This is a German hospital," I told him. "They're pumping us for information. I don't know what the hell we've got, but they're after something."

"Hell, no," Walby said. "This is a genuine American hospital in France."

"It's a kraut hospital, I tell you. Let's look for a chance to break out of this place."

Bill sat up in his bed, with a look of mild worry behind his smile.

"You don't want to break out of here," he said soothingly.

"Yes I do, and I'm getting ready for it."

"What do you mean?" Bill asked, now concerned.

I looked around, making sure none of the German orderlies was near enough to hear, and whispered in a barely audible rasp.

"I've been swiping a knife here and there, and I've got some other kitchen utensils. I have a big fork. If we get enough of that stuff, we can do a pretty good job on some of these guys, and then we can get out of here."

Surreptitiously, I lifted my blanket so only Bill could see the collection of knives and forks I'd hidden at the foot of my cot.

I don't know how I got the notion that I was in a German hospital. I suppose it was because the last thing I remembered was being surrounded by the Germans in Hatten. I figured they'd captured me, and now they were trying to pry information out of me. I intended to slash my way to freedom with eating utensils.

Bill turned me in. He was looking out for me again. I was crazy enough at that time to hurt somebody, and get myself killed in the process.

The nurses confiscated my weapons stash. They kept all sharp utensils from me, and after that I had to eat my meals with a spoon and a standard army mess kit. But I still knew all the doctors, orderlies and nurses were Germans, so I never trusted them. That delusion stayed with me until it was time to go back to the front.

I guess I spent a couple of weeks in that hospital. I can't be sure, since I wasn't thinking clearly. I don't believe it was long enough, because I never did get over some of that battle shock. After the war, when I started to feel safe again, a lot of bad memories from the war — especially being buried alive in Hatten — invaded my dreams. You never quite shake something like that.

A year or so after I returned home, I saw a doctor about it. I'd known the man before the war, so I trusted him. He'd taken up residency at a veteran's hospital in Reseda. At that time, I'd returned to work as a teacher, and I was suffering from terrible stomachaches. After a month under observation in the hospital, the doctor diagnosed it as a spastic colon. He said it was related to my combat experiences, and to the PTSD that grew out of them. He operated, trying to reduce the spasms.

But the advice this doctor gave to me was more beneficial than any surgery. He told me to change myself, to alter my behavior, and relax my ambitions. He told me to tone down everything I was doing, and warned me against getting too wrapped up in my teaching work. He cautioned me to avoid anything that might cause excitement, and especially to avoid anything that involves competition. This meant competition for higher positions and salaries in my career.

All of the aspects of PTSD were inherent in his suggestions. He told me never to try to be the top person in anything.

"Even if you're close, don't try," he said. "Just be happy with your place in things. If you push too hard, you'll develop ulcers."

I did develop a couple of small ulcers, but they never became serious, because I followed the doctor's advice.

During my stay in the hospital in Nancy, none of this was relevant yet. I was stuck inside of my delusions, always suspicious of the doctors and nurses. Bill Walby was very understanding. I guess it was because he'd been through it himself. All the guys in that hospital ward had experienced something similar to what I was going through, so no one made fun of my condition.

Besides, there were more radical cases of shell shock in that hospital ward. One guy used to jump out of bed in the middle of the night, comb his hair and shave. He did this every single night that I was there.

Each morning at about six, we'd all stand by our beds in a formation of sorts, just to keep some semblance of military bearing. And each morning during this ritual, the guy jumped out of bed, and stood stiffly to attention. Then he'd salute and shout, "Corporal so-and-so, serial number such-and-such, reporting for action, sir!"

No one said anything. It didn't strike us as strange. It was just the way we started our day.

The strangest thing I saw during my hospital stay was when I walked into an adjacent room and discovered a grizzly picture. A group of dead bodies lay on tables, uncovered, pale and stiff. They looked like mannequins in a department store warehouse.

I guess the doctors had tried to save them, but couldn't, so they left the bodies for the graves registration guys. It was probably foolish to leave such a sight where shell shock cases could stumble upon it, but it didn't bother me. Dead bodies are ubiquitous in combat zones, and I guess that's still where my head was.

I looked carefully at one body. The guy had no apparent wounds, outside of a small blue mark on his right cheek, below his cheekbone. His face was frosted from the cold weather. He looked like he could be alive, but he didn't seem to be breathing. I made sure by checking the tag on his toe, which pronounced him dead.

Some time later, when I was back at the front, I ran into a guy who looked familiar. We started chatting, and he told me he'd been wounded, and knocked unconscious.

"Next thing I know, I'm in a bag full of stiffs!" he continued.

Then I realized why he looked familiar. He was the dead guy with the blue mark on his cheek. The graves registration guys had stuffed him into a body bag with other dead bodies, and were dragging it for burial when he woke up. He fought his way out of there, which must have scared the hell out of the burial crew.

Turns out he'd been hit in the cheek by a bullet that knocked out a tooth. The concussion put him into a deep state of unconsciousness. There had been no blood, probably because the bullet didn't nick any capillaries, or because it was just too cold to bleed from such a wound. The cold weather may have produced a type of suspended animation, where his breathing wasn't noticeable, either.

In any case, I was thankful that I woke up in a hospital bed, and not in a bag full of dead bodies. That probably would have sent me over the edge.

My condition was only good for a couple of days of rest and rehabilitation, because in that time, the Army decided it needed me again. The Germans had broken through our lines on the Moder River on January 25, and established a bridgehead in the Ohlungen Forest. At least, that's what the visiting officer said.

None of that meant anything to me. I still thought I was behind enemy lines. In fact, I thought it was some kind of trick when this officer said the breakthrough was an emergency situation which required "the servicing of walking wounded," as he put it. That meant anyone who could walk and carry a gun was returning to the front lines.

There were about twenty-five or thirty of us in the hospital who could walk, and among those, the only guy who didn't go back into combat was our spit-and-polish neighbor who "reported for action" every morning. They shipped him to Paris.

"Damn," said Walby. "Who the hell is crazy now?"

We were sorry we didn't "report for action" every day, too.

They mustered us out of our hospital garb and into some rags they called uniforms. We threw on some aged British helmets and moth-eaten overcoats to protect against the bitter cold. There was no modern American equipment to be had there, so someone had scrounged about a hundred old Lee-Enfield rifles. These were vintage World War I bolt-action infantry weapons, which were obsolete on a modern battlefield. They required you to work the bolt between each shot. By the time you could bring the thing around to bear, the target was gone. You might as well fight with a broomstick.

The rifles had bayonets attached, which made them even more ungainly. The British seemed very proud of these weapons, but I didn't think much of them. They had a peculiar front sight that reminded me of Mickey Mouse's ears. As far as I was concerned, they weren't designed for fighting in a war zone.

They also gave us two bandoliers of ammunition, and loaded us into a truck headed for the front lines. I never did fire the Lee-Enfield they gave me. When we dismounted, I found an old Springfield Model 1903, and used that instead. It was vintage World War I, too, but it was a much better rifle in my opinion — deadly accurate, and with a better rate of fire. It's what Sergeant Alvin York used when he wiped out dozens of Germans with his sniping in the First World War.

Thus armed, and wearing those odd soup bowl-shaped World War I helmets which the British continued to use, Bill Walby and I took up our positions in a house with a few other guys. I have no idea in what town or at what part of the lines we were located. We simply aimed our obsolete rifles out of the windows and fired at everything that moved. For some reason, I was thinking more clearly in combat than I had in the hospital. I knew now that I was among American soldiers, and not kraut interrogators.

Apparently, our division counterattacked the Germans with a lot of force, because they melted away quickly in our front. When the shooting died down, Walby and I left the shelter of the house and walked among the fallen enemy soldiers. We prodded them with our rifle barrels, to make sure they weren't pretending to be dead.

It was no silly gesture, because we'd heard often about Germans feigning death, and then hopping up after our guys had passed them to make a getaway. Sometimes they were shot, as our troops reacted to the sudden movement. Sometimes they shot us. It was probably the oldest ruse in warfare.

Unlike some of our soldiers, I wouldn't use a bayonet to prod the fallen Germans. It seemed like it would be a bloody mess to do that. I simply nudged the bodies with the barrel of my Springfield, or bumped them on the head with the rifle butt. I had no live ones that day, but one of our guys prodded a "dead" German trooper, who immediately sat up and surrendered to him. We called somebody to haul him to the rear, which was standard operating procedure.

While waiting for an MP unit to pick this prisoner up, we kept him in a house with the rest of us. He was wounded, and kept asking for water. The guy standing guard over him shouted, "You ain't getting any *Wasser*, Fritz."

"Oh for God's sake, let him have a drink," one of our other troopers said, approaching with his canteen.

"Get the hell out of here," shouted the guard, actually turning his rifle toward the approaching GI, but not pointing it at him. "He can suffer the way his kind made my friends suffer."

That was the logic of war for some men. It was a never-ending series of revenge opportunities, to pay back the enemy for dead and wounded friends. It was hard to argue with it, but the GI with the canteen persisted. It took a long time, and some ragging from the rest of us before the guarding soldier relented, and allowed the German a sip of water. The guard couldn't resist letting us all know what a bunch of idiots we were.

During the battle around Hatten, there were rumors that the Germans had used some of their crack Waffen SS units. They were incredibly good soldiers, but they were fanatics, and we trusted them about as far as we could throw them. It wasn't surprising that they received "preferential treatment" when we captured some of them. We'd heard about what happened up north in Malmedy during the Battle of the Bulge. The SS units there had captured about two hundred American soldiers and simply executed them in the field. They left their bodies to freeze in the snow.

Something similar had happened in Hatten, where about fifty of our guys from the 242nd Infantry were executed after they'd surrendered. All of us assumed it was the SS, but after the war, the onus for that atrocity fell on a regiment from the German 7th Parachute Division. No war crime trial ever took place, so I guess we'll never really know who was responsible. But at the time, we automatically blamed the SS for any atrocity in the field.

For this reason, whenever we knew we were up against SS units, we ratcheted up our fighting intensity. That had been the case in our recent action. One of our outfits captured an SS platoon during the Moder River fight, and was marching them down a road toward the stockade. Our guys were covering them with .50 caliber machine guns. One of the machine gunners just opened up and shot the whole procession of SS prisoners to pieces.

I couldn't take that. There are plenty of reasons to repeat the mantra that "war is hell," and I knew that shooting prisoners wasn't confined to this present struggle. My background as a history instructor taught me that even our own troops in the Revolutionary War had an episode where they killed British soldiers attempting to surrender. The British in this case had been led by Banastre Tarleton, who himself had ordered the murder of colonial troops who had surrendered. To our troops, it was simply turnabout. They called it giving the prisoners "Tarleton's Quarter."

I suppose that's what the machine gunner gave to the SS prisoners: Tarleton's Quarter. But it didn't make me feel any better.

STRASBOURG—
Allied Advance Renewed

After we forced the Germans back across the Moder River, Walby and I climbed into a half-track and joined the long line of vehicles driving down the river road. I was just taking in the scenery while standing in the back when suddenly the half-track in front of us swerved and tumbled down the steep bank into the river. The current was swift, and I could see the driver emerge. He wore thick glasses, and I saw them fall off and sink. He and the others in the vehicle began to swim, but unlike the rest who swam toward the near bank, the driver swam in the opposite direction. We called out to him and a few guys ran down to the shore to help. But the guy kept swimming in the wrong direction, and finally disappeared. I guess he was blind without his glasses. They never found him, and he was officially listed as MIA, Missing in Action. His family probably received notice, saying he'd died bravely in combat.

We were somber during the rest of the trip, as the half-track brought us back to our own unit. When we arrived, there was plenty of back slapping and some playful insults hurled our way. It was clear the guys were happy to see us. I actually was glad to be back with them, too, even though it meant returning to the danger zone. It's one of the odd psychological byproducts of war. You become so close to your guys in the unit that you prefer being with them than being where it's safe. This is why so many soldiers feel lost on leave, even those who get to go home.

A bunch of the guys joined Walby and me, telling us what had happened while we were away. As we sat above the river, a few peeps arrived. One of them stopped in front of us.

"Hop in," ordered the sergeant behind the steering wheel. We did, and the peeps sped, bouncing and jarring, to a temporary depot. We got out and happily surrendered our obsolete World War I equipment. I managed to keep the 1903 Springfield, however, and sent it home to Pauline for safekeeping. It was one of dozens of weapons and artifacts that I sent to her.

The new equipment we received was impressive — uniforms, bedrolls, helmets, weapons and ammunition. We also received a new combat jacket. I think they called it an Eisenhower jacket. It was short, coming only to the belt, and lightweight, but it was warm and allowed easy movement of the arms. This is vital if your life depends on firing your weapon before someone fires at you.

The helmets were improved, too. They came in two pieces, the outer steel helmet and the inner plastic liner with webbing that acted to cushion your head. This took some of the shock away. If I had been wearing this helmet when the house collapsed on my head, I probably wouldn't have been knocked out. But the new pot was still inferior to what the Germans used. Theirs was stronger, and better designed.

The supply people must have realized suddenly that it was winter, because we also received fur-lined caps, mittens and new shoe packs. The shoe packs were like a big overshoe, a combat boot that was a combination of rubber and leather. You laced it up to your shin, so it was easy to get them on and off. They kept your feet dry and prevented trench foot, which was a big problem for our troops up until then. You still could get trench foot in the new boots, but there's no way to prevent that when you spend a week in your shoes. The new boots were a great improvement.

Better equipment wasn't confined to our creature comforts, either. Our division received the latest improved version of the Sherman tank, designated M4A3E8, which had thicker armor, so it wouldn't light up on every strike, and wider tracks to handle better in the mud and the open field. Apparently somebody was finally paying attention to the complaints of the tankers.

You could see that the designers were copying the features of the superior German tanks. There was more room for recoil behind the guns on the new tanks, and they had a lower silhouette. They also could shoot accurately on the move, and they were pretty fast. The improved models also came with additional weaponry, like rocket launchers.

This model, which mounted a contraption called a Calliope on a medium tank, definitely was not one of the Army's shining successes. The Calliope was a multiple rocket launcher mounted on the tank's turret. During a demonstration, one of them blew up. Fortunately, our division only received two or three of these things.

It reinforced my opinion of the tank. They were just big junk piles as far as I was concerned, and I was glad I didn't have to ride in them.

West poses for a photograph he sent to his wife, Pauline, in 1945.

We still had our light tanks, of course. They had been the signature of the Mechanized Cavalry, because they had aircraft engines and were fast. They needed to be. They were made of a thin, flat steel plate with rivets all along the borders, and when hit by an 88-mm shell, those rivets would fly around inside the tank like angry bees. Their speed was their best defense against panzers.

We would use all of our new finery in a general attack that was being organized at that time. The entire Allied front hoped to regain the initiative it lost during the Battle of the Bulge and the Hatten-Rittershoffen fights.

In our sector, the attack jumped off on February 1. This time, the heavy armored units led the way, instead of our cavalry outfits. We already knew exactly where the Germans were, and how many units they had.

The battle opened with the rumbling of artillery, ours and theirs, in the distance. I was glad to be listening instead of ducking. All of our guys were still exhausted, and the break gave us a chance to gather ourselves.

For the first time, we heard loudspeakers near the front broadcasting in German, urging the *Wehrmacht* troops to surrender. The Army was making a concerted effort that included propaganda and psychological warfare.

Our artillery fired shells filled with surrender leaflets into the German lines. It was our turn again to claim victory, even though we hadn't won much in this latest surge. We knew from our returning wounded that German resistance was stout, and that they were getting behind our front lines and creating problems whenever they could.

Many of the returning wounded had been horribly mangled by mines. The Germans had taken advantage of their long possession of this ground by literally covering it with "Bouncing Bettys," Schu mines, and other nasty surprises. But that was the concern of the troops fighting on the front lines now.

What were we doing through all of this? Many of our guys ran around in the snow, hunting rabbits. I didn't partake in that sport. I never could understand why anyone would want to shoot a little bunny. I didn't think highly of eating one, either, so I certainly didn't bother to shoot one. I would have been ashamed to shoot something like that.

Instead, I liked exploring the countryside. It soothed me to be away from the towns and cities, because they were so bombed out. It was depressing to see all that damage. In some country areas, you'd hardly be able to tell that there was a war on, or that anything out of the ordinary had happened.

I liked looking at the flowers when the weather was warmer. The country people were great about raising flowers. Along the Rhine, the German generals had greenhouses full of flowers and plants. I enjoyed going through them.

When I could, I collected seeds from these flowers, and especially from the vegetable plants, and mailed them home to Pauline. She planted them, and raised an impressive garden of flowers and vegetables particular to Alsace and Germany in our yard at home.

I wrote to Pauline every chance I got, thanking God that I'd made it through another day. My letters usually started off with, "You wouldn't believe what happened to me today...." I also used the letters to let the families of others soldiers here know that their men were doing OK. My friend Ernie, who also came from Ontario, rarely wrote to his wife, so I made sure Pauline would tell Ernie's wife that he thought of her all the time.

Getting mail from home was like a magic elixir, and I received mail almost every day. The one I remember most was the telegram I received from my dad in January 1945. A civilian riding a bicycle delivered it to me when I was in the field, which was very bizarre. The telegram said: "Haven't heard from you in some time. Greatly worried about your division. Hope you're doing OK, and write when you can."

The telegram arrived at the low ebb of the war for me, because it seemed like that month of January was all bad. Every time you would lift your head, someone took a pot shot at you. So the telegram really raised my spirits. My dad always had a knack for knowing when I needed his help.

I received another uplifting letter from Reg Manning, the cartoonist for the Arizona *Republic*. I'd known him when I was at Arizona State University. He'd wangled me an Associated Press pass back then, which I used to get into the football games. I'd written him a letter, saying how much I would like to have one of his cartoons, and he sent me one by V-Mail. The cartoon showed Hitler being chased by General Patton, spurring a mechanical horse with the words "14th Armored" written on it. I sent it home, and after the war I had it enlarged and framed it to hang on our wall.

My travels during this period of rest and relaxation took me to Sessenheim. The town was proud of one particular achievement — so proud that they'd painted it on a sign: "Welcome to Sessenheim, hometown of Vincent Van Gogh's mistress."

I stayed in a house there, and felt fairly safe since it was somewhat removed from the fighting. I'd hear a distant shell burst occasionally, but nothing serious. One night I heard some of the guys moving around inside the house and on the street outside. Suddenly, the ground jarred like an earthquake, and there was a tremendous explosion. Its concussion blew debris everywhere.

I jumped out of bed. All of us piled outside into the pitch darkness, and heard men yelling. We realized the shouts came from the latrine. It was made of brick, and the explosion had blown the roof off.

All of us figured the latrine had suffered a direct hit by German artillery. Later, we learned that gas in the latrine had ignited while two guys were sitting on the toilet. Both of them survived to suffer our running taunt: "How did you get your Purple Hearts?"

Judging that Sessenheim wasn't completely safe, I moved further away from the front lines.

One of the true oddities of life in the rear is the ubiquitous army band. Every division had a concert band, and ours was made up of MPs and medics. They'd go from unit to unit and perform. It was strange, because often you could hear artillery booming in the distance, and you knew men were dying every moment while you listened to bouncy brass band music.

They always performed with a bunch of flags, which seemed to mean a lot to the band members. Sometimes these concerts were a change of pace, but I wasn't too eager to attend them. I never liked martial music. It didn't stir me, and they always played it out of cadence anyway.

But we were forced to attend these concerts. It was a standing order. It was the same with attending church services. I don't know if refusal to sit through a band concert brought the same kind of punishment that some guys received for failing to go to church, however. Those guys had to take a five-mile hike.

One of them was a preacher. Praise the Lord, and pass the ammunition.

We received other entertainments. The USO shows were pretty good, and always a delight to see. They were like something from another world. But they kept you in touch with that other world, if only a little. In our sector, we didn't get any of the top-billed shows that included Bob Hope and Betty Grable. We got shows with lesser stars, but they were much appreciated just the same.

A few of the units received passes during this period of R&R, and many soldiers headed straight for Paris. I avoided the so-called City of Light, because it seemed like a closed-up place. I'm sure it had its high points, like the architecture, but I didn't really care for the city. Besides, my French was not very good.

That got me into trouble during my stay in Strasbourg. I'd befriended a lady professor there. She was Alsatian French, but we had to communicate mostly in the pigeon German that I'd managed to learn.

One day, a corporal pal of mine returned from leave in Paris with dozens of bars of Parisian soap. He swore that it was better than any American soap. He tried to offer it to my professor friend. I hoped to impress her with some French, so I asked the corporal how to say that this soap was good for washing your face. He gave me a flurry of French, which I repeated to the lady.

"*Ach, du schlechte Mann!*" she spit, and walked away angrily.

Turns out the phrase he gave me meant, "This soap is good for washing your butt."

The corporal fell down laughing at my stupidity.

Strasbourg had another nasty surprise for me. I was staying in a nice hotel, enjoying the luxury of sleeping in a bed with sheets, and being able to eat a warm meal. Explosions suddenly tore up the lobby, the outer walls and the whole area around the building. I hit the floor, thinking it must have been some delayed fuse bombs going off, because I never heard any gun reports. You almost always hear the firing before the explosions.

When I ran outside, there was broken glass and chipped concrete everywhere. People were scattering for shelter in all directions. Then I heard a whistling screech that was completely foreign. I looked up.

Three German ME-262 jet fighters were diving at what seemed to be me. I'd never seen anything move like those damned things. They were on top of

West poses beside the wreck of a German ME-262 fighter jet, similar to the one that nearly killed him during the war.

the town in no time, strafing with their cannons, but I heard their firing only after the shells hit.

I dove back inside. The place erupted again, and suddenly it was silent.

When I went back outside, they were gone. I hoped that the Germans didn't have many of those jets, because I knew our best prop fighters like the P-51s wouldn't stand a chance against them. Fortunately, the Germans did not have many, so they didn't influence the outcome of the fighting. But they created quite a buzz among all of the troops. They made us wonder what else the krauts had up their sleeves.

I returned to my unit after about a week in Strasbourg. There were a lot of new faces. They were replacements for the many men we lost in the Hatten-Rittershoffen ordeal.

Unlike many outfits in the U.S. Army, we didn't give our replacements a hard time. We tried to bring them in as gently as possible, and not scare them to death. They received basic pointers from us, like never to salute anyone in the field. German snipers targeted officers. Aside from that, the best advice was to volunteer for nothing, keep your head down and your bowels open.

Determined to help the new guys, I passed along the best advice that I'd received: don't be too eager to act. Sit and observe for a while. Following that rule made sure you avoided an ambush, which the Germans frequently set up. It also applied to German attacks. Often the enemy seemed to be attacking from a certain direction when it really was a feint to get us to commit ourselves, so they could cut us off.

Sometimes we'd mess with the new men when they were on guard duty, however. One of the guys would sneak up behind one, and shove his knees into the replacement's knees so he'd drop down. The replacement's first reaction usually was to whirl around with his rifle. When replacements did that, we gave them a going over, telling them they had to accept it, like an initiation.

Most of our replacements did well in combat, and survived the war. After all, they'd been in basic training for so long it was a relief for them to get into combat. And we were glad to have anyone who could fill our ranks and shoot well. We welcomed them gratefully.

Many of the replacements had gone through Army Specialized Training, so they were a high-caliber bunch. We had some from Medical Training School, and other advanced programs. They all seemed bright and literate, so we had a lot in common with them — especially their shock and dismay about army food in the field.

We rated our field cuisine as "bad" and "worse." Bad was when we were behind the lines, and our so-called field kitchen had a chance to prepare hot meals. It was just a half-track with a gas griddle and some burners set up in the rear compartment.

Our cook was a French guy named Nadieu. He couldn't cook worth a damn. He made the standard stuff, like dried eggs with Spam. We called it "Heartburn-briand," and some other things that don't bear repeating.

At first, I suspected that Nadieu would hand out better food to the people he liked, but I learned that he didn't like anybody. Often, he simply cooked up C-rations.

Our cuisine achieved "worse" status when we were close to the fighting. We ate from our ration cans. If it was safe to build a fire, we'd heat the rations right in the can. But you had to be careful about this. You had to keep it over the fire only long enough to warm the food inside the can. If you heated it too long, the can would explode like a bomb. If the food squirted out when you screwed off the top of the can, you knew it was ready to eat.

Among other things, this is what separated the veterans from the new guys. I was among the ranks of the Ration Can *Illuminati*.

Once these lip-smacking treats were cooked to our liking, we poured the contents into our metal cups and ate. When we finished, we dipped the cups into a fifty gallon garbage can filled with boiling water to clean them. It's a wonder we didn't all die from ptomaine poisoning.

The standard contents of our ration cans included beef stew, pork and beans, canned eggs or Spam. K-rations came in an elongated box, which contained a little of this and that, including a couple of cigarettes, chewing gum, and a laxative.

The German civilians liked these awful things, so I wound up giving most of mine away. It helped to establish a *quid pro quo* with the civilians, because sometimes they'd cook for me on the fancy stoves in their homes. We were always looking for some self-serving civilian who would cook us something fresh to eat — if they had it. The meals we got from them were delightful, compared to what we'd been eating.

The biggest culinary bonanzas occurred when we obtained local livestock. Sometimes we'd pay for a cow, and sometimes we'd just "requisition" one. It depended on the farmer's attitude and level of Nazi fanaticism.

Our unit was fortunate to have a guy who was a butcher before he was drafted. He'd dress the livestock we obtained. Everyone was thankful, because there's a big difference between a cow on the hoof and a steak on your plate.

We also had some guys who could cook biscuits without baking ovens. I guess they used Dutch ovens, like in the Old West.

But for the most part, we had to depend on canned rations when we were close to the front. Everyone complained about them, except one member of our troop — Morehead. For some odd reason, Morehead loved the dry biscuits that came in the C-ration cans. He stuffed his pockets with them, and he nibbled on those big round biscuits all night. It sounded like someone walking over crusty snow — crunch, crunch, crunch. It got to the point where no one wanted to stand guard with him, because we were sure the krauts would hear him. We even feared that we wouldn't hear them coming over all that crunching.

Water was another concern when we were in the field. The small amount in our canteens went quickly, since we used it to heat for shaving as well as for drinking. Every unit had a small truck that carried a cylindrical water tank, but many of our troops preferred to find fresh water in the local wells. I thought that was a good idea, too, until someone pointed out that many of the wells were surrounded by graveyards. After that, I left the well water to the cows and horses, and I stuck with the rusty, foul-tasting stuff from our water truck. If I was lucky, I could eschew that for wine that I'd found in a local cellar.

Although we were temporarily out of the fighting, we still had to deal with the weather. It was February, in the heart of one of the most severe winters Europe had seen in years. Just keeping warm was a daily obsession. Whenever we could, we'd billet in a house or a barn. It was the first thing we sought whenever we moved to a new venue. When we found one, we set up our CP, our Command Post. The standard operating procedure in this process was: "CP no good? Get new CP."

Often, CPs were no good due to rat infestation. If we saw that our current place was crawling with rats, we didn't hesitate to scout around and find another place that was much cleaner and nicer. When we couldn't find one, we had a fall-back procedure — our sure cure for rats. If we heard them running around in an attic or in the hayloft of a barn, we'd rake them with a .30 caliber machine gun. That usually worked, but it was amazing that we never burned everything down.

One of the main prerequisites of a good CP was the quality of the food cooking on its stove. The French families were glad to welcome us. The Germans were less enthusiastic. We'd enter their houses, thank them for their courtesy, and tell them the neighbors next door are waiting for them. They weren't very happy about it, but they went peacefully.

Finding a CP was not always possible. Fortunately, we had plenty of gasoline. This was thanks to the pipeline that General Patch had set up. Not only did it provide us with all the fuel we needed for maneuvers, but we had plenty left over to make bonfires that kept us warm at night. Generally, we'd pour the contents of a five-gallon gas can on a pile of old tree stumps and sticks we'd pulled from the ground. It blazed all night, surrounded by men snoring in their mummy cases.

Since we were a mechanized outfit with so much gas to spare, I often slept in the cab of the half-track with the motor running all night. There was a nice spot behind the driver's seat where I could lie crosswise and warm up my backside near the manifold while I ate my C-rations.

The Germans weren't so lucky regarding fuel. Our bombing campaign against their oil refineries and fuel infrastructure made them gasoline paupers. Their situation wasn't helped by the large amounts of gasoline we captured from them during our advances. General Patch wanted us to scrounge every gallon of gas we could find, and it hurt the German mechanized divisions.

It wasn't unusual to see German tanks being towed by oxen. They'd travel at three to four miles per hour, until they reached a spot where they could be brought to bear. Only then would they turn over their engines. But even with that disadvantage, they still put up an incredibly strong fight. God help us, I thought, if they'd had plenty of gas and ammunition.

Finally, we received orders to move. Our destination was the area near the towns of Maenholsheim and Wolsenheim. A Troop also received a new commander, since we'd lost all but one of our officers in Hatten. He was Lieutenant John Kraker, someone we already knew and admired for his excellent leadership of another troop of the 94th Cavalry.

Kraker was from New York, and he lived up to it. He was tough, and he expected his men to be the same way. Under him, we knew we'd be looking for trouble, but we also knew he wouldn't waste our lives needlessly. He was a good officer, and after the war, he became a particularly good friend of mine. Everyone admired him.

Another fortunate change in command put Major George England in charge of our combat command group. He was meant to be a great military leader, having been born in a Missouri barracks to a career army officer.

George Washington England grew up on military posts in China, the Philippines, Texas, Alabama, New York and Washington, D.C. It was a tough military upbringing, and if George or his brothers misbehaved, their father came down hard on them. One time he put George — still a boy — in a military stockade.

Major England was West Point all the way, and in the course of this war, he received two Silver Stars, a Bronze Star and a Purple Heart. After the war he paid us the highest compliment: "The soldiers I commanded were like brothers." We were lucky to have him.

Our new posting still wasn't involved with the enemy, however. Mostly, we rested, worked on our vehicles and trained. Later we would get patrol duty for the 1st Armored Group. Then we received orders to move up to the Moder River at Phalsbourg.

We had our new equipment or new weapons, our new replacements and our new commanders.

A Troop was loaded for bear again. We were about to learn how we'd use that.

ACROSS THE RHINE—Fighting through the Last Barrier

A blind man could see what was happening. The endless convoy of deuce-and-a-half trucks bringing up ammunition, the troops stacking it in enormous piles on the roadside, the heavy artillery being towed into position, the new tanks and mechanized guns, the new divisions numbering tens of thousands of men taking their places near the front—the U.S. Third and Seventh Armies were preparing to deliver a haymaker.

We threw it on March 15. Even the dead must have heard it. Every gun, howitzer, mortar, plane engine and bomb coalesced in a typhoon of noise without pause. A great spring of American might which had been coiling since it arrived on the Rhine the previous December was cut loose.

The immediate effect was shock and awe. The Germans in our sector offered little initial resistance. They fell back to their Siegfried Line. Not even the night protected them from our tracers. We stole the night. We created "artificial moonlight" with dozens of our anti-aircraft searchlights pointing straight at the enemy on the ground.

Our units rolled through Hatten and Rittershoffen, the scenes of such intense fighting and death just a couple of months before. There were no signs of German soldiers in these bitter places now. Farmers tilled their fields instead, preparing for the onset of spring planting. We saw them filling in foxholes, so they could plow evenly over the detritus of those who had died there. They were getting on with their lives, confident the maelstrom had passed them by.

Seeing them returning to normalcy gave me a dark feeling as I rode past in the half-track, knowing that I was following that maelstrom. There would be more death and maiming in my future here, perhaps even my own.

Our units rode through Hatten ahead of the Free French Infantry. The FFI had already earned a reputation as glory grabbers. They often rode around on bicycles and showed up after we'd paid a dear toll in blood to take a town, parading through its streets like they'd done something great. Every time we had a victory parade in a town we'd liberated, they were right there to take credit they didn't deserve. Then they'd disappear quickly into some local bar, where they celebrated.

We didn't think much of them. Their training was not very good, but they were hell on the French civilians who'd collaborated with the Germans. If you wanted to get rid of a collaborator or a German spy, you gave them to the FFI. They usually took it upon themselves to shave the heads of any women in town who'd slept with a German soldier. They took it a step further with the men, hanging them from lampposts. We Americans weren't always the shining light of humanity, but I thought we usually brought peace and human decency back to these liberated towns.

As we stopped briefly in one Alsatian village, we watched in amazement as the FFI troops set up a series of machine guns with a wire attached to them. It was designed to fire all the machine guns at once, sending the bullets to the same place. I figured they meant to use it as a warning device, but every hour all the machine guns began sputtering. It was a friendly fire danger, and it wouldn't have been the first time the FFI accidentally shot at us, thinking we were Germans.

The U.S. Army gave tanks to the FFI, but they never showed the French how to use them. Not only did we have to watch for Germans shooting at us, we had to be careful of these clowns, too. They had a lot of deadly equipment, and they shot in every direction. We were scared to death of them.

Everyone was happy to leave them behind as we pushed on for a second crack at the Siegfried Line. Its fortifications were just as formidable as they were before.

Our infantry probed for weak spots, while our artillery and tanks hammered the pillboxes. Anyone trying to crawl among the anti-tank obstacles was caught in a deadly crossfire of machine gun, mortar and artillery. Bullets ricocheted murderously off the concrete, tearing from one obstacle to another. Bits of cement and lead filled the air just above their heads. I saw a man drag a wounded trooper to relative safety.

I was relieved our unit wasn't at the point of this attack. Instead, I watched from our position as three platoons of infantry from the 68th and the 25th wormed their way forward under the cover of smoke. But when the smoke dissipated, the enemy machine guns cut them up. Survivors had to take cover in nearby houses, cut off from the rest of their outfit.

The German artillery and pillboxes poured fire into those houses, where someone undoubtedly was directing our counter-fire. We cheered when one of our tanks knocked out a pillbox. It went on like this until dark.

At first light the next morning, we were jolted by a powerful explosion. I peered over a wall and saw that the engineers had blasted a gap in the dragon's teeth. They must have planted charges in the night, even though a nearby burning warehouse illuminated the place.

Another roar, this one constant, announced our incoming artillery. It was a fearsome barrage, smashing pillboxes, knocking out periscopes and creating huge craters. A round struck what appeared to be an ordinary house, tearing away part of the façade and revealing a six-foot-thick, reinforced concrete wall. Inside were 88-mm guns, one for each "window," primed to fire flat-trajectory, high-velocity destruction at any tank that dared to approach.

The infantry moved in again. Most of the action was lost in smoke, but I caught bits of the drama. Our troops moved past the pillbox that had been knocked out, and it started firing again. Apparently, the Germans had re-manned it through some underground passage. The infantry turned around and took the strong point again, tossing fragmentation and phosphorous grenades through the firing slits.

Then I witnessed a beautiful sight. Here and there, Germans stumbled into the open, their arms in the air. A few of them waved white cloths. At first there were two, three, five. Then they came in groups of ten. The "impreg-nable" West Wall was breaching.

Fighting continued into the night again, which brought the inevitable German counterattack. It was desperate and violent, but it only led to more surrenders. The deep darkness of that night also allowed our engineers to plant more TNT among the enemy battlements. They hit the detonator, and 300 pounds of dynamite lit up the night.

The next morning, it was our turn. We moved toward the Siegfried Line in our vehicles, accompanied by tank dozers. When we were within range, we dismounted. Lieutenant Kraker ordered us to advance.

Like the rest of Troop A, I crawled on my belly, worming through the dragon's teeth. Although most of the Germans had been cleared, there still were pillboxes firing at us. I was frightened, until I saw Kraker driving up and down our column in a peep. He barked commands as he studied the terrain.

Here and there, he found lingering German resistance, and he ordered us to these spots. We crawled up to every suspect pillbox and lobbed grenades through the firing slits. We got one pillbox to surrender by telling them they were cut off from the rest of their people. We told them that we'd bury them alive with the tank dozer if they didn't surrender. Seven of them emerged meekly from the pillbox, their arms aloft. We tossed off their helmets, frisked them, and put their hands behind their heads.

Kraker ordered us to move on. When we hit towns, we dismounted and searched the houses. It was nerve-wracking. I never knew whether an enemy soldier was waiting around a corner, ready to blow my nose off as soon as I poked it around. You even had to watch where you stepped. The places could be littered with mines and booby traps.

I'm sure our commanders clung to the hope of capturing a Rhine bridge intact. There was one at Germersheim. The race was on.

Along with about half a dozen heavy units, we surged toward the river. If we could capture the bridge, our orders were to hold it until the rest of the command arrived. The nearer we came to the prize, the fiercer German artillery became.

The town of Germersheim lies in the open country of the Rhine Valley. There aren't even many trees. Any attacking force has to run through that landscape with no cover.

And the Germans were taking no chances. By the time our forward units came within sight of the town, the bridge had been blown.

Our Corps artillery poured shells into the town anyway, almost out of pique. P-47 Thunderbolts dove on it, dropping bombs that flattened houses. Suddenly a column of white smoke roiled skyward, followed by a terrible, persistent roar. A P-47 had scored a direct hit on an ammunition dump.

It seemed as though the Germans finally had been cleaned away from the west bank of the Rhine. German soldiers now surrendered in the hundreds. Germersheim was ours.

But the enemy continued firing at us from across the river. Mortars and artillery rounds landed in our positions all of that night. They must have figured we were concentrating there.

Moving forward in the din, we somehow heard chickens clucking inside a barn that we passed. One of our guys jumped off the back of my half-track and ran into the barn to look for eggs. A minute later, he emerged holding his helmet in front of him like it was a holy sepulcher. It was filled with eggs.

He ran back towards the vehicle wearing a broad smile, and some of the other guys hopped out to grab eggs for themselves. All of them returned with helmets full of eggs. But as they got close to the vehicle, mortar shells landed all around, practically on top of us.

I told the driver to get the hell out of there, and looked back at the men. One of them carefully set down his helmet full of eggs, and only when he decided they were secure did he dive for cover. He didn't care about getting killed so long as those eggs didn't break. It was a lesson in a soldier's priorities during combat.

The Germans shot at everything that moved. I dismounted and headed for the nearest cellar. The deeper, the better. It didn't matter whether the house was on fire. A fire would be preferable, because it would keep me warm on this frigid early spring day.

As I entered a cellar and took cover, inevitable memories of my entombment in Hatten returned. I tried to banish them, because I knew I was in the only safe place in Germersheim during the bombardment. All of us were cellar rats in that town. You never wanted to come out unless you absolutely had to.

But sometimes we had to find a volunteer to crawl up and peek outside, to see what might be coming. Those sojourns were quick, because it simply was mad to be above ground.

Two shells landed near the cellar in close succession. They hit so hard, the ground shook and I felt like an invisible fist had knocked my head into the cellar wall. My face was already pressed tight against it, so the concussion broke my nose. I didn't realize it at the moment. I was too busy burrowing for cover. Later, after the war, I needed an operation for a deviated septum, thanks to that particular barrage.

But we set up our own artillery beyond Germersheim, and that night the Seventh Army fired its first salvo across the Rhine. It was followed by many others, and the German gunnery slackened.

When we emerged from our caverns, the town was little more than a rubble heap. We took stock of our outfit, and I learned that I'd lost a good friend in that bombardment. His name was Tom Lavenduski. He was a nice guy, and a good soldier. A shell had killed him, landing directly in the cellar where he hid. The shells got you sometimes, no matter how safe you thought you were.

After Germersheim, we moved to Schleithal. It looked even more dangerous. The town was surrounded by thick woods, which provided a lot of cover. At night, those woods were so dark that we often walked face first into a tree.

But we had to patrol every inch of those woods, because the Germans were good at camouflaging their positions. We already had firsthand experience of stumbling into the crosshairs of an enemy anti-tank gun that no one saw until it opened fire on us. There was no warning. You'd be walking, and suddenly a PAK gun would blast you from point-blank range. When that happened, all you could do was bury yourself in some fold in the ground, and call in the heavy stuff like artillery or an air strike. Then you begged the deity that your guys would get them before they got you.

Whenever we entered a town and its surrounding woods, we deployed outward to protect our flanks. It made sure all of our units were in position to support each other. If the Germans attacked one of our flanks, we could send troops around and counterattack them from their rear. Mutual support and close air support were the linchpins of our recon operations. But on a night patrol in pitch-black forest land, we were on our own.

A friend of mine got the surprise of his life in the woods near Schleithal. His name was Richard Horney. Naturally, we called him Dick. He was a redheaded farmer from Nebraska, and a really great guy. Dick was slinking along in the darkness, squinting to see what was ahead when he stepped on something soft. It moved. It sat up and yelled.

Horney jumped backward and fired, killing a German. The soldier had been sleeping when Dick stepped on him.

Sometimes, after one of these missions ended, the guys would discuss what had happened. It was a way to relieve the tension. Horney was a little shaken by his experience, but he did the right thing. Under night patrol conditions, it was necessary to silence any Germans as quickly as possible.

We told Dick that shooting the kraut was a lot better than letting him stick you with a bayonet. All of us knew that anyone could have had the same crazy experience as Horney, because there wasn't anything we hadn't encountered by this time. Sure, it was scary, but we knew the Germans were scared, too. That never stopped them from trying to kill us.

Dick lost his life later in the campaign. I didn't hear about it until well after it happened. We moved so fast that it was impossible for us to keep track of our casualties. Sometimes a guy would be gone for weeks before anyone noticed it. But I missed Dick, and still do to this day.

The troop moved on to Kapsweyer. It was familiar territory. Now we were returning after it had been brutally blasted by our artillery.

The air was still thick with powdered plaster when we arrived. Buildings blazed. So did the bodies of men and livestock. There were women and children among the forms that littered the streets. A few of them writhed on the broken ground, suffering their final, agonizing death throes. We couldn't do anything for them. We had to keep moving.

There were more dragon's teeth, as Kapsweyer was a Siegfried town. Kraker ordered us through. We moved from cover to cover, until we were beyond the tank traps. No shots were fired. The enemy had cleared out.

I used that as an excuse to "patrol" the Siegfried Line. It gave me a chance to inspect the abandoned pillboxes. Some of those constructions were so good, I thought they should be preserved as war memorials. They provided unusual comfort for the defenders.

One of the pillboxes I inspected had seven levels, each with a different function — ammunition storage, food storage, hospital, living quarters, mess hall. There also were underground passages that allowed the defenders to move to other pillboxes when necessary. It was ingenious, but we broke through it anyway.

We didn't spend much time in Kapsweyer. The Germans were in general retreat toward the Rhine, and we wanted to keep them moving.

The roads were jammed with tanks, trucks, half-tracks, armored cars and mechanized artillery. Peeps and motorcycles weaved in and out, sometimes zipping along the side of the road. Engineers frantically filled in craters and removed roadblocks while traffic backed up in a snarl of idling motors.

When we moved, we passed through German villages, every house bearing a white sheet from a window. Usually, the civilians abided by those symbols of surrender, but sometimes we heard about them taking a pot shot at our guys.

In one town, a civilian tossed a phosphorous grenade into a half-track and killed two of our troops. Everybody knew it could happen again, so we were on guard, our machine guns aimed at all windows and ready to fire, white sheets or no white sheets.

As we traveled in the countryside, the sights changed. Bare-headed German prisoners, dusty and dazed, marched in the dirt beside the road, going in the opposite direction.

Were we looking at a defeated army? I doubted it. This was April Fools' Day, 1945.

It was also Easter Sunday, and it brought good news. Some units of our division had crossed the Rhine.

It happened at a single pontoon bridge that engineers had built under heavy fire at Worms. Now endless columns of American armor and trucks clogged the roads leading to that bridge. They were crossing the last daunting natural barrier to the Third Reich.

It didn't seem very daunting to eyes that had seen the Arkansas River in flood. At this point, the Rhine was only about five hundred yards wide.

Just keeping the traffic flowing across a bridge is challenging. It was vital to get our tanks and guns on the other side of the river, so any vehicle that stalled was simply shoved off the road. Anything that stalled on the bridge went into the river.

The riverbanks were speckled with our anti-aircraft guns, pointing skyward. We knew the *Luftwaffe* considered this little collection of rubber boats and bridge tracking a high priority target.

My outfit occasionally had to guard this bridge. Pontoon bridges always frightened me, because I knew the Germans only had to hit one end with an artillery round, and the thing would float down the river. And I knew from our experience with the flood in Arkansas that any large debris like floating trees would crash through the bridge and take it downstream. I was sure the Germans knew that, too. It was only a matter of time before they dumped heavy debris into the Rhine somewhere upstream to destroy our makeshift bridges.

It didn't help matters that our air force had blown up a number German dams far up river. This brought a lot of flooding our way, and a lot of debris racing toward the flimsy bridge I guarded. Sometimes our engineers had to drive north, and try to intercept the floating trees and bits of houses before they got to us.

On the opposite bank of the Rhine, there still was strong German resistance, even though our division had established a decent bridgehead. The Germans were fighting for their Fatherland now.

We could hear the firing to the east, and we knew our advance units were taking the brunt of ferocious counterattacks, as they defended the bridgehead.

When my troop received orders to move out, they sent us north, toward Berlin. This excited everyone in the column. We pictured ourselves rolling into the Nazi capital and grabbing Schicklgruber before he could make a getaway.

The first place we went was Bad Neustadt, located on the main road going north in that area. The Germans were in full retreat, but the heavy units ahead of us caught them out in the open. I heard what sounded like a distant thunderstorm, and recognized our 155s and eight-inch guns blasting in rapid fire. The closer we drove, the more I felt the road shaking beneath the half-track. On the horizon, great columns of smoke boiled upward, obliterating the blue sky.

I couldn't be sure what had happened until we arrived on the scene. The road was covered by wrecked German vehicles. Some were so twisted and fragmented I couldn't recognize what they had been. A large number of them blazed furiously, sending clouds of thick black smoke along the breeze.

German soldiers and horses lay everywhere in tortured poses. And yet, in the fields off to the side of the road, surviving horses peacefully grazed.

There were places where the road was completely blocked by destroyed vehicles, and we had to call for bulldozers to shove them aside so we could proceed.

Our war colleges would call this scene "an efficient use of artillery." It looked more like a massacre.

I didn't know the whole story of this bombardment until after the war, when a German general said that during the thirty-minute barrage, he lost seven thousand men. He'd never seen such an array of artillery, he claimed. And he'd been a veteran of the Russian front. It was just one episode in the drama that was unfolding.

Our division traveled a hundred and fifteen miles in the first three days following the surge across the Rhine. The 14th Armored poured into every town, leading an army of one hundred twenty thousand men in a column about a hundred miles long.

It was an astonishing change, after the static fighting we'd had for the entire winter. We were bypassing strong points, charging into the German rear areas.

On our way to Bad Neustadt, we came upon the aftermath of an amazing story that concerned General George Patton. We passed through Hammelburg on the Saale River about a week after one of the most daring commando-style rescue operations of the war took place.

Hammelburg was a training and target range site for German tank crews. It also was the location of a POW camp in which the Germans kept a wide variety of prisoners, mostly Americans. One of the POWs was George Patton's son-in-law.

Captain Baum of the Patton's Third Army put together a task force from the 4th Armored Division to go behind enemy lines, attack Hammelburg, and liberate the POWs. When Task Force Baum attacked, they came under deadly accurate fire. Since it was a target range, the German gunners already had every inch of the battlefield meticulously bracketed. They badly shot up our troops, and wounded Baum.

But he pressed the attack, and his troops reached the camp. Some of his tanks simply rammed through the fence, causing the amazed prisoners to erupt into a tremendous cheer. The Germans retreated. The POWs were free.

With the help of a major who could recognize him, Patton's son-in-law was located and tossed into an artillery spotter plane that was flown by a friend of mine. The plane took him directly to London.

The wounded Baum was miffed that they neglected to take him as well. He had to stay in a local field hospital. But he was well rewarded for his heroism. General Patton visited him in the hospital and presented him with the Distinguished Service Cross.

After the war, I met both Baum and Patton's son-in-law. Baum gave me an autographed book in which he recognized how the 14th Armored Division had arrived in time to get him. The son-in-law also gave me an autographed book, thanking the 14th Armored Division for its assistance in getting him out of there. He lived to raise a good-sized family.

When my unit arrived in Hammelburg, the remaining POWs were being gathered for transfer to the rear. I was amazed to find some of them were from my outfit. One, Ted Perkins, had been a cavalryman in B-Troop. The Germans had captured him in Hatten.

Ted was an old friend of mine, and when he disappeared I thought he'd been killed. When I saw him here, I couldn't believe my eyes. Ted was a big guy, but I could see he'd lost an astonishing amount of weight.

When he recognized me, Ted broke into a big smile, revealing a huge gap in his teeth. He explained that the German guards had beaten him, and knocked his teeth out. I could see he didn't want to talk about it, so I didn't press him for details. But it made me furious that the Germans would treat their American prisoners that way, when we were sending our POWs to sunny southern California.

My mood wasn't improved by the condition of the other American prisoners. Some of them had donned different uniforms so the Germans wouldn't take them east to another POW camp, and prevent their repatriation when we arrived. This was especially true of the American officers, who the Germans were determined to keep as prisoners. I saw American officers dressed in Serbian army uniforms. Some of them had even wrapped themselves in bandages, pretending to be too injured to travel.

But the thing that bothered me most in that POW compound was the execution wall. It was made of lead, and it was filled with bullet holes and smeared with dried blood. Next to it was a small building that I took to be the place where prisoners waited to be shot. On the wall was a picture of Jesus with the inscription, "I am the hope and the life." None of the guys in my unit felt sorrow for German suffering after we left Hammelburg.

As we drove north, the scenery changed drastically. We were suddenly in a heavily industrialized region. All around us were bombed-out factories. Most of them had been making anti-aircraft guns and ammunition until our B-24s dropped their payloads on them.

The further north we went, the more eager we were to shoot straight into Berlin. But when we arrived in Erfurt, our orders had changed. We had to turn around and head south, toward the Brenner Pass in the Alps. That took us back toward southern Germany.

We were way out front, doing what we'd been trained to do. Our job was to run into German resistance and draw fire. If the enemy was too strong for us to handle, we called in the tanks, artillery and air force to take care of it.

My platoon practiced these tactics on a smaller scale, too. We had a corporal who was half mad, and impervious to danger. He just didn't seem to notice bullets flying at him. Whenever we came upon a suspicious situation, the colonel sent this guy ahead to draw fire. If the enemy shot at him, we got a read on their positions and their strength, and we'd send reinforcements to take care of them.

The eastern side of the Rhine is heavily wooded. The Germans knew how to take advantage of that cover. They fortified a lot of strong points, and they gave them up reluctantly.

For us, it was a case of fighting in the sticks and trying to outlive the other guy. I didn't hate patrolling in the woods, but I was always dirty and wet after those episodes. Creeping along through the dark underbrush, your senses reach a state of sharpness that you never suspected you possessed. It was because you never knew what you would find in the woods. Sometimes you'd encounter wild animals, like boar. Sometimes you'd come upon local people picking berries. This was not rare. The civilians in this part of the country were beginning to starve.

When we came to a village or a farmhouse, we didn't expect a welcome. We knew where we were, and the civilians were not glad to see us. We told them we were sorry about that, and gave them a few minutes to clear out the stuff they wanted to keep before we blew up the whole neighborhood. Then we made ourselves at home.

I was often amazed by what people chose to take with them when we informed them they had to leave. They'd hitch a horse to a cart, and fill it with stuff like a grandfather clock and other ridiculous items. You'd see them coming down the road, hauling wagons loaded with junk when they should have packed food, water, shoes and anything else necessary to help them survive. Many of them suffered and some died because of their misplaced priorities during an emergency.

Inevitably, we ran into towns that were still occupied by German troops who refused to leave without a fight. This meant that civilians would die.

In war, there's no way to avoid civilian casualties, but we did our best to avoid them anyway. In 1945, there was no smart weaponry. Our planes dive-bombed, which was about as accurate as we could be from the air. Artillery was even less accurate, depending on how good the spotting planes or forward units were at directing fire. Our own troops often suffered casualties from friendly fire, so civilian casualties were assured.

It's very disheartening to see civilians killed or wounded. We tried to give them medical help whenever we could. We used a lot of our own medics to treat them, and later, when the shooting stopped, we called in the Red Cross. But often we just couldn't get them help quickly enough.

Seeing children killed or wounded is the worst. It tears at your heart. I always looked away as soon as I caught just a glimpse of a child lying in the street. Some of the other guys became hardened to such horrors. I never could.

Every now and then, when we had to shell a town the Germans were defending, we'd receive unexpected help. The first time this happened was right after my troop started moving south. I was helping to direct artillery fire on a town, the name of which I no longer remember. Through my binoculars, I saw a villager running toward us. He appeared to be unarmed, but we raised our rifles when he arrived, just in case.

Out of breath, he started chattering in broken English that our shells were landing on civilian houses, and completely missing the places where troops were hiding.

I believed him, so I called in some firing adjustments on the phone. Soon our shells were landing on the *Wehrmacht* anti-tank guns and troop concentrations. The barrage killed many of them. The surviving troops cleared out, and we entered the town safely.

I heard of the same thing happening several times to other units. In one case, it was a small boy who came out and helped American artillery placement.

This was especially true when the defending troops were SS. The German civilians knew about the SS, too. The hardcore Nazi fanatics were not that popular with the people who already knew that the war was lost. For the most part, they just wanted to get the fighting over with. They'd had enough.

We passed through many towns on our way south, some defended, some not. We moved fast, and occasionally we got lost. This usually happened when we drove through areas that recently had seen combat, where all the road signs had been shot away.

It was always interesting, trying to find our way back on a sector map that we'd run completely off. Sometimes we blundered into German units that were far behind the front. They always seemed as astonished as we were. Our guns would blast them, and they'd scatter.

Often, they left everything behind, which made for good souvenir hunting. I liked to gather up what I could, before they could recover and come after us. We tried to be gone well before that.

Sometimes we used radios when we were lost. Every one of our vehicles had a radio, which was vital since this was how we called for air support or directed artillery when we ran into trouble. As often as not, the radios didn't work, and it got tiresome, changing vacuum tubes again and again. I'd have to take out the tubes, blow the dust and grit off them, and put them back in the radio sets, with my fingers crossed that they'd work again.

By this time, our radios were using multiple frequencies, so we could shift around on them, and find the best broadcast band. They just never were dependable.

There was usually a backup Morse Code radio, and I hated that thing even more. If it was cold, I had a lot of trouble keying the signals. I wound up doing it with the palm of my hand.

The best way to get help was by landline. The Germans often eavesdropped on our radio frequencies, and could hear everything we said. Using a telephone was much safer. We could lay a phone line from a spool on the back of a peep quickly, and do it for miles.

I liked the German phone wire much better than ours, and used it whenever I could get some. It was more flexible, and you could lay wire from the back of a peep at twenty miles per hour. The kraut phone boxes were better than ours, too.

But racing around Germany as we were doing, sometimes behind enemy lines, laying phone wire was out of the question. So when we got lost, we hoped to see GI signs on the buildings we passed. Often our troops made a V-symbol with machine gun bullets on the side of a building, indicating which way they'd gone. My troop used paint or chalk to leave markers. Somehow we blundered through it all without being captured.

Not long after we entered Germany, I discovered a place called the Deutsche Champagne Company. It didn't take us long to locate the warehouse, which was packed with cases of very good champagne. Every bottle had a swastika on the label.

I told a captain what we'd found, and said, "It sure would go good with those K-rations."

It didn't take much persuading for him to give us permission to collect the booty. We gathered some volunteers, and drove half-tracks and peeps to the warehouse. Each vehicle received at least one case of champagne, and sometimes two or three. After everyone loaded up, we took what was left and put it in the back of our half-track. That champagne lasted us nearly the rest of the war.

Souvenir hunting is probably as old as warfare, and a victorious army commonly takes advantage of that privilege. I raised it to the level of a science.

Whenever we entered a town the Germans had occupied, I made a point to visit the former headquarters of the ranking officer, and checked out his personal quarters. Some of those officers didn't scrimp when it came to their creature comforts. I usually found a lot of signals equipment, along with little niceties that were worth keeping.

In one officer's quarters, I discovered a beautiful silver lighter. It was about the size of a water pitcher. It had a trigger that fired out a butane flame to light cigarettes and cigars. It even had a special part for lighting pipes. I used it for as long as the butane lasted, then traded it for something else.

While I had the lighter, it came in very handy for the Turkish cigars I discovered in another officer's quarters. Each cigar was in an aluminum tube. I don't know how old they were, but they were as good as the day they were made.

With more booty than we could use, we liked to invite some of the guys in other outfits to join us for dinner. We'd have champagne with our pork and beans, and then light up a big cigar. This showed everyone that A Troop knew how to live in a war zone.

In the course of the war, I captured twenty-one rifles and pistols. I sent most of them home as soon as I could find the means. The majority of the rifles were standard *Wehrmacht* Mausers, although I found one Model 1897 Mauser that had two triggers.

I also had a number of Luger pistols. One of them was silver plated with pearl handles, but it was no good for firing. All of the rifling had been shot out of the barrel, so I sold it to a Navy guy for three hundred dollars.

Whenever we entered a German town for the first time, we collected all the rifles and pistols. The townsfolk were ordered to bring them to us in their city hall. There often were piles of rifles and pistols, and the ones we didn't keep as souvenirs had to be destroyed.

The first time we did that, someone had the bright idea to pour about twenty gallons of gasoline on the pile of guns and light it. Half of the guns turned out to be loaded, and they started firing. Not only were bullets whizzing around our heads, but pieces of the firearms were flying like shrapnel.

That was the last time we burned any guns. From that day forward, we simply laid the guns against a curb and ran a tank over them to bend all of the barrels.

West sports a collection of German Army medals which he "liberated" from a *Wehrmacht* prisoner. Beside him stands one of the new recruits to A Troop.

My souvenir hunting kept me occupied as we barnstormed south toward Bavaria. In one abandoned German headquarters, I found a couple of oil paintings that I liked. I had to figure out how to send them home safely, and I eventually hit on the idea of cutting off the frames carefully. Then I rolled up the paintings tightly, padded them with paper and wrapped them in a blanket to be shipped out. Those paintings hung above the fireplace in my home for many years.

I sent just about everything that seemed interesting home to Pauline. I shipped her everything from German vegetable seeds to simple mementos, like the program from an opera or a stage show, or advertising fliers. I even sent home canned food.

The souvenirs also came in handy as items of trade. Aside from the usual soap, cigarettes and chocolate, which were always in demand, I habitually had a few pistols stowed in the half-track cab. They were as good as gold at that time.

Whenever we found a souvenir that wouldn't fit inside the half-track cab, we'd either put it on top or we'd tow it. That was the solution when I discovered a German staff car, which they used to call a *Kugelwagen*. It was a small

Volkswagen convertible which they sold years later in the States under the name of The Thing.

My Thing was painted red. I don't know why it was red, but it was a nice-looking car, and it was in mint condition. We towed it behind one of the half-tracks, and when we stopped, I used that *Kugelwagen* to run errands.

I only got to enjoy the vehicle for a few weeks, however. During the next German counter-offensive, we had to turn around and head back toward our lines. I was driving the *Kugelwagen* when we came upon an American strong-point. They opened up on me, riddling the road with machine-gun fire.

"What the hell are you doing?" I yelled.

"We're going to shoot the hell out of you, you goddamn kraut," came the response.

"This is no kraut vehicle."

"Well it sure doesn't look like one of ours," said the soldier.

I managed to avoid getting shot to pieces by friendly fire, but it was clear that I had to get rid of my *Kugelwagen*. I would have loved to hang on to it, but I believed in bad omens. I threw a thermite grenade into it, and watched it blaze.

The one souvenir we did not collect was German money. We had no regard for it. We made this known to the German populace by dumping it into the streets from the backs of our vehicles. We didn't realize at the time that those *Reichsmarks* would be worth something after the war, because it was the only currency the Germans had.

It wasn't all souvenir hunting during the breakthrough, however. We still had to deal with some German resistance in towns like Weissenbach, Modlos, Ober Leichtersbach, Breitenbach, Schondra, Mitgenfeld and Schildeck. Mostly it amounted to a few shots from stragglers, although one time our tanks had to take out a pair of civilians toting a *panzerfaust*.

We were literally high-balling down the autobahn at this time, trying to capture as much ground as we could. There were a few attacks on our column by German fighter planes, but we sent up such a wall of lead with our .50 and .30 caliber machine guns that they didn't stay too long. We shot a couple of them down.

Our advance was probably the fastest of the entire war. Everyone said they'd never seen so much territory covered so quickly. We blasted through Windheim, Burglauer, Niederlauer, and Heldburg so fast that I don't remember much about those places.

Windheim was unusually peaceful, although there had been a lot of activity there before we arrived. But the German resistance was non-existent by the time my outfit got there. We went through the place without incident, because the Germans were retreating. We moved so fast that we didn't give them time to organize, or dig into any sort of defensive positions.

In Burglauer, we captured a bridge intact, which was a major accomplishment. The Germans were meticulous about blowing bridges.

The operation took place under the leadership of a British officer named Hull. He was odd in several ways. Firstly, the fact that he was British and serving in our outfit was strange. Hull also was a history scholar. He amazed me by comparing this bridge capture to Morgan's similar feat in the Revolutionary War.

The bridge helped my unit maintain its lightning advance. When we reached Heldburg, the Germans were shocked, and surrendered in large numbers. They simply weren't expecting us for many days. The front was shifting so quickly at the time that neither army knew what side of the lines it was on.

We captured an extraordinary number of enemy soldiers during our advance. Many of the German prisoners were stragglers in a retreat that had turned into flight. They were disorganized, and their interest in continuing the fight seemed to be gone.

Our construction battalion built a POW stockade near the front, and in no time it was crammed with more than fifty thousand German prisoners. It was a miracle how our supply people managed to feed all of them. The ones we captured were put to work quickly doing KP duty.

We limited their work to cleaning, and kept them away from food preparation, so they couldn't poison us. They washed dishes, pots and pans. A lot of passing troops enjoyed the sight — German soldiers washing dishes.

I spoke to a few of the prisoners with my smattering of German. They were happy to be out of the fighting, and in our hands rather than the Russians. I said goodbye to one of the prisoners as he was being loaded on a truck bound for Cherbourg, where he would be shipped to a camp in the United States.

"Hope you make it," he said.

I almost wished I was going with him.

"Do you want me to say hello to anyone?" he added as he waved goodbye. I didn't take him up on his offer.

These interludes were rare, because we never stayed in one place for long. We only slowed down when we met a little resistance, and our tanks, artillery and planes pounced on it immediately. Since we had powerful forces covering our flanks during this breakout, we could dash through the German lines and hit them from behind.

Riding in half-tracks, light tanks, and armored cars, we covered an unprecedented amount of enemy territory. We didn't want to stop, and the only time we did was to refill our gas tanks. Once we did that, off we'd go again.

One day we came across a Swiss Red Cross column. There were many German wounded in the ambulances, driven by Canadian POWs. We immediately freed the Canadians, and sent the Germans back to our own POW stockade.

Our column barely stopped long enough to chat with the Canadians, and we drove into Pegnitz, where we captured a huge number of German troops. They were so shocked by our arrival, they looked at us as if we'd come from the moon.

When we arrived in Wombach, the Germans finally were waiting for us. My platoon was not on point, so we didn't receive direct fire. But I could see that our guys had been pinned down by AT fire and mortars on a muddy hillside. They had no cover, and they were taking a lot of fire.

Many times, in situations that seem desperate, the only way to escape is to attack. This was true in 1863, during the battle around Chattanooga, Tennessee. I recalled from my history lessons that Union troops were pinned down in the rifle pits below Missionary Ridge, receiving murderous fire from the Confederate soldiers above them. Without orders, Arthur MacArthur, father of General Douglas MacArthur, led a charge into the face of all that fire, and routed the Confederates from their stronghold.

Now I was watching Sergeant Martin Roark do the same thing. He led an attack that captured fifty-six German soldiers, including three officers.

Even though I knew Roark, I couldn't believe my eyes. Roark was an attorney from Baltimore, and a really nice guy, but under fire he was another one of those totally fearless men who always seem to know what to do in an emergency. When he returned from his attack, he brought more prisoners than we could count at the time.

Following this heroic episode, our outfit moved on to Rossbach, and cleaned the Germans out of there. It was no easy task, because they'd heavily fortified the place. Still, we bagged fifty additional German prisoners.

I talked to a few of them as they marched past me toward the rear, and I learned that most of them simply had run out of ammunition and other supplies. More importantly, they seemed glad to get out of the war. That made quite an impression on me. It would be important in a very short time.

We were working close to George Patton's Third Army now, so we had to keep moving. Next on our list were the towns of Gefall and Geroda. My unit joined with the 3rd Infantry, so we had the manpower and the equipment to win a nasty firefight there.

We gained a big advantage by bringing up the 155-mm self-propelled guns. They blasted everything that shot at us. They weren't very crew-friendly, because those soldiers had to work in an open-topped vehicle with some frontal armor protecting them. The gun was a stubby-looking tube, but when it fired it recoiled about six feet, which would obliterate any crew member foolish enough to be standing behind the breech when it fired.

We used the self-propelled 155s as tank destroyers, and there wasn't a tank in the world that could stand up to them. I'd seen them knock a Tiger tank sideways. Firing them on a flat trajectory at point-blank range gave them a terrible wallop.

Our attack on Geroda was led by Lieutenant Kraker and Sergeant Froeschner. We fought our way around the town's outskirts, surrounding it as best we could without getting into some bloody Stalingrad-style house-to-house fighting.

Both Kraker and Froeschner spoke German fluently, so once we were in position around Geroda, they called upon the *Wehrmacht* troops to surrender. I held a bazooka, loaded and aimed, waiting for an excuse to fire it. Any single rifle shot would have sent my rocket flying. Instead, I was surprised to see a throng of grey-clad German soldiers filing down the street toward us with their arms held high.

We took Geroda that day with a total of one hundred forty-three enemy prisoners. Both Kraker and Froeschner received Silver Stars for that action. I knew both of them deserved it, because they were extremely brave.

Froeschner's heroism was a bit confusing to me, though. He was such a religious person that he always said grace before we ate — even when we were sitting down in a mud hole to crummy C-rations. He always gave thanks for what he had. All of the guys thought he was a bit crazy, but no one said anything about it.

Throughout the war, Froeschner was a buck sergeant, and he was brave in every battle. But he was always interested in theology, too. I never worked up the nerve to ask him about that dichotomy, killing enemy soldiers single-mindedly on one hand while spouting the doctrine of Jesus on the other. I just shrugged and went with it. After the war he became our divisional chaplain.

The enemy troops that didn't surrender to us in Geroda tried to retreat. We caught them in the open and phoned for artillery support.

It was another massacre. The whole column disappeared in billowing smoke and loud bursts. The road leading to Gefall became a terrible killing ground.

This allowed us to enter Gefall without much resistance, although there was some scattered shooting. A few of the guys followed my lead to explore the town, and we headed straight for the first Gasthaus we saw, hoping to score some good wine and spirits. We were disappointed to learn that the krauts had cleaned out the place.

The first time my unit really stopped following the breakout was in Langenleiten. We ran into heavy fire, and actually had to withdraw. The Germans were hitting us with a lot of rounds from their Panther and Tiger tanks, which had been dug into the ground so that only their turrets were visible.

Basically, we had done our job by drawing fire and pinpointing an enemy stronghold. The brass ordered us out of the town so they could send in the heavy armor to deal with those tanks. I saw that it was not easy to knock them out, since they were small targets. Our tanks and TDs started firing high-explosive shells into the ground just ahead of the turrets, and that produced instant results.

The TDs were deadly to all German tanks. Their 90-mm guns fired on a fairly large German armored column we encountered on the open road outside Langenleiten. They were exposed, driving single file on a mountainside.

We brought up four TDs. They blasted the lead vehicle and the rear vehicle in the column. The Germans were trapped. For about half a day, our TDs picked off everything they had, while their troops dismounted and scattered everywhere. We fired machine guns at them.

One by one, the TDs destroyed every enemy vehicle in that column — tanks, armored cars, half-tracks, trucks, motorized artillery, staff cars — about fifty in all. We let the Germans who wanted to surrender enter our lines, and we shot anyone who wanted to stay on the mountainside and fight. There was no escape for them. The ones who tried to go over the hill were clearly exposed, and we cut them down with machine guns.

We thought our 90-mm guns were about the finest in the war. They probably had been fashioned on the German 88-mm gun, because they had the same recoil and sounded the same when fired. This got us into trouble occasionally, because our own artillery would hear them fire and think it was an 88. More than once we had to duck to avoid salvos from friendly artillery, so we learned to move our TDs immediately after firing them. We figured that we'd receive return fire from both the Germans and the Americans.

After the enemy column was destroyed, we moved onward. As usual, we went as far as we could while still being maintaining security, and then set up for the night. We dug in, and ran telephone wire to various points on our line, so we would be in constant touch with our sentries in all sectors. If the Germans attempted a night attack, we could move reinforcements to the flash point quickly.

Cigarettes played a vital role on our watches at night. Just about everyone in my platoon smoked cigarettes, and they used them as a means to catch a few minutes of sleep. Whenever someone intended to go to sleep, they put a lit cigarette between their fingers. That way they knew they wouldn't be asleep for more than eight minutes, because that was how long it took for a cigarette to burn down to their fingers. When they felt the burn, they'd wake up and look around to be sure everything was secure. It was always a good idea to see what was happening around you every eight minutes.

That was the cavalryman's technique — to sleep in a peep with a lit cigarette. Of course, that meant that every cavalryman had burn marks on his fingers. It also meant that every cavalryman was sleep deprived.

Some of the guys basically lived in their peeps, and almost never got out. They slept sitting up, cigarette in hand. They loved their peeps, because they were fast and could get them out of trouble.

The peeps didn't offer much protection, however. The Germans came up with the despicable idea of stringing thick metal wire across the roads at night. They stretched it right at head height of a man riding in a peep, so anyone who drove with the windshield down would be decapitated. The razor-sharp wire would take off a head with ease if you were driving at fifty miles per hour, as we often did.

One day we were moving at a good clip. A fellow we called Pancho was driving a peep that had a machine gun on a stand behind the driver's seat. The wire hit the machine gun, snapped, and struck Pancho in the side of his head. He was lucky it didn't kill him, but it destroyed his optic nerve, blinding him.

After that, we welded solid steel poles vertically to all peeps, right at the front fender, so we could catch any wires and break them before they broke us. Of course, then we had to pray that the broken steel wire didn't hit us as it whiplashed around.

Years later, I ran into Pancho again. I had been admitted to a hospital to remove a fish bone lodged in my throat. I guess I was chatty after the removal, because Pancho recognized my voice, and came over to greet me. He was a patient in the hospital, and recovered only a little vision in one eye. But his spirits were high. He told me that he'd been tending bar at his uncle's restaurant in Tucson.

Pancho's misfortune

Doug Prindle, Paul Shotola and Sgt. Froeschner sit in a peep, somewhere in France, 1944. Note the pipe welded to the front bumper, which was intended to break steel wires strung across the roads by the enemy.

was sobering, but wire booby traps weren't the only things that occasionally slowed us down. At times we became caught in the inevitable traffic snarls that fully mechanized armies suffer at important crossroads.

One day in May, we hit a jam-up and our lightning advance slowed to a crawl. Our unit had just been transferred to Third Army at this time.

As we inched toward the intersection of two roads, I noticed that a full general was standing on an oil drum, directing traffic.

It was George Patton. He looked like a big city traffic cop, performing balletic moves and shouting expletives as he kept the vehicles moving.

Two of Patton's armored divisions were chasing two German armored divisions. The directions that the enemy divisions took were causing Patton's columns to run into each other, so the general directed each division to turn about and trade their enemy targets with one another to avoid entanglement.

Although I couldn't know it at the moment, the solution worked beautifully. Both German commanders panicked, because they became convinced that two American armored divisions were after each of them.

As our unit crept to the jammed intersection, Patton looked at us and stopped his traffic cop gesturing.

"What the hell is that?" he shouted, pointing at our vehicles.

All of us were mystified, until he made it clear that the sandbags we'd placed in racks on the sides of our vehicles did not please him.

"They look like a bunch of bums!" he yelled, as an aide tried to explain the protective purpose of the sandbags. "I can't have my armored outfits looking like bums."

Patton's temper was famous. He was a spit-and-polish commander, and when any man or unit violated his sense of military bearing, his punishment often was severe. We expected the worst, but his aide came to our rescue.

"Those guys are with the 14th Armored Division, General," the aide said. "They were at Hammelburg. Don't be too tough on them."

Reminded that our division was on hand when his son-in-law was liberated, Patton's rage mellowed.

"All right then," he said. "Just have them pull off to the side of the road and remove all that crap from their vehicles. It looks like hell. And get rid of that damned rocking chair!"

Patton referred to one of the booty items that we'd stashed in the back of the half-track. I have to admit that we did resemble a refugee column at times, with odd items strapped to the back of our armored cars.

He made us dump all of it, including the kettle hanging from a hook on the back of one of the armored cars. We'd been using it to boil water for coffee and for shaving. Now we'd have to return to boiling water in our helmets.

We were losing protection for the sake of appearances, but that was George Patton's way, and all of us admired him as a fighting general. But those sandbags were with us for many weeks before we joined Third Army and had our Patton episode. A Troop and 14th Armored still had a lot of ground to cover while under the command of Seventh Army.

We sped through the countryside, all of us taken with its beauty in the full blush of spring. Flowers bloomed and trees were turning green. It was impossible to digest so much natural beauty and realize we were in a war zone.

Then we'd roar through some anonymous town and see the ruin, where gutted buildings still smoldered, and bulldozers had piled rubble fifty feet high to clear the roadways.

Our mission was to keep moving fast, and keep the enemy in flight. All of us sensed that the Germans were finished now.

We should have known better.

CREUSSEN—Another Deadly German Counterattack

Even a lowly private like myself could see the signs. The German troops were surrendering now in the thousands. We watched long lines of them trudging west, obediently heading for internment with just a few MPs guarding them.

We heard stories, too. There were tales that the SS units were killing *Wehrmacht* troops that tried to surrender. Someone told me that a *Wehrmacht* captain shot an SS officer who had captured Americans, and then turned his pistol over to the former prisoners, surrendering.

There was no front line to speak of. We drove past patches of white phosphorous lobbed by our artillery to mark the front lines, but these signposts had become meaningless.

Phosphorous was an effective weapon, but you had to be careful around it, since it had staying power. You didn't want to get any of it on yourself. Sometimes our artillery units fired phosphorous shells with proximity fuses, so they would burst at treetop level, and descend on anyone below. The trees would catch fire and the phosphorous would drop from there.

We had to drive through wooded areas which had been raked by phosphorous fire, and if any of it dropped on your uniform, you had to peel the clothes off immediately. It even made snow hot where it landed, and if you grabbed the wrong handful of snow to treat a phosphorous burn, you'd just make it worse.

I was burned badly by phosphorous on this advance. I was in an open jeep when several globs of it dropped on me from a tree, burning the surface skin off parts of my forearm and my head. Some of those burns never healed, and I bear the scars today. But a medic gave me quick aid in the field to reduce the pain, and off we went again.

The speed of our advance never seemed to slacken at this time. When we passed regular infantry units as they rested on the roadside, they called out things like, "Goodbye, you poor bastards." They knew we were shooting ahead, looking for German strongpoints. Of course, once we found them, we'd call up the infantry, and when they passed through us to fight the Germans we'd say, "Goodbye, you poor bastards."

Being so far out front meant there was always a danger of being hit by friendly fire. We came to expect it, and though we didn't like it, we had to accept it.

Our only casualty at this time came from friendly fire. It hit one of the guys who'd been separated from our column. I watched sadly as someone lifted him, and carried him on their shoulders to the medics. I never learned whether he made it, because we just kept moving.

We were heading due south, in front of everyone. We knew that sooner or later we'd have to run into some kind of fight, but for now we were high-balling down the autobahn into Bavaria. The road was a superhighway, six lanes wide. It reminded me of the freeway in Los Angeles, complete with underpasses and clover-leaf exits. On it, we were able to capture towns with almost no trouble.

The supply units kept us gassed up, so we never stopped. When we arrived in Heldburg, we started picking up German stragglers. I figured we must be getting close to the main enemy units, but as we crossed a dam bridge below Lichtenfels, there was still no sign of trouble. It looked like we'd punch across the Main River at any moment.

The Germans seemed utterly shocked by the speed of our advance. One of our units charged into a German officer training school, and bagged two hundred candidates who were just returning from an exercise. They must have been astonished when our vehicles sped around them, as they were looking forward to a hot meal in what they considered a secure zone.

While we laughed at this story, our unit entered a town and surprised a German military wedding that was in mid-ceremony. Our half-tracks and armored cars pulled to the front of the church, and we saw about forty German officers standing in two rows, their sabers raised above the bride and groom as they walked down the church steps. The groom, another German officer, walked his bride right into us, and their smiles disappeared.

We captured all of them. Motioning with our machine guns, we chased off the civilians in the wedding party, and marched the German officers to the town square. Four half-tracks surrounded them. There were female German officers present, too, and all of them were in full parade dress for the wedding.

I approached the groom and took his pistol. Then I noticed that he carried a fine Exacta camera, so I liberated that, too.

"*Nichts military*," he protested.

"That's all right, buddy," I said. "It has military applications."

I eventually sold the pistol, but I kept that camera for the rest of the war, and brought it home. It's the best camera I've ever used. Spoils of war.

Soon, we sent the officers to the rear with an MP detachment. I was glad to get rid of them. I wish I could recall the name of the town where this happened, but we went through so many towns so fast that I never knew some of their names. Even if you had a good map, which we didn't, it was difficult to know the names of some towns.

In no time, we'd captured seventeen towns while encountering only sporadic machine gun and small-arms fire. We had our TDs with us, so these nuisances quickly were dispatched.

In just a few days, the 94th had cut off the major cities of Bayreuth and Nuremberg. We'd collected so many German prisoners by this time that we had to detail two of our platoons to set up a POW cage at Linderhardt. It immediately was filled by fifteen hundred defeated *Wehrmacht* troops, including our wedding party.

When we arrived in Creussen, we dismounted and did some exploring. We found an underground factory that made anti-aircraft weapons. We waltzed in and freed six hundred slave laborers the Germans had been using there. The factory also made old small arms for use by the *Volkssturm*, the national militia that now was made up of old men and young boys.

The slave laborers were ecstatic to see us, but we weren't too pleased with how they looked. Most of them were gaunt and emaciated, dressed in rags. They pointed out the factory's German owner and employees, and we took them into custody. It was mostly for their own protection, because the laborers wanted to tear them apart.

Since German military units were putting up resistance around the town, we armed the slave laborers with the old weapons we'd found. The rifles weren't much good, but the laborers were so eager for revenge, they made fine use of them.

I found a rifle that fired .22 caliber ammunition. It was just an old bolt action piece that looked like a Mauser, but it was amazingly accurate. I gave it to one of the Polish laborers, and he eagerly shot Germans with it.

All of the armed slave laborers went after it with a passion. They marauded throughout Creussen, shooting every German they could find. You heard rifles cracking in the town all night long. They shot German troops, local civilians, and even collaborators among their own ranks.

Our commander, Major George England, did what he could to keep their fighting directed toward the German military. The laborers were very effective. We began calling them "England's Irregulars."

A good number of them were Poles who had been in captivity since 1939. The Germans had been working them to death at starvation level for six years. It was a miracle that so many of them had survived.

I learned from them what a terrible number had not survived. This is why we turned a blind eye when the laborers looted the stores in Creussen. One shoe store was cleaned out because the owner had been a Nazi. I saw one laborer emerge with about eight pairs of shoes in his arms. He figured he deserved them, after the Germans had made him work for years with no shoes at all. The laborers took as much as they could.

We fed them with our canned rations. They were so hungry, they stewed the cans in water so they could get all of the contents out of them. They didn't leave a speck of food big enough for a fly.

Upon further inspection of the factory, one of my pals discovered a huge cache of alcohol, which the Germans used to fuel their buzz bombs. Someone had the bright idea to mix it with the canned pineapple juice we found in the factory kitchen. We made gallons of buzz bomb punch and had a party one night.

The stuff was like white lightning. In no time, all of us were dancing in the streets. A good number of our guys got very sick. But the poor laborers were so skinny and run-down that the punch knocked them for a loop. Most of them became ill, and a few actually died.

During all of this, we knew the larger German units weren't far from Creussen, so Major England decided to consolidate his forces. He ordered all troops of the 94th to gather in town, and called division for reinforcements. It was clear even to us that he was expecting trouble here. What we didn't know was that just fifteen miles outside of town there was a large, active training center for German panzer troops.

But on April 15, we got an education. The Germans attacked with about fifty of their most modern tanks, Tigers and Panthers, and surrounded Creussen on three sides.

When the shells started landing, I headed for cover. It felt like Hatten all over again. A hurricane of blasts and machine gun fire raged above me.

We had plenty of TDs with us this time. Major England had set up defensive positions in the town, with the TDs covering all routes of approach.

Now I really was thankful for the help of the slave laborers, who took up positions alongside us. I knew that our outfit simply didn't have enough men to hold off the German attack by ourselves, because the enemy had added another concentration of tanks from Bayreuth. They wanted us out of Creussen, because it was located on the autobahn directly between Bayreuth and Nuremberg.

When the column of panzers came down the road toward town, one of our TDs fired a round that exploded just in front of the lead tank. The panzers started shooting back, and we had to get out of the area.

As I ran, I felt sick. I felt like giving up. Just the day before, it seemed like the war was over. Suddenly I was running for my life. I thought I certainly would be killed or captured in this fierce fight that came out of nowhere.

By this time, we had only about one hundred twenty men scattered around town in graveyards, woods and houses. We used every able-bodied man we could find to help us—slave laborers, MPs, medics, even civilians.

I was stuck in the graveyard, trying to keep covered behind a thick headstone. It was the strangest place I'd ever fought during the entire war. Bullets ricocheted off the tombstones and bits of granite and shrapnel flew all around me.

The cemetery was surrounded by woods where the enemy used good cover to fire on us. I ducked and fired haphazardly. I couldn't see anything other than blinking muzzle flashes in the dark woods. I tried to shoot at them and then hide again behind my tombstone. It was a big marble cross, and the German bullets were chopping holes in it.

This went on for a couple of hours, and then I heard the drone of airplane engines. I thanked God for Major England and his good rapport with the Air Force brass, because I knew he'd called for support. I glanced skyward at the noise and watched P-47s scream down out of the blue. They plastered the woods surrounding the cemetery. The whole forest erupted in noise, smoke and shattering trees.

It was over in less than a minute. We rose carefully from behind our headstones and moved into the woods. We didn't find a single body. I figured the Germans just wanted to let us know they were still in the fight, and then got out of there when the big stuff started landing on them. The few who didn't make it probably were vaporized.

Walking back through the cemetery, I suddenly thought of Hatten again, and the tiny cemetery I'd come upon shortly after that battle. It had been used for soldiers as well as civilians. In its corner, I found a mass grave where the Germans had buried about a hundred American soldiers. The grave was marked by a wooden chapel about twelve feet high that the Germans had built. They'd posted a sign on it, saying, "*Amerikanische Soldaten,*" and hung strings of bailing wire from its sides. On the bailing wire were the dog tags of the dead Americans, left there so our Graves Registration units could identify them.

It touched me that the Germans could be so thoughtful and courteous, and still be so capable of barbarism. It made me think that all of us might have the same dichotomy, a capacity for the angelic and the bestial.

All of this took place during the lull after the battle in Hatten, when both sides were exhausted. I think all of us would have quit then if we could have. But that was another battle, in another cemetery.

The fighting still raged in this battle. We learned from observation planes and patrols that two German armored divisions were headed our way, down the road from Bayreuth. There would be no way for our small unit to stand up against that kind of power.

On orders, I stationed myself in a house on the edge of town with a radio to call in artillery fire.

"If you see anything that moves, shoot it," Major England said.

I was alone, every sense sharpened to the level of a feral dog. I heard the drone of p-47s again. The German armored divisions were clogging the roads and the fields around them, a real concentration of tanks. It was the kind of target that airmen dream about.

The planes dived, strafing and dropping their bombs. Two or three waves of them attacked the column, slowing it down. Then the artillery went to work.

Every time the krauts broke through our lines, I noticed they tended to concentrate their tanks in one sector, so I directed artillery fire there. I used a simple map with numbered grids to guide the barrage. When they were on target, I told them to fire for effect.

This went on for two days. We sent shells down on the German column every thirty minutes. Some of the explosions landed around the house where I was spotting. I couldn't be sure which side they came from.

But the German column was being immolated. Their tanks fired in every direction, because they couldn't tell where the shells were coming from.

I witnessed the most frightening use of Corps artillery that I would see for the entire war. The shells landed in predetermined sectors, saturating each in turn with deadly blasts. After one of those blasts, there was nothing left in that area. One salvo alone knocked out seventeen German tanks.

As I watched, I realized there could be nothing worse than being under fire from our Corps artillery. The Germans were getting everything our army had, from 240-mm guns on down to light field pieces. When all of those shells land at once, the ground boils. After a couple of days, there was nothing left to destroy.

I exited the house and climbed a hill above the graveyard where I nearly lost my life just two days before. I peered into the distance at where the panzer column had been. Half-tracks and bulldozers were towing the shattered remains of German vehicles off the road. The dozers were busy filling in shell holes, so we could use the road again.

The barrage had stopped the German counterattack cold. I don't know if we lost a man. That was the point. It wasn't about the amount of shells you expended. It was about the number of lives you saved, and how quickly you got the job done. In Creussen, we got the job done in a few days.

My unit returned to patrol duty around the town, since there still were remnants of enemy troops in the area. It was on one of these patrols that I had the strangest experience of my life.

I was hiding alone in some bushes, keeping watch when I heard some rustling behind me.

"*Hände hoch*," said a voice.

I turned to see a German soldier leveling a pistol at my head. I don't know how, but he got the drop on me. He'd been wandering around like he was lost, so I paid little attention to him, until now.

I raised my hands and stood slowly, leaving my carbine on the ground. He told me that I was his prisoner, and ordered me to walk with him toward his lines. I started to obey. A feeling of relief passed over me for a moment. It was cold that day, and I actually thought it might be a nice thing to get out of this damned war.

But then I thought of George Bailey, how thin he looked after being freed from a POW compound. I remembered his missing teeth, the product of a beating by the German guards. I wasn't sure how the krauts would treat me in captivity.

I don't know where it came from, but suddenly I became eloquent.

"You look like a smart guy," I said, my hands still behind my head. "I'm sure you understand what's going on. This war is just about over. Your side will lose, probably in a matter of weeks. Germany will surrender. You haven't got a chance in the world, and you know it. Why should you give up your life for a lost cause?"

He said nothing. He just stood there, listening to me.

"Isn't it better to be alive than to be a dead hero?" I continued. "Think. You can spend the rest of the war in comfort. You'll be safe, away from the fighting. Far away. You'll be in a POW camp where it's warm. Scottsdale or Phoenix. We have POW camps there. They'll give you great food. They'll feed you ice cream and chocolate every day. You'll get a ration of cigarettes."

He remained silent, but his pistol lowered slightly.

"What does the German army have to offer you?" I asked. "If you give me that pistol, I'll take you back, and turn you over to our MPs. They'll escort you to our camp, and in a few days you'll be on a boat to America."

By some miracle, he bought my pitch. He handed me the pistol, and we walked back toward Creussen. There, I handed him to the MPs to be taken back to the POW stockade behind our lines.

I kept the pistol. It was a 9-mm Browning, manufactured in Belgium. When the Germans captured Belgium they took over production of these pistols, and made them conform to their 9-mm Luger ammunition, so they could use them easily in the war. The one I captured had wooden handles, like the Model 1911 .45 automatic, but it carried thirteen rounds in the clip. It was very similar to the current standard-issue NATO pistol.

I had that pistol in water and mud, and it never failed. It was very easy to strip and clean. I wore it on my army belt, because it had a clip.

And it was accurate. I used to take target practice, firing at birds sitting atop a barge on a lake. If I had to choose a pistol that I'd need in the field for a long time, I'd take that Browning. I dragged that pistol all over Europe with me. I was a little scared of being captured again while carrying it, because the Germans didn't look too kindly on American soldiers in possession of their equipment. But it had precious meaning, so I took the chance and kept it.

Just about everyone in my unit had captured weapons, anyway. Whenever we knew action was imminent, and there would be some risk of capture, we'd all dump our booty into the cook's half-track. He had a stove on board, and we'd all throw our captured guns into the back.

"Those damned things in here will get me killed," the cook always protested, but we didn't pay attention.

After the action was finished, we'd all return to the cook's half-track to reclaim our items. Sometimes fights would break out over who owned what.

But I made sure no one had a chance to swipe my Belgian Browning. I kept it on my belt through all actions, and brought it home with me after the war. It's still in my family to this day.

Our unit had a lot of other captured German equipment, because we found that it often was better than our own. We used to watch movies on a nice projector that we'd found. We connected it to a German power generator, which was a great piece of machinery. It had a relay overload switch, so with a little rheostat rewiring, the thing could light up a whole house. We never managed to overload that generator.

We weren't adverse to using captured German vehicles, either. Aside from the little red *Kugelwagen* I enjoyed, the unit had a wide variety of tracked and wheeled items.

In Hilpolstein, we found all kinds of abandoned German and European vehicles. Incredibly, about half the vehicles in our column were German by this time. We tried to paint them olive green with a white star on top to avoid friendly fire or air attack.

The rest of them became like toys. We had road races in them, right through the center of town. I thought the German motorcycles with sidecars were the most fun to race. They were amazingly fast, thanks to the high amount of horsepower they possessed.

Some of the guys made a big deal over who won the races, but it was basically a free-for-all. We had so much fun just driving wild and fast that we didn't care who won. In fact, our contests were less like races and more like demolition derbies.

One day I hopped into a large German truck, the kind that could transport a whole platoon. I gunned the engine, got it up to speed, and rammed it into a bunch of cars. When I got out of the smoking, twisted mess, I tossed a thermite grenade into the truck, and watched it burn. I nearly burned down the whole town.

It wasn't like we needed the German vehicles. We had plenty of our own. But we knew the Germans needed every truck, half-track and armored car they could get, so we were doing the right thing by destroying them. We just added a little fun to that military necessity.

If we saw a good German blanket, we'd appropriate that, too. The only problem with the German blankets was that they were too short. Their beds weren't as long as ours, and they habitually slept with their heads sticking out of one end and their feet sticking out of the other.

Sometimes we even stole equipment from our own side. It wasn't unusual for some guys to pile into a peep during a rest period, and drive to Paris looking for booty. One character from our outfit drove by the officers' quarters, and exchanged our old beaten up peep for a newer model parked outside. He just swapped the hoods, because that was the only place where the vehicle identification number was stenciled.

Many men in our unit were gifted thieves who had a talent for finding things that we needed. They were always looking, always scrounging in every town for items we could use.

We lost a few of these men to booby traps. Luckily, I never had to deal with a booby trap, because I always stayed clear of anything that looked too inviting. But it's a wonder we didn't lose more men to the infernal devices, the way some of our guys went after souvenirs.

During the lull after the fight in Creussen, we started seeing a lot of German refugees. Everywhere we went, we had to deal with them. There were thousands now, and they clogged the roads.

We moved them to the roadside so they wouldn't bog us down. But we did what we could for them, because these people were in a mess. They all were hungry, so when we came along it was like a godsend. We were the reason why some of these people survived.

But it was organized confusion. We set up refugee camps where we could take care of some of them. Occasionally there would be a character who'd try to steal from the others, but for the most part they were trustworthy people. They just were homeless and hungry.

They all craved cigarettes, too. It was common for a civilian to approach me and say, "*Haben Sie Stumpf?*" I always was glad to share my cigarettes with them.

These people had no chocolate or sugar, so that was another golden item. Dairy products were almost nonexistent, except among the farmers.

I especially enjoyed giving things to the kids. Some of them had never even tasted chocolate. The looks on their faces were indescribable when they bit into a candy bar.

Pretty soon I had a flock of kids following me every time I showed my face in the street. They always clustered around me, shouting, "*Herr Hugo! Herr Hugo!*" They couldn't pronounce the word Hugh.

An officer witnessed this exhibition one day and approached me. He suggested that I could easily get elected *burgomeister* here.

"Who needs that?" I told him. "I'm already Santa Claus."

Sometimes we were lucky enough to find civilians who had food, wine and spirits to share with us. The town *burgomeisters* often wanted to treat us to schnapps, or other types of drink. But we weren't ever sure whether they intended to poison us.

Several times our guys actually were poisoned, and became extremely sick. We never knew what the bastards had put into those drinks, but we assumed it was rat poison. They didn't use a dose strong enough to kill, but it incapacitated a few of our men.

Ernie Wharton was our official liquor tester. Ernie could drink just about anything, and he always volunteered to sample the drinks offered to us. He'd take a snifter, swallow it, and after about twenty minutes he'd say it was all right. Then we'd all drink.

Ernie only got poisoned once. We got him to a hospital quickly, where he recovered.

Ernie could outdrink anybody I'd ever known, and he was also one of the best poker players I'd seen. He had a reputation throughout the Seventh Army.

One time I passed through the 45th Infantry Division. When some of their men saw my 14th Armored Division shoulder patch, they said, "We don't like you guys."

"What's the matter?" I asked.

"Some little guy came through here yesterday, and cleaned out the whole division in a poker game." That was Ernie Wharton.

A destroyed German 88mm anti-tank gun. These weapons were instant death to all tanks they hit.

I would have been thrilled to spend the rest of the war in Creussen, but we received orders to move out. When my unit re-equipped and topped off our gas tanks, we left Creussen and continued heading south.

I liked to pass the time in my vehicle listening to the radio. We picked up the German propaganda broadcasts featuring "Axis Sally." She had a sexy, deep, whispering voice, and she played great music.

Between records, she'd say things like, "Hello there, members of the 14th Armored. Hope you're having a happy day. Just down the road from you there are twenty 88s waiting to say hello.

"You probably won't get very far, but there are a lot of boys training right now in the United States who will take your places when you're gone. So there will always be a 14th Armored, even though most of you will be scattered all over the battlefields of Europe."

We didn't pay attention to what she said. We just enjoyed the music.

The weather was turning cold and wet. It was just our luck that this April would be the wettest that Germany had seen in years. And after miles of vehicles, the roads became muddy quagmires.

We had winches and cables on most of our peeps, armored cars and half-tracks, so we spent a lot of time pulling each other out of mud several feet deep. In some places, the mud was so bad that my half-track sank five feet into it. Our traffic probably set the roads back one hundred years.

Eventually the engineers came to the rescue with tank recovery vehicles and special half-tracks. They attached bulldozer scoops to the front ends, and scraped the mud completely off the roads. In some places, they scraped it right down to the ancient Roman road surface.

My outfit had to stand guard over these roads as they were being cleared, because sometimes kraut snipers fired at the bulldozer drivers. By this point in the war, we went into a bloody rage when a sniper fired. We became absolutely determined to kill him.

The standard procedure was to send a few men forward to take the shot, while the rest of us provided cover fire to keep the sniper's head down. Once we figured out where the shots had come from, we fired with everything we had while our guys moved into the building. From there, it was a cowboys-and-Indians type of thing, except it usually was inside a house or church instead of the open range.

There still seemed to be snipers in every town at this late stage in the war, which infuriated me. When they fired at our bulldozer drivers, however, they never hit them. A steel bulldozer scoop makes a great shield when it's raised.

We performed our highway patrolling in peeps. I drove down the road at a good clip while another fellow sat in the back, manning the mounted machine gun. I drove at fifty to sixty miles per hour down those roads, while my gunner fired in every direction. It sprayed a lot of bullets and used up lots of ammunition, but we didn't care. The Germans didn't know what to make if it, though.

There were times when we knew where a German sniper hid. We liked to dupe them by pretending to do road repair work, while sending a small unit around and behind the sniper to get him. This worked more than once.

It was always a good feeling. No one liked snipers. We didn't even like our own snipers.

When it was time to move again, we headed south toward Ingolstadt. My unit picked up prisoners all along the way.

In Hellingen, we captured sixteen German troops after a brief firefight that claimed the life of my friend, Sergeant Faye Miller. It was an especially bitter loss, knowing that we were so close to the end of the war.

This was on everyone's mind now — not to be the last to die in this campaign. But we knew some of us would indeed die. The Germans hadn't quit yet.

At one point on the road we came upon a village. Lieutenant Kraker ordered our column to stop and dismount. He was suspicious of what he saw.

There was a large barn ahead of us. We surrounded it.

Kraker ordered me and Corporal Ray Oestrich to run up to it and open its doors. I trotted carefully forward, half-expecting a rifle crack to drop me at any moment. The unit had the barn completely covered by machine guns, but I knew that wouldn't matter to some fanatic who had a beautiful, clear shot at my head.

I arrived at the barn door. Taking one hand from my carbine, I grasped the handle and flung it open. Instinctively, I raised my carbine at the gaping, dark doorway.

My heart stopped. A sea of field grey uniforms moved toward me.

About a hundred German soldiers walked out of that barn. Luckily, they were surrendering. I gestured with my carbine, and they put their hands behind their heads. Nobody fired.

The surrendering horde was a combination of soldiers, Red Cross workers, and civilians, including seven officers and two nurses. The barn had been a field hospital, and a sort of final fortification.

Familiar faces from my unit joined us, covering the Germans. Together we marched the prisoners to a nearby church courtyard where we'd parked our half-tracks.

Three of our men stood in the ring mounts of those vehicles, covering the throng with .50 caliber machine guns. By the time we gathered all of our recently captured Germans, we counted nine hundred fifty-seven of them. The prisoners sat, and there they remained under cover for three days until the MPs came and took them to the stockade.

Many of the troops inside the barn were grounded *Luftwaffe* fliers. There weren't enough planes to make use of them as pilots, so they were awaiting a shipment of rifles to join the fighting as regular infantry. It was just another sign of how desperate things had become for the Third Reich.

Adding insult to injury, we captured the convoy bringing rifles to those grounded fighter jocks. Of course, the scarcity of planes didn't mean that the *Luftwaffe* had disappeared. The ME-109s and FW-190s still made appearances, strafing us for two or three runs before our combat air patrols descended on them.

They also sent light bombers at us during the nights, usually Junker 88s. We called one of these planes "Bed Check Charlie," because it bombed every night around the same hour.

There wasn't much damage done by the bombings, but missions like that forced us to maintain our blackout procedures in all bivouacs and vehicles. Driving at night with just a thin strip of light coming from the head lamps caused dozens of accidents, and claimed a lot of lives. Being non-combat fatalities so late in the war made the losses that much more tragic.

But we had a piece of good news at this time. Kraker had been promoted to captain. We were glad for him, because no one deserved it more. He'd done a great job and he looked out for us. Everyone admired him.

Kraker ordered us to mount up, and the column continued moving south. We roared through a series of nameless towns.

While in Hellingen, I sat and watched as our vehicles drove across a concrete bridge that we'd captured intact. One of our TDs got to the middle of the span, and suddenly I heard a loud cracking noise. Apparently the TD was too heavy for the bridge, because it fell straight through the bottom and into the water below.

Luckily the water was only deep enough to reach the base of the turret, and it was only about a ten-foot fall. But to me, it looked like the thing had just disappeared. We couldn't use our prized bridge after that, but it didn't stop the column.

We liberated our own POWs along the way. In Schomfeld, we freed two hundred five of them, including three officers and six Australians who'd been incarcerated since the battle of Tobruk, three years earlier.

I was happy to hear at this time that George England had been promoted to full colonel. We all felt fortunate to be under his command throughout the campaign.

New orders took the unit off the autobahn. We were to clear the woods at the side of the superhighway, between it and a railroad line.

This was a maddening detail, not only because that forest was crawling with snipers and small enemy units, but because after we cleared them out, more of them would infiltrate the woods behind us. They'd set up machine gun nests, and we had to clear the same area again.

Night patrols in these woods were especially tense. To help us see better, someone in our supporting units had the idea to place giant anti-aircraft searchlights on top of the hills behind us, and shine them down on the area we had to patrol. It illuminated the woods with an eerie kind of light, not very bright, but a soft, white luminescence. The beam was invisible, since it was coming our way from a higher altitude.

I'm sure the Germans hated it, because it robbed them of concealment in the darkness. The problem was that it did the same thing to us. We became stark shadows silhouetted in white light, and therefore beautiful targets. While we enjoyed having the light to prevent any German from sneaking up on us, we felt like clay pigeons in an arcade as we crept forward looking for trouble.

We were used to night patrols, because we'd been conducting them on and off for months. We nearly always went out at night, and the patrols were always ticklish, having to crawl around in the dark woods. But we learned to depend on the Germans being exactly where our intelligence people said they would be.

They had them pinpointed by this time. We took some prisoners, shot up some enemy vehicles, and blew up several of their ammunition dumps. We put some Compound-X plastic explosive on key places in one of the dumps, set the detonation timers, and got the hell out of there. It was quite a fireworks show when it went up, and I felt good to know that we destroyed their materiel before they could use it against us.

During one foray, we found a stash of benzene tanks. The Germans were using benzene because of their critical gasoline shortage. We blew those tanks and pushed on.

There were inevitable firefights in the woods at night. They usually were short, nasty affairs. We were often accompanied by light tanks, so we had a hammer that we could use against snipers and machine gun nests. The small tanks were vulnerable to *Panzerfausts,* however.

On one patrol, a kraut stood up and fired his rocket, scoring a direct hit on the front of our light tank. It burst into flames. I saw one of the crew men struggling to escape, so without thinking I climbed aboard and helped him out of there. We weren't more than a few yards away from the tank when the ammunition began cooking off, sending bullets and shrapnel out like an enormous Roman candle.

Sometimes the night patrols lasted almost to dawn, so we had to grab sleep when we could. On one of these patrols, we bedded down in a turnip field that seemed secure. But at first light, I opened my eyes and saw the muzzle of an 88 looming over a dirt bank just a few feet away.

My heart pounded as I slowly picked up my carbine and crawled to the edge of the bank. When I topped it, I brought my rifle around, ready to blast anything that moved.

There were no troops. The gun had been disabled and abandoned, but it scared me pale to think I could have been snoring peacefully beneath the business end of a fully crewed AT gun.

Following the miserable days in those enemy infested woods, Combat Command was confident that most of the threat had been eradicated. They ordered my unit back to the autobahn.

We were speeding south once again. Our division's goal: the Blue Danube.

It was April 20, Hitler's birthday. We had a major party in mind for him.

MOOSBURG—Freeing Thousands of Allied POWs

After three days of weaving in and out of traffic, and sometimes using side roads, the unit was back on point with orders to patrol on the right flank of the general advance toward the Danube.

Everyone was thrilled with the news of what had happened during that time. The 14th Armored Division officially had been transferred from Seventh Army to George Patton's Third Army. We were under the whip of a real cavalryman now.

The 94th Cavalry Recon had developed a proven system in our race from town to town. We sent out a single man in a peep who would drive ahead of the main body into every town and tell the *burgomeister* to surrender if he wants any of his town left. We always used a man who spoke German somewhat fluently, like Sergeant Froeschner, who was effective at getting them to cooperate.

Colonel England and Captain Kraker spoke German, too, and they often used loudspeakers to urge *burgomeisters* to surrender their towns. Most of them did, but when they didn't we called in the heavy stuff and fulfilled our promise to blow the town to hell. Early in our tour, the Germans developed a system where they'd let our lightly equipped recon units drive through unmolested, and fire on the larger infantry units that followed. In those cases, we had to turn around and help by hitting the Germans from behind. This caused a lot of confusion, since our units and the infantry fired in each other's direction, although it also cut up the enemy badly.

All of that was different now. England and Kraker made sure we traveled with 90-mm TDs, and when the Germans saw three or four of them in column with our armored cars, they didn't allow us through any longer.

Even though it was late April, the weather was still cold and wet. It rained almost every day. It actually snowed one day in early May.

I didn't pay attention to it. By this time, I had become impervious to the weather. We could always stay dry in our vehicles, anyway. I felt sorry for the infantry guys, who had to slog through the deep mud, soaking wet all day and all night. We could get cleaned up and shave once in a while. It was a picnic, compared to what we'd been through.

As we raced southward, the Germans were moving that way, too. Whatever troops they couldn't get north, they sent south, with the apparent intention to defend the Brenner Pass in the Alps.

At this time, we started hearing rumors that the Nazis planned to mass troops in the mountains, and set up a "National Redoubt" there. They would be extremely difficult to defeat in that terrain, and could continue resistance almost indefinitely.

We also heard rumors that the SS planned to create "Werewolf" units in those mountains, trained to fight a guerrilla war in which they would hit-and-run, and launch sabotage operations that could continue for years.

I learned later that General Eisenhower and his staff had become completely paranoid over this possibility, which was why they ordered our units to travel so far to the south. We were to prevent any German concentration of troops in the mountains of Bavaria.

The rumor sounded reasonable to us, the rank and file soldiers. We intended to see to it that the enemy never was able to organize enough force for a National Redoubt, and we like to think that our units had something to do with the fact they never did.

Our Air Force was determined to prevent it, too. They attacked all German trains in the area. When the Germans began using electric trains, our pilots got wise and fired on the cars instead of the locomotives.

I don't know how hard the Nazis tried to fulfill their mountain defense plan, but they couldn't pull it off. It was simply too late.

The heavy units of our division meanwhile had reached the Danube River. German resistance there was vicious. All bridges were blown, one of them with an American lead tank charging across it.

We anticipated joining the charge across the Danube, but all units in our vicinity received a new order. There was a large Allied POW camp near Moosburg, housing thousands of Americans—some of whom were from our own unit.

Intelligence reported that the Germans intended to move them eastward, and perhaps even shoot some of them. Every unit within striking distance of Moosburg was to head for that POW camp, and rescue the prisoners. We turned our vehicles, and joined the stampede.

Before we arrived, the German commander of the camp sent a major to parlay with American and British officers, requesting that Moosburg become a neutral zone and for all Allied troop movement in the vicinity of the camp to stop. You can guess how that went over. Our response: unconditional surrender, or suffer the consequences.

German SS troops took up positions outside the city of Moosburg, and the fight was on. It was less a fight than an extermination, because in half an hour just about every SS soldier was dead.

Our tanks rolled through Moosburg, which was an ancient city with beautiful cobblestone streets. Two of our lieutenants hopped into a peep with a .30 caliber machine gun mounted in the back, and drove to the POW camp. They stopped among the German guards outside the gate, and one of them stood and shouted one word.

"Achtung!"

The Germans laid down their arms, surrendering the remainder of their six-thousand-man garrison in Moosburg. More importantly, one hundred ten thousand Allied prisoners were free.

When I arrived with my unit, it was the biggest mess I'd seen in the whole war. How do you fly out more than a hundred thousand men? How to you treat so many of them who needed medical attention and nourishment? Our Air Force tried to fly them out as fast as they could.

The celebration of the prisoners was unforgettable. Some of the poor men had been imprisoned for years.

Thirty thousand of the total were Americans, but there were Norwegians, French, Poles, Dutch, Greeks, Romanians, Bulgarians, Italians, Russians, Serbs, New Zealanders, Australians, South Africans, British, Canadians — even a few Brazilians. It struck me that the Nazis had tried to lock up the whole world.

There were twenty-seven Russian generals who had managed to survive the cruelest incarceration. There were sons of four American generals. There were women, three of whom were Russian doctors.

The city of Moosburg itself was filled with slave laborers, also newly freed. The crowds of thankful prisoners pressed our vehicles so tightly that we were almost afraid to move.

They cried. They shouted. They patted the tanks like they were living things.

I watched one giant Aussie run up to a peep driver, and almost crush him with a bear-hug.

"You damned bloody Yanks!" he shouted. "I love you!"

Some of the women had flowers. I have no idea where they got them, but they threw them on our vehicles.

I saw a Serbian soldier weep, and simply touch the face of one of our men, as though to be sure he was real.

All of the POWs I talked to were ecstatic to get out of there. We gave several of them their first bath in three years. They couldn't get over it.

One of the prisoners had been the Commandant of West Point, so we cleaned him up and used him as a speaker to organize the POWs. This man would later become Commandant of the Air Force Academy in Colorado Springs, where he had an entire room dedicated to the 14th Armored Division.

Everyone we could move out of there, we moved. The ones who were worst off physically flew directly to England. We scattered the rest everywhere behind our lines. It turned into a giant transportation headache with so many rolling out of that prison at once.

Some of them stayed with us, and joined our unit. Many of the Australian POWs didn't want to go home. They wanted to keep fighting, and get revenge against the Germans. We gave them weapons, and fixed them up.

They rode on the backs of our tanks for a few days, but the brass put a stop to it. They said it was a violation of the Geneva Convention to put former POWs in combat, and if they were recaptured, the Germans would execute them.

I personally thought that was nonsense. From what the prisoners told me, the Germans already had done a hat dance on the Geneva Convention — especially in the case of the Russian prisoners. But orders were orders, and we sent them home.

The Aussies were certainly a game bunch. They made as much fun of the British as they did of the Germans. They accused the British of stopping in mid-battle for tea.

We kept about seven of the *Einsatzgruppen* guards with us to help find the Germans who'd escaped into the nearby woods. The rest of the guards were formed into a column and marched away.

It galled us to see that nearly every one of them carried several loaves of bread so they'd have enough to eat in captivity. A bunch of our guys leaped off the tanks, grabbed the bread, and tossed the loaves over the fence to the prisoners. The Germans didn't utter a sound.

Stories began to circulate. I heard that one fellow in another of our units was reunited with his son, who'd been a prisoner. I also heard that some of the German troops were as young as nine years old, and that there were female guards still in their teens.

All of them had been armed. Now all of them marched in a mile-long column toward their own imprisonment, a light tank in front of them and one in the rear with their guns aimed down the line.

That first night in Moosburg, I was afraid of a repetition of the Hammelburg tragedy. The prisoners broke into everything, finding food, clothing, and of course, alcohol. In no time the streets were filled with drunken revelers who hadn't had a decent meal in years.

It looked like a surreal carnival of souls, all of them dressed in whatever garb they could find, no matter how outrageous or grotesque. There were men in tall silk hats and tails shouting in foreign tongues. There were men in long ladies' coats carrying crossbows, live geese, rocking chairs. Everyone seemed to have found a bicycle, and they wobbled through the cobblestone streets, crashing and falling.

The German citizens of Moosburg hid in their homes that night. For many, hiding did no good.

My unit moved out. We were tasked with protecting the local airfield in Landshut. We did round-the-clock guard duty, so the air flow would not be interrupted.

There were still enemy units in the vicinity, especially around the airport. The Landshut airport was large, probably as big as the one in Munich, so it was vital for flying prisoners to England. Our orders were to guard the airport at all costs.

The Germans were retreating from Landshut when we arrived, so our unit swung ahead of them and cut them off. Once we had them surrounded, we called for tank and artillery fire to hammer them in the pocket.

I observed the barrage, stationed with my unit to make sure no enemy troops would sneak around us. We had a good vantage point, but the Germans had built some large towers in the hills. They looked like forest service towers, and they used them as observation posts.

Every now and then we took a pot shot at one of those towers with a 90-mm gun to knock it down. We also used a .50 caliber machine gun, but we fired it just one shot at a time, like a sniper rifle. We aimed through a pair of binoculars for each round. The high explosive and armor piercing bullets did terrible damage.

We held them in that pocket for as long as we could, watching the puffs of smoke rise from the artillery rounds. When the smoke cleared, I saw that everything had been blown to smithereens. Our spotter planes had done a great job directing the fire. They were just small, single-engine observation planes, no bigger than a crop duster.

I guess the enemy units called for some air support, because a few German fighter planes attacked us. There were a several anti-aircraft guns stationed at Landshut airport which fired flak at them.

Unfortunately, one of the flak rounds came down on us, and I lost another friend, Warren Fry. We all knew it happened occasionally — that spent ammunition came down. We knew it was still lethal, and it was a wonder that we didn't lose more men to it. But that didn't ease the pain of losing Warren.

After dispatching the enemy in the pocket, we drove up and down the airport flanks, shooting at marauding Germans. We also were able to protect the prisoners as they boarded the planes for takeoff. Some of the men being flown to England were Germans who our officers thought might be useful to Allied intelligence.

It occurred to me that all of our training, going back to the camps in Tennessee and Arkansas, was aimed at preparing us for this kind of fighting. Our training also prepared us for collecting and organizing prisoners, both the Germans that we captured and the Allies that we liberated.

While we stood guard, all of us had a good feeling. Our work freeing the Allied POWs reinforced our nickname, the Liberators. We'd received that nickname while still in the States, and we never really understood it until now.

We also could hear the rumble of battle while we stood guard at the airport. The rest of our division was forcing the Isar River at Moosburg, heading for the Inn River.

As they moved deeper into Germany, our tankers began to make startling discoveries. I only heard about it at first, being at the airport where a lot of men passed through. It was hard to believe, but so many people said the same thing:

The Germans had been mass-murdering Jews.

A guy from the 47th told me that in Ampfing, his outfit found a concentration camp where two thousand people had just been cremated. He said the Jewish inmates revolted when our tanks appeared, and beat the camp commandant and some of the guards to death. Then he saw them run to a team of horses that had been killed during a fight with a German convoy, and tear at their flesh with teeth and hands. Later they ran to the American soldiers and kissed their boots.

I heard another tale from the same place, which housed a slave labor plant that made explosives. The guy told me that the Germans kept hundreds of Jewish women there as prostitutes for the slave laborers, and gassed them when they became pregnant.

It was hard for me to grasp — educated, twentieth-century people from one of the most modern nations in the world, committing that kind of barbarity. If it was true, I thought this war had been elevated to new moral level for our side. Later I would learn firsthand that it was, indeed, all true.

THE DANUBE—Racing into Austria, VE Day

When the MP battalions arrived, we handed airport security duty to them, and hit the highway. We drove to Velden ober-Bayern, a tiny village with a dark secret. There was a company of enemy troops defending the town, so we charged around the edges, and hammered them with our TDs and light tanks. It wasn't long before the procession of field grey trudged out of town, waving white handkerchiefs and holding their arms in the air.

We collected about two hundred prisoners there, and as usual gave all the town's buildings a good inspection. Along with the usual cache of wine and food, we discovered a poison gas dump. It was a large pile of metal drums with black skulls and crossbones stenciled on them.

I didn't know what it was, but I got out of there. Later, I thought it might have been the poison gas the Nazis were using in the concentration camps. But after the war I learned that we might have found a cache of sarin gas, a deadly nerve agent the German scientists had invented.

Fortunately, the Germans never used it. I guess Hitler was afraid that we'd retaliate. He knew how terrible poison gas was. He'd been gassed in the First World War.

Following our gruesome discovery, we mounted up and headed for the next town. We cleared four towns that day. I don't recall any of their names, because we blew through them so quickly.

I do remember the fifth town, however. When we arrived at Lauterhofen, four Tiger tanks prevented us from entering.

The Tigers were hard enough to knock out in ordinary circumstances, since their armor was so thick. These Tigers were dug in, buried up to their turrets, and we couldn't get a good shot at them with our 90-mm TD guns.

Their 88-mm guns and machine guns pinned us down, so we went to step two: call for artillery. I helped to spot the barrage over the phone, walking it right on top of the tanks. All of them were destroyed.

The next day we moved toward Eidelberg, and encountered a roadblock that seemed to be freshly built. When we approached, one or two German anti-tank guns opened up on us at point-blank range.

One of the shells landed near a half-track and destroyed it. The driver wasn't killed, but the concussion of the blast knocked him unconscious. We got angry about that, so after we knocked out the AT guns, we grabbed civilians from the town and marched them to the roadblock.

"You built it," I said to one of them. "You take it down."

They had no choice but to obey us, and the Germans couldn't fire at them. Maybe it wasn't in the spirit of the Geneva Convention, but the men who wrote that set of gentlemanly rules weren't in the war right then. After all, now that we were in Germany, we encountered civilians fighting us with small arms and *Panzerfausts*. That wasn't in the spirit of the Geneva Convention either.

In Eidelberg we received orders to reconnoiter for crossings over the Danube River at Inglestadt. But on the way there, speeding along the autobahn, we smacked into a pair of SS companies, complete with self-propelled guns and tanks.

They had us outgunned, so once again we called for artillery. This time, a friendly round landed in our midst, killing two of our men and wounding four more.

Captain Kraker decided that our general orders took precedence, so he told us to bypass the fanatics, and we moved on to our goal. That night we stayed in Brunau, caught a few hours of sleep, and moved out the next morning. We plowed through four towns, encountering only light resistance, until we hit Unter Rodel. The Germans there hit us with a lot of small-arms fire, including MG-42s, and a lot of their excellent assault rifles, called *Sturmgewehrs*.

Our battle reaction to this had become a kind of template. We called in artillery, watched the columns of smoke inundate the town's structures, then moved in cautiously.

There were German dead and wounded, as usual, and a handful of unharmed troops who'd had enough. And just as if following the same template, we spread out into the buildings looking for trophies and treats.

I walked down the street and stopped at a crazy sight. One of the artillery rounds had scored a direct hit on a bank, and I suddenly was walking knee deep in paper money. Soon I was joined by curious, eager comrades, and we sifted through the currency.

Most of it was *Reichsmarks*, which we ignored. But some of the bills were South American money. I filled several barracks bags with the South American currency, and shipped that home.

I had the foresight to collect some of the *Reichsmarks,* and keep them with me. They would come in handy when the war ended, because the *Reichsmark* was all Germany had for monetary exchange at that time. Only later did the new German government make an official *Reichsmark,* this one without the swastika.

I hoped to find some coins in the street outside of the blown bank, but there weren't many. People had been hoarding them.

In the course of the war, I picked up coins wherever I found them. All of us did. By the end of the fighting, I'd collected enough of them to fill a big woolen sock. Among them were modern coins from Germany, Austria and

Russia, but I also found old coins from the Holy Roman Empire, and even a few from ancient Rome.

One day, we emptied all of our coins on to a cot and divided them up. One guy would take one, then I would take one. I went for the older coins, while he specialized in the larger denomination coins.

I was quite pleased with myself. When I got them home, I had them assessed.

They all were counterfeit.

The next morning, we were on the road again, traveling with the 47th Tank Battalion. My unit took the point, and we ran into strong resistance at Alferhausen. We stood by and let the tanks and infantry take care of them. They made an enormous racket, but it was over in a few hours.

We drove through Alferhausen to Ingolstadt, and there it was: the Blue Danube. But it wasn't the Blue Danube I'd always heard about, and I imagined no tones of a Strauss waltz when I first saw it.

There was a lot of fighting up and down that river, which was in flood stage at the time. Some ice still floated in its current.

We rode along the banks, looking for a place to cross. There was stiff fire coming from the other side. They knew that if we bridged the Danube, they'd be finished.

Once again, American artillery and air power crashed down on the enemy, driving them to cover while our engineers tried to build a pontoon bridge. My unit was holding a flank in this action, and the Germans kept probing us for weak spots. They wouldn't find any.

We were surrounded by American mechanized artillery, tanks and infantry, all of them moving up to the riverbank. It seemed like the whole American Army was piling up in a great, terrible tsunami, about to break on Austria. It was April 29.

During the stop on the Danube, our squadron report summed up the previous few days:

"A Troop moved out, capturing twenty-one towns. Firefights at Pfeffenhauser, Oberneuhauser, Glain and Ergolding. Liberated two POW camps.... A Troop met enemy column attempting to escape from Landshut at Glain, and dispersed it by calling for tank and artillery fire. Cut enemy escape route."

We had reason to be proud of ourselves, as our troops now were about to cross a river that would help to end the war.

When the engineers finished the bridge, our job was to guard it. We knew the SS would do anything to destroy it. Even the *Luftwaffe* made an appearance. Several fighters swooped in trying to bomb and strafe the pontoon bridge. They cut a few holes into the boats, but those were easily repaired.

There were never many German planes involved in the attacks by this time. Our Air Force had destroyed most of their airfields. But it seemed like every barn in Germany had a plane hidden in it.

Once they revealed themselves in an attack, however, they didn't have a long life expectancy. Our P-51s were on them immediately, and the aging *Luft-waffe* fighter designs never matched up with that plane. Now, with so few in the air and being flown by untrained, young pilots, they didn't have a prayer.

While we were stationed on guard duty at the bridge, a bunch of guys from my platoon stayed in a decent German house. At night, when off-duty, we drank whatever spirits we could find and played poker.

We sat at a wooden table in the main room of the house, while in the back room, one of the gang toyed with an old Italian-made .32 revolver that he'd captured. He was spinning the cylinder, checking the action on his new prize.

Suddenly there was a loud pop. Before I could dive for the floor, I saw the man opposite me pitch forward. His head hit the card table with an ugly thud.

Everyone rose cautiously. One of the men went into the back room and snatched the revolver away from the fool who'd been playing with it.

Apparently the hammer accidentally had come down and the pistol fired. The .32 slug hit the poker player in the back of his head.

I don't remember the poor guy's name, but I'll call him Rivata. We checked out his head wound, and saw there wasn't anything we could do for him, so we put him into a peep on a stretcher that was attached to it, and sent him off to the hospital.

The guy who shot Rivata received a reprimand for his stupidity. That was all. The Army seemed to understand that soldiers are always fooling around with a variety of weapons during war, some of them captured and unfamiliar. It was a wonder that we didn't all kill each other.

The day our unit finally crossed the Danube, Captain Kraker and Colonel England were right in the middle of it. I rode across the pontoon bridge in a peep, wondering what we'd find on the other side.

I soon found out. When we stopped in a town called Jsen, I billeted in a *Gasthaus* room on the third floor, overlooking the front door. I could see people going to church — mobs of them — and it wasn't even Sunday.

The news reached me when I picked up a copy of *Stars & Stripes*, the U.S. Armed Forces newspaper.

Germany had surrendered. The war was over.

I was still alive.

It was hard to believe that, after what had seemed like a mad eternity, the damned thing had finally come to a conclusion.

I taped the front page of *Stars & Stripes* to the wall in my room, and photographed it with my trophy Exacta camera. I did it quietly.

Nobody cheered or carried on at all. We didn't raise hell. The news sobered us. We did more reflecting than celebrating.

All of us wondered what we were going to do next. Some of the guys had been in the war for years, and never got to college. They didn't know what would happen to them when they got home.

In some cases, guys were afraid to return home to their wives. Everybody worried about going home.

Some men feared making the adjustment to peacetime. I was fearful about adjusting to peace, too. I was grateful to have been spared, but everybody lost something in that war, and I would be haunted by it for a long time. It would interfere with my family life.

I would be a hard guy to live with for a while. I wouldn't have patience for people who didn't get things done. I would be too demanding. I would lose control over my children and my wife. I would have to change.

West poses in the shadows of his *Gasthaus* room in Jsen, Germany, following VE Day. Like most of the other American soldiers, West celebrated the occasion quietly and thankfully.

My family behaved commendably by putting up with me during my troubles. I couldn't explain to them that death has a smell. It's all over a battlefield, and I brought it home with me. It was my family who guided me back to some kind of normalcy.

But for now, on this joyous VE Day, I simply was numb.

Southern Europe—
Postwar Military Details

For the next few days, the endless columns of German prisoners that shuffled along the roads made me think of the Biblical Exodus. The division processed more than one hundred fifty thousand of them in just a couple of weeks.

Along with the defeated armies came the armies of displaced persons, so miserable and sad as they blankly walked on spindly legs and stooped frames. Most of them had been in German camps or factories, being worked and starved to death. Now they were going home.

At least, they were going where home used to be. In most cases, home didn't exist any longer.

Our supply people did everything they could to feed these wretches. Many of them, young and old, wore US Army issue olive drab clothing to replace the rags they'd arrived in.

Our transportation units supplied hundreds of two-and-a-half-ton trucks to ferry them to processing points, where they could be nursed back to health, deloused, and sent to their destinations.

My unit had the sad task to help organize the situation in one of the satellite camps of Dachau. We were among the first to arrive at the camp. When we drove to the gate, I saw that the fences, guard towers, barracks, "showers," and crematoria were still there.

So were the inmates. They were busy burning their own dead in the crematories. In their striped uniforms, they pulled box carts piled high with corpses, dumping them at a loading point to be transported to the ovens.

The stench hit me like a club. You could smell the burning human flesh twenty miles away. Nothing can prepare a person for that, not even combat. For a long time afterward, I couldn't eat.

Some of the prisoners were too weak to move. They'd gone down to nothing. Our medics had a tough time separating them from those who were healthy enough to be sent away for better care. We used every resource to feed these people, and keep them alive.

I spoke to some of them, and it seemed to me they couldn't talk about their experiences. They simply were too horrible to remember right then. They said our arrival, and the prospect of getting out of this camp, was like daylight after darkness. Some of them had spent many years in that darkness.

I walked through the camp and arrived at one of the "showers," where the Germans had gassed these people. The ceiling was at least twelve feet high, thick concrete, and yet it was scored by scratches from human fingernails. Countless desperate men and women had climbed atop each other trying to claw their way out.

In the nearby town, we came upon a store that sold lampshades made of human skin. The shades had tattoos on them. We trashed the place immediately. If we had found the owner, we would have done the same to him. We were enraged.

Dachau. West obtained this photograph, which was taken by an SS Guard during the exterminations in the camp, after his unit helped to liberate it.

Our duty at this Dachau death camp didn't last long, and we were thankful for that. We returned to Jsen, where there were a good number of former slave laborers.

Orders came down to use many of them to do spring plowing in the fields. They joined the local farmers, filling in foxholes and trenches, and plowing the fields for planting. They knew they had to do it, because soon their lives would depend on that harvest.

These poor people had to plow fields filled with mines and unexploded shells. It was not uncommon to suddenly hear a blast that took the lives of a farmer and his plow horse.

There was shrapnel everywhere. Even the trees were peppered with steel fragments from all of the air bursts and proximity fuse shells that had burst at treetop level.

In the Black Forest area, most of the trees were still alive, but they were filled with steel fragments. The locals who cut down those trees for lumber learned that as soon as they took those trees to their saw mills. The shrapnel destroyed their saws, and the lumber business was devastated for a long time.

The town of Jsen was only about thirty kilometers northwest of Munich. Although it was Germany, the locals were nice to us. The town hadn't been bombed, and there were kitchens where we could get hot food.

The citizens still used *Reichsmarks* for money, which surprised me. I guess they had no other means of monetary exchange. For me it was lucky, because I'd stuffed my pockets full of that currency at the blown-up bank.

Dachau. The ovens as they appeared in 1990, when West revisited the former concentration camp with his family.

By local standards, I was a rich man. I decided to use some of those riches to get a haircut. The guy in my unit who usually cut our hair was named Buche, and as a barber he made a great butcher.

Buche usually gave a terrible haircut, but if you got into an argument with him and made him mad, it could be fatal. The madder he got, the more he snipped. Pretty soon you were hairless and bloody. You were lucky if you still had ears.

But I always felt good after a haircut and a shave, so I found a barber shop in Jsen and walked inside. A beautiful woman gestured for me to sit in the barber chair. I'd never had a woman barber before, and never even had heard of one. But I figured it would be nice to have an attractive female working on my head, even if she didn't know anything about barbering. She couldn't be any more dangerous than Buche.

She did a fine job, and when it was over she asked for two *Reichsmarks* as payment. The smallest denomination I had was a fifty-*Reichsmark* note, so I gave that to her.

She balked, and sputtered about not having enough to change it. I told her that she deserved a good tip.

I walked out of there, and a line of soldiers were waiting to have their heads coiffed. But the lady barber pulled down her shades and went home.

"What the hell did you do to her?" one of the soldiers protested.

West poses with two new friends in Jsen, Germany, 1945. West's popularity with children was buoyed by his generosity in handing out chocolate. The German children called him "Herr Hugo," because they couldn't pronounce the name Hugh.

I just shrugged and walked on, figuring the lady had earned her whole weekly wage with me. That's how long the barber shop remained closed.

My riches allowed me to help out a few of the locals, who repaid me by cooking excellent meals, and having me as a guest in their homes. The fare wasn't five-star, but it beat the hell out of C-rations.

I made a habit of giving the local kids candy, or money to buy it. Word spreads fast along the starving-child grapevine, and soon I had a hoard of little ones following me like the Pied Piper, with the familiar chants of *"Herr Hugo!"* My pals in the platoon couldn't get over it.

"West," said one of them. "Your German isn't very good, but it's a pleasure walking down the street with you."

All of us were learning that the Germans were only people, and if you treated them right, they were good people. There still were some bad ones about, though.

We had orders to study the identification papers of anyone passing through the checkpoints we'd set up on all road junctions. A lot of high-ranking Nazis and war criminals were trying to escape.

The intelligence branch gave us a list of people to look for at the checkpoints, usually with a photo attached. Once in a while, we'd catch one of them.

I never knew what happened to them once the MPs came and hauled them off. If they had anything to do with abominations like the one I saw in Dachau, I only hoped their punishment would fit their crimes.

It was disappointing to learn years later how many of them had slipped through our net. A lot of them escaped through the Italian Alps, and used false passports supplied by the Red Cross to leave the continent, or to disappear inside Europe.

There was a second list that the intelligence branch gave us. We were to watch for German scientists, *Abwehr* (German intelligence) officers, fighter pilots, and any other person who might help us now that the war was over. Even rank and file dog faces like myself appreciated the high level of German technology, so it wasn't surprising that our government had placed a high priority on harvesting the brains that created it.

My other duty was to take charge of the motor pool. For some reason, Captain Kraker decided that I was the only guy he could trust with this duty, because I was fastidious. He knew I'd always make sure to get signatures whenever someone checked out a vehicle.

But I didn't want all of the guys coming up to my room to sign for vehicles. I was still on the third floor of the *Gasthaus,* next door to the town church. We worked out a system where guys who wanted a jeep or a truck just stood in the street below, and yelled at my window:

"Hey! I need a car!"

I lowered the printed order to them on a string attached to a pebble. When they signed it, I pulled it back up, and if it looked all right, I tossed down a key.

The system was bizarre, but necessary, because a lot of guys ran off with vehicles or stole gasoline. Everybody wanted gasoline at this time. So I had to have forms and signatures, insuring against any nefarious behavior. When they returned the vehicle, I had them check it in and closed the account. Since the fighting had ended, we received a lot more leave. I took advantage of my motor pool position by taking out a peep, and driving into the countryside.

Bavaria was beautiful, practically untouched by the fighting. I enjoyed taking pictures of it. There was one breathtaking vision of a meadow with a stream running through it, the mountains looming in the distance. Rose bushes dotted the meadow and livestock munched grass as if nothing awful had ever happened. It was a nice change from getting shot at all the time.

We liked all of the towns in southern Germany. They were clean little communities, and the populace treated us right. No one tried to kill us.

The people were religious, and only a few had been Nazis. Bavaria had always been heavily Catholic, and quite separate in culture and history from the rest of Germany. Of course, its capital, Munich, was also the birthplace of the Nazi Revolution.

I returned to Munich during one of my leaves. I rode there in a German electric train, which whisked from stop to stop, much like a New York subway. I got hungry about halfway through the journey, so at one of the stops I ran like a sprinter to a food vendor, grabbed something, paid the man, and hopped back on board as the train pulled out.

Later, when I was riding one of these trains with some of my platoon pals, we discovered it was carrying a load of K-rations. We loaded up on cigarettes, which we used to barter for food at the next stop.

When I stepped on to the station in Munich, I was glad to see it had made it through the rest of the war without being bombed. My unit had been there during our race around Bavaria in the war. We'd roared on to the tarmac of the city's small airport, and shot down a German plane that was trying to take off. I guess we surprised them.

There were enemy troops in the control tower, too. We tried to talk them into surrendering, but they wouldn't cooperate. We had to bring up one of our TDs, and blow off the top corner of the tower. After that, they were very cooperative.

Now I noticed a lot of our troops were guarding the water supply in Munich, because we would need it. We didn't know how long we would be here.

The Germans were skilled at putting their water reservoirs underground, insuring that minimal bacteria would get into them from the air. They also had built extensive waterworks in the nearby mountains that brought water down into Munich. Wasserburg was the control center for all water going into Munich, and there was a heavy contingent of GI guards manning the place.

I spent as much time in Munich as I could. The beer halls were excellent. Ladies served at outdoor tables, carrying an amazing number of filled beer mugs in each hand. I bought a few very decorative mugs and sent them home. The atmosphere was festive again — loud talk, laughter, music from *oom-pah* bands. It made me pause and wonder how such a happy, deeply religious people could have spawned an Anti-Christ.

In my wanderings around the city, I came upon a factory that had manufactured experimental German aircraft. It was unsettling to see the strange airframes. Many of them had a big Messerschmitt engine in the front and a four-bladed propeller on the tail.

Someone told me the prop added a couple of hundred miles per hour to the plane's speed. It reminded me of my encounter with the ME-262 jet fighter, and I was thankful the war ended when it did. If the enemy had time to manufacture these incredibly advanced weapons in numbers, we'd still be fighting them in France.

During my leave, I also journeyed to Berchtesgaden, and the "Eagle's Nest," Hitler's spectacular private lair in the Bavarian mountains. This was where he plotted a world war, where he approved the murder of millions of civilians, where he dallied with his mistress, Eva Braun.

The place was a shambles when I arrived. It had been bombed, and the living room was blown out through the front window. There had once been a forty-foot-wide glass window facing the spectacular mountain peaks in that room. Now the whole thing was burned out, much like the rest of the Third Reich. But I marveled at how the place had been built, high atop a steep mountain. Despite the damage, it was the most beautiful place I'd ever seen.

My extended R&R allowed me to spend a good deal of time in a nearby Bavarian resort called Eipsee. It was on a large lake right at the base of a mountain. It had been a resort for German generals, and there was a stable of horses with all types of mounts. Some were meant for pulling carts, some for jumping in shows.

I had fought an entire war as a cavalryman, and never once sat a horse, so I thought I should have the experience now. I chose one horse, not knowing anything about how to judge the equine character. This particular horse ran, but only uphill. When we climbed, the thing would break into a gallop that nearly unseated me. It refused to obey me when I tried to make it walk going up a hill. And going downhill, I couldn't make it run. It also would never stop when I said, "Whoa."

West poses in front of a Munich beer hall, following the war. Munich was fairly well preserved, since it had escaped the intense bombings that other German cities in the north suffered.

I figured, being a kraut horse, it didn't speak cowboy. Soon I learned that it stopped only when you shouted, "Halt!" But I never mastered the language that would make it run or walk when I wanted.

There were a number of sailboats moored at the lakeside that were available to us. One day a few of the guys and myself took one, called *Prinz Eugen,* for a jaunt. Not one of us knew anything about sailing, but we learned after a while without drowning ourselves.

I enjoyed fishing on the lake. It soothed me to take one of the motorboats out to the middle, and just sit there with a line in the water.

The German motorboats had a long propeller shaft that almost lifted the craft completely out of the water, so I had some fun hydroplaning on the lake surface at high speeds. Everyone urged me to go faster, and it's a miracle we didn't flip the boat and kill ourselves.

The resort was crowded with Red Cross nurses, and we traded a good deal with them. They also graced the nightly dances that were held there. So did many of the locals, all of whom looked hale and hearty. It seemed like every one of them was young, and they loved to sing and climb mountains.

Sometimes we danced all night.

It was a week of pure, cushy living, and everything was on the house.

When I returned to Jsen, the unit was beginning to get back some of its wounded, who'd spent varying times in rear echelon hospitals. It was good to

West rides a German cavalry horse during his R&R stay in Eipsee. Figuring he'd served the entire war as a cavalryman, West felt it was necessary to ride a horse at least once. Unfortunately, this horse only obeyed orders in German.

see these guys, because once they were gone, we had no idea what had happened to them.

One day a familiar face sauntered up to me on the street.

"How's it hanging, Westy?"

It was Rivata, the guy who been accidentally shot in the head during our poker game. I thought for sure that he was dead when we loaded him on to the peep stretcher. Now here he was, looking fine and healthy.

"Great to see you," I greeted him, patting his shoulder. "They must have worked a miracle, taking that thing out of your head."

"No, the bullet's still in there," he said. "The surgeons were scared to operate, because it's in such a dangerous place. They said maybe I can have it removed stateside, after we get home."

The bullet lodged in his brain didn't seem to affect him at all when he went back on duty with us. For all I know, he spent the rest of his life with that bullet in his head.

Soon, I received more surprising news. The 14th Armored Division was being deactivated.

It seemed so premature, so unnecessary. Our outfit had existed for just three years, two in training and one in combat. But during that last year of its existence, we made all of the training count.

Since arriving in Europe, the 14th Armored Division captured eighty-four thousand enemy soldiers, liberated two hundred thousand Allied POWs, captured a thousand cities, towns and villages, and had freed more than a quarter of a million displaced persons, earning its title, the Liberators.

Between its arrival in Europe on October 29, 1944, and May 8, 1945, our vehicles traveled an average of two thousand miles. In that period, the division destroyed or captured five hundred enemy tanks, a hundred self-propelled guns, five hundred artillery pieces, and a hundred thousand small arms.

West sails a boat on a lake in Eipsee, following the war's end. His unit stayed at a resort there for R&R.

The outfit destroyed or captured fifty thousand tons of German munitions, took two thousand railroad cars, captured or destroyed two hundred factories, destroyed four hundred anti-aircraft guns, and captured or shot down four hundred enemy aircraft. Not bad for a bunch of green citizen soldiers.

The division had a final review for General Patton and General Smith. The supply unit issued us fresh uniforms, and we wore our unit patches for the last time. When it was over, I was transferred to E Company of the 218th Regiment, 80th Infantry Division.

I had to join my new unit in Czechoslovakia. The occupying forces there were in the midst of dividing the country, half of it supposedly going to the Soviet Union, and the other half to the U.S.

It was a mess, with throngs of Czechs fighting to get into the American sector so they wouldn't have to live under the Russians. I dealt with scores of pleading civilians, begging us to take them before the Red Army arrived.

One woman begged to be permitted just to ride on the fender of my half-track when we left the sector that had been given to the Soviets. I told her the Russians can't be that bad, and she responded with a story about one Soviet soldier who stole her wristwatch. She said he held it to his ear, and when he heard it ticking, he smiled. In return, he gave her six watches from his pocket. None of them worked.

There were stories that were much more grim. Stalin's government had made it official policy for its soldiers to rape German women. Russia's greatest poet exhorted the Red Army to the task, saying, "Soldiers of Russia, the women of Germany are yours." Apparently some of the Red Army took that exhortation to include Czech women as well.

The Russians already controlled the eastern half of Czechoslovakia by the time I got there. The flood of refugees pouring out of that sector, and trying to get into our sector produced an administrative nightmare.

Adding to the problem was Stalin's insistence that we return all of them. The Americans were still trying hard to be good allies of the USSR, so we had orders to cooperate.

It was a heartbreaking task. You could see that the Czech people were very democratic in their ideals, and we were leaving them in the clutches of another dictatorship.

Aside from dealing with desperate locals, I was assigned to join the office that sold US Savings Bonds. The brass decided to make one last big push to sell them to the troops while they still were in service in Europe. It was a job that nobody wanted, so I got it.

Many of the guys in my new outfit were in the Signal Corps, which meant they could get hold of anyone in the Army. If you needed to reach any US soldier, they and the cavalry unit were mobile enough to go out and find them.

We used this advantage to sell the war bonds. I sat in a crowded office all day, where lines of soldiers came to buy them. I had to keep track of all the transactions on an adding machine that didn't work. None of them seemed to work.

When we finished one day, an officer asked me if I had signed for all the money. I told him I hadn't, because I was just an enlisted man who agreed to sell bonds. I told him it was up to an officer to take care of the rest.

He loaded all the money into a barracks bag, tossed it into a jeep and went to Paris. For all I know, he started Xerox with that loot, because there was absolutely no written record of the cash.

Like most of occupied Europe, Czechoslovakia was in ruin, physically and economically. A pack of cigarettes sold for fifty dollars American on the black market. For US soldiers, who received liberal supplies of cigarettes, the packs were like gold bars in barter. A GI could pick up a priceless painting or family heirloom for two packs of Chesterfields.

But I wasn't too interested in bartering for souvenirs at this point. I'd been suffering from a nasty case of trench foot for months, and it kept getting worse. By the time I entered Czechoslovakia, my feet were numb all the way to my knees.

A doctor who inspected my legs gave me a medical leave, and sent me to Marienbad. It was near Constantinsbad, where the Roman Emperor Constantine had set up his personal mineral baths. I was going for the Emperor's Cure.

The bathtubs in Marienbad were about three feet deep, and all lined up. I sat in one and ran the sulphur water over my legs and feet. They called it "radium water." I soaked for hours in that warm mineral spring water, and when I came out I was so limp that I barely could crawl.

I made it to a wooden bench, and the attendants dumped a bucket of ice water on me to close my pores. It was like an electric shock. I almost jumped out of my skin. But in a very short time, those mineral baths healed my trench foot.

I was capable of working again, so the Army assigned me to the regimental headquarters in Marienbad. The local population was eager to do whatever they could to help us, so we hired many of them.

We came up with a payment process where we gave them *Reichsmarks* for work completed. The *Reichmarks* were redeemable only in our outfit, and they used them to buy supplies from us.

The work was typical Army drudgery, but after-hours I had a lot of fun in Marienbad. I went to floor shows, which were held every night, and there were dances with live music that played American Big Band tunes.

The local women were becoming skilled in all of the Yankee dance moves. They ate up everything American.

There also was a lot of local color — Bavarian singers, Czech violinists — and spectacular restaurants. Our dinners were served on tables with linen tablecloths. This was culture shock to a dog face who'd been eating out of a tin can for months. We had it so good that a lot of my friends begged me to get them transferred to Marienbad, and I managed to pull that off for a couple of them.

All of us shared information about the local places of interest and attractions. I'd heard about the famous Passion Play that nearby Oberammergau holds every ten years. I traveled there on a short leave, and enjoyed the Biblical paintings and murals on the sides of buildings. The whole town was decorated for the occasion.

It was a tradition that began in the seven-

West receiving one of his two Bronze Star medals from General A.C. Smith in Gars, Germany, June 7, 1945.

teenth century during the Thirty Years' War, after the plague had claimed the lives of countless citizens. The *Oberammergauers* swore an oath then that they would perform a play about the suffering, death and resurrection of Jesus every decade.

The first play took place on a stage built in the town cemetery, above the graves of their plague victims. The performance I watched continued the tradition of electing someone from the town to play Jesus.

I didn't want to leave Czechoslovakia, but the Army had other ideas. They were assigning men to places all over Europe, trying to get the most out of what was left of our service time. My new assignment would take me north, to a place where I wouldn't need to struggle with the language — at least, not very much.

EDINBURGH—Stationing
in Scotland

The Army had to find something for me to do with the rest of my time, so they sent me to Scotland. I went to the airport holding a thick stack of paper orders stapled together. The orders had such high priority that they kicked a colonel off the plane to make room for me.

My new top-drawer assignment? I was to train civilian agencies under a program called TWCA. It had to be the easiest job in the Armed Services, I thought, until I arrived at my new post.

A corporal greeted me like a Tasmanian Devil.

"I am the commanding officer of the Edinburgh TWCA," he barked. "If any of you sons of bitches screw up, I'll kick your ass back to wherever you came from. I may be just a corporal, but I'm in charge here!"

I forgave him for his manner. He'd been a professor at Dartmouth before the war.

My new station was called TACA-Edinburgh. I dealt with the city government and the school districts there.

I had an opportunity to meet some of the government officials, and study their court methods and higher procedures. Before long I realized that the city was under something resembling a military government. It seemed inappropriate to me, but I was just a stranger in a strange land. No one really cared what I thought.

The top man in Edinburgh was called the Lord Mayor. He wore a wig to denote his office, just like the high justices there. It all seemed very foreign to a Yank like me, but the people were very nice, and they seemed to like the same things that I did. It reminded me of a comment by George Bernard Shaw: "England and America are two peoples separated by a common language."

One of the local people I frequently met was Ann Patterson, the chief psychologist for the Edinburgh schools. The district had an incredible number of schools—one hundred sixty-seven in all—everything from boys and girls high schools to trade schools.

Ann Patterson's job was to select which children would attend which schools. Her decision was based mainly on a single test, which I thought was a terrible weakness in their system. Any child who didn't do well on that test simply didn't get a good education and a chance to get ahead.

Having been a teacher in the American system, where advancement was based on long-term merit, this seemed outrageous. But since I was just a foreign interloper, I had to keep my mouth shut.

Another person I worked with was the Edinburgh Director of Art, George Scott. He had access to all of the student records, and he worked with them throughout the entire district. His plate was full, because this represented an enormous number of kids.

There were some Russian children among his students, and one day he asked them to draw pictures. It was a standard test that he also gave to Scottish students.

In comparing those drawings, I saw right away that the Scottish kids had a much brighter outlook on life. The Russian kids were repressed, much less flamboyant. It made me realize that any attempt to allow Russian youngsters to cut loose would have to be done very gradually.

I still had to perform regular Army functions. One of those

West dressed in a Scottish kilt, to blend into his new surroundings after being posted to Edinburgh. Photograph was taken on May 10, 1945.

duties was to distribute PX supplies each week to the troops. I was like a supply sergeant, passing out cigarettes and other things to the military personnel stationed there.

But the military bearing of our troops in Scotland was very loose. We could stay wherever we wanted. You only had to tear off a sheet showing where you were staying, and hand it in to a sergeant.

Most of the time, I stayed in a nice hotel on Princess Street, near the old opera house. From there, I took excursions to see the countryside and nearby towns.

I learned to be careful with the Scottish taxi drivers, who liked to take advantage of my initial ignorance of local geography. They would take the long route, and jack up the cab fare if they thought they could get away with it.

A lot of the local Scots invited American soldiers into their homes for meals and good company. Some of it was sheer kindness, but I also knew that it had much to do with the sugar ration books all US soldiers possessed. Those books were our ace in the hole, because sugar was in such demand in Scotland.

I'd never seen a more sugar-starved people in my life. They were overjoyed to have me as a guest in their homes, so they could get their hands on that sugar.

Like all of the American troops, I always carried a lot of sugar ration books and gave them out wherever I went. It went over big with the people I stayed with. And if they were happy, I was happy.

There were other barter items that had great value. I brought some of my captured material with me to Scotland, including a Luger pistol. But I knew that when I arrived, I would have to go through an inspection similar to customs at any airport. The inspectors took everything out of your bags.

I figured the Luger was fine by itself, but I was worried about the ammunition, which I carried in the bottom of my barracks bag. So before I hit the inspection station, I went to the toilet and flushed away fifty rounds of 9-mm ammunition, one bullet at a time. It took about an hour.

When I emerged, some people looked at me like I was diseased. I guess they thought I had dysentery. But I got to keep the Luger.

The Army gave us passes that allowed us to use all modes of transportation throughout the British Isles, and I did a lot of wandering in England. I used the railroad to go sightseeing. I liked the River Clyde. I liked the city of York. It reminded me of some of the medieval games I played when I was a kid, because the city was walled.

The desk man at my hotel there warned me that I had to be in by a certain hour, because they locked the city gates at night. I don't know if they still feared a Viking invasion, but one time I was late and had to ring the bell just to enter the city.

Edinburgh had its own medieval flavor. There were a lot of old structures around the city, including medieval castles. I explored them. One castle had a cannon that they fired every day at noon. That meant every day at noon, all of us combat veterans dove into a cellar. The boom reverberated throughout the city, and we hadn't shed the instinct to find cover at the sound of artillery. I never got used to that cannon. What your body has learned in combat leaves you only very gradually.

My excursions took me to London a couple of times. It was a matter of passing through more than anything else. I didn't want to stay there, because it was bombed out, and reminded me so much of the towns in Alsace and Germany. I didn't need reminders like that at this point.

Looking at all the destruction, I wondered again how ordinary people could withstand such a horror. The Londoners I spoke with seemed so nonchalant about it all. They said the same thing: they'd hear the sirens, walk down to the tubes, and wait it out — sometimes all night. They didn't speak of the thousands who drowned in those subway stations when the water mains fractured and flooded them.

A lot of familiar places were missing, too. I went to look up someone I knew at the Eveready Battery factory in London, and when I got there it was gone. It had been blown apart by German bombers.

I did find a beautiful old tobacco shop on Bond Street. I was looking for a Mershon pipe and some good tobacco, but all I could find was a bag of pipe tobacco called "Baby's Bottom." They had no Mershon men's pipes either, so I settled for a small ladies' pipe they had in that brand. I brought it home, but eventually I gave up smoking after the war, because my wife had ruined all of my pipes by washing them out with soda water.

London was depressing, so I hopped a train back to Edinburgh. When I arrived at my hotel, there was a message bidding me to see the staff officer. I went, and he handed me a thin slip of paper.

It was hard to believe such a puny sliver of parchment could have so much power. The paper informed me that I had reached the requisite number of points for deactivation.

They were sending me home.

America—Home and Wife

The C-47 transport was loud and uncomfortable, still rigged to carry crates and hard cargo. Now I was the cargo. But I didn't care about the hard floor beneath me, or the droning engines.

The plane landed in Munich. My orders directed me to meet up with the 799th Infantry, which had just arrived from Italy. This outfit was legendary. All of the soldiers were Japanese-Americans, and the deeds they accomplished against Field Marshall Kesselring's army in Italy had made them one of the most decorated units in the entire US Army. I think every one of them had at least one Purple Heart.

I would be traveling home with these heroes, because the Army was grouping soldiers by the amount of points they'd accrued, instead of by unit. The point system was based on time served, combat, decorations, wounds, and some other considerations that required a slide rule to decipher.

I rode an electric train to Marseilles, to meet up with the 799th and our Liberty Ship. The city hadn't changed since the 14th Armored Division landed in its port more than a year before. It was still a rough town.

But we had changed. Now we called it "Little Dachau." It was December 1945, and it was freezing, as winter set in on southern Europe once again. I saw kids scrounging for coal.

We weren't much better off. They packed us into tents, six to eight guys in each. We huddled around an old pot-bellied stove trying to keep warm, but I never got warm in my tent.

I only had to spend a week in Marseilles before boarding the boat. It was going to be a long, difficult crossing. I knew that from past experience—the rolling and dipping with its attendant seasickness, the airless conditions below, the rows of hammocks, the sheer boredom.

I celebrated Christmas 1945 on the Liberty Ship. They served us turkey that day and it was so old it had turned green. I think they probably loaded the turkey into the refrigerators when they built that ship, and just saved it for us.

We spent most of the voyage quietly reflecting on everything, and trying to visualize what it would be like when we got home. Many of the guys who had things on their consciences—things they did in and out of combat—let it out in the course of our journey.

They really were scared of peace, because they'd become so accustomed to war. Peace actually had become a dark specter to them, and they didn't know how to handle it. They wondered what they would do.

The Liberty ship *Henry Middleton* which brought West home from Europe.

A number of them had contracted venereal disease in Europe. They'd taken penicillin, which was roundly regarded as a wonder drug. But about half of those guys on the boat came down with renewed outbreaks of the disease. We learned later it was because a lot of the penicillin administered overseas had been diluted by black marketers. I felt bad for those men, not only because of their physical pain, but because of the shame they had to face in front of wives, girlfriends, mothers, sisters. But I felt good that I wasn't like them. I was happy to be going home to peacetime.

When the ship entered New York harbor, everyone was on deck. I saw the Statue of Liberty again, this time from the opposite direction, and in the opposite state of mind. My heart pounded so hard I thought I was going to faint. I had to steady myself on the rail. It was the greatest feeling I can ever remember.

I was home. I was alive.

There were so many times when I was sure I would never get back. America always seemed like a remote dream when I was in the field, and if a thought about home entered my mind, I tried to banish it right away.

Now I stared at the shocking reality. The statue looming before me made it real. It represented my home.

I stayed only a couple of days in New York. The Army was doing its best to get us on our way. American Airlines flew troops out of the city in four-engine civilian passenger planes. It was such a foreign experience, sitting in a padded seat, chatting with your neighbor like nothing unusual had happened in your life during the past year.

We were on high priority, and flew right into Phoenix. I peered out the window at the Arizona landscape that I knew so well from my youth, while the plane refueled. It occurred to me that a lot of enemy prisoners got to spend the last year of the war in this beautiful place, while I was dodging bullets in the mud of Germany. Some of them had been sent here by me.

Pauline as she appeared when West returned home following the war.

The plane flew straight to Los Angeles from Phoenix. I grabbed my gear and walked down the steps into the gate. There was a crowd of strange faces. It seemed like all of them were holding their breath, their eyes hungrily consuming me for a sign of familiarity.

I scanned them, traveling from face to face. My eyes came to rest on Pauline. She ran to me, and threw her arms around my shoulders, weeping. I didn't know how to react.

It was just so amazing to be in this place with her — that I could be so far away for so long, go through a war, and still get back in one piece. Now my wife was crying and clinging tightly to me.

For some stupid reason, it made me feel uncomfortable and self-conscious. I thought everyone was looking. I simply didn't know how to handle so much emotion at that moment.

The first thing I did when I got home was take a bath and go to bed. I think I slept for two days.

I don't remember what Pauline served for my first home-cooked meal in more than three years, but I devoured it. My table manners from before the war had been discarded, and replaced by pure animal hunger. Like so many other things, it took time to get back into being my old self during meals.

But I never really did get back to that old me. The Hugh Warren West who left our lovely Ontario, California, home in 1942 was obliterated somewhere in those muddy fields and ruined towns of Europe. What came back was a man who looked somewhat the same on the outside, but who had undergone a sea change on the inside.

The same drama was taking place all over America. Sons, husbands, brothers, lovers — all were back, and yet none were all back.

It had been an episode of dying. Now it was time to try living again.

Epilogue: The Return—
1990 Tour of ETO Battlefields

In 1990, I turned seventy-four years old. I'd finished a long and enjoyable career as a school teacher in Ontario, California. My two children were grown adults. My wife and I lived the comfortable life of retirees.

Over the years, I had told my family about some of my experiences during the war in Europe, but I knew they never could grasp them completely. I decided to show them myself.

We booked a trip to Europe and toured the places where my unit had lived, died, laughed and cried. My son and daughter accompanied Pauline and me to places that I no longer recognized, but still were branded into my memory.

We went to Waldersheim. Through all the years following the war, I had corresponded with the Gantzer family, who had been so kind to us in sharing their home and their lives. I'd sent them aid packages in the mail whenever I could, and our relationship continued to grow.

It was through the mail that I notified the Gantzer family we would be coming, and when we arrived, the whole town turned out to greet us. The local newspaper even printed a story announcing our arrival and telling the citizens who I was. And to my amazement, the Gantzers had saved every one of my letters.

We visited Barr. I reunited with the doctor I had met in the hospital there so many decades before. He still was running the hospital.

One of our group of veterans thanked this doctor and the people of Barr for taking care of him when he was wounded, more than forty five years ago. He revealed that, because of their kindness, he'd named his first son Barton— after Barr.

We went to Creussen. We were guests of the mayor, and all of the town officials greeted us. They thanked us for our kindness and consideration to the civilians there during the war. I made a speech. I talked about how wonderful it was that the German people had become such good friends to America.

And we visited Hatten. I was happy to run into my good friend Ted Perkins there. He was doing the same thing as I, showing his family the physical places that had become so indelible in our lives.

The city had planned a big parade for the reunion, featuring a mixture of troops from NATO and the USSR. When we learned that there would only

The West family in 1990 during their return to the sites of the war. Standing left to right are West, his wife Pauline, three members of the Gantzer family, and West's son, Alan. Kneeling is West's daughter, Carolyn.

be twenty-five American troops as compared to one hundred each from the Soviet, British and French contingents, Ted got on the phone.

Suddenly there was an extra one hundred American soldiers in the parade. Ted pulled some strings through his connection to then President Bush. They were lifelong friends, going back to their days at Amhearst.

The tour was the best investment I have ever made. It brought my family together. It gave my children an idea of what happened in the war. You can read about it and hear about it, but no one really can understand it without directly experiencing the places where it happened.

My children saw some of the war terrain that had been preserved. They walked through the Maginot Line. They met some of the people they'd heard me talk about for years.

At one of our stops, a woman approached me, and thanked me for saving the life of her husband. I don't know where she came from, or how she found me, but after speaking with her I realized her husband was the German soldier who had given me the Browning pistol. He had remembered my name, and apparently he talked about me after the war, which showed up in a German newspaper article.

She thanked me again and again. I told her that it was I who should thank her husband for sparing my life. He'd held that pistol on me first, before handing it over.

She explained it would be impossible for me to thank him, because he had passed away.

As this is written, I am ninety-two years old. I trust that soon enough, we'll be able to thank each other in person.

Index